THE FIRST EVIDENCE

THE FIRST EVIDENCE

A Memoir of Life in Iraq under Saddam Hussein

by Juman Kubba

McFarland & Company, Inc., Publishers
Jefferson, North Carolina, and London

Library of Congress Cataloguing-in-Publication Data

Kubba, Juman 1965–
    The first evidence : a memoir of life in Iraq under Saddam
Hussein / by Juman Kubba.
        p.   cm.
    Includes index.
    ISBN 0-7864-1580-0 (softcover: 50# alkaline paper)
    1. Kubba, Juman, 1965– 2. Women—Iraq—Biography.
3. Iraq—Politics and government—1979–1991.   4. Iraq—Politics
and government—1991–   I. Title.
[DS79.66--]   2003
956.7044'092—dc21   2002155762

British Library cataloguing data are available

Cover photograph: ©2003 PhotoSpin

Manufactured in the United States of America

*McFarland & Company, Inc., Publishers
    Box 611, Jefferson, North Carolina 28640
    www.mcfarlandpub.com*

In dark underground dungeons,
in mass graves in the desert,
and in many alleys of Baghdad,
thousands of young men and women
vanished at the hands of the regime
between 1971 and today.
I dedicate this work to their souls
and
to the memory of my parents

Acknowledgments

It is a pleasure to thank the outstanding friends who kindly encouraged me and believed in my work. I am so grateful to F. Faraz, K. Razi, S. Hale and G. Gliesman. I thank these wonderful friends and colleagues for their encouragement and for patiently reading various parts of this work. I am exceedingly grateful to J. Lee for her comments on my work, her support throughout this project and at other times, and for being a true sister and friend. I wish to thank my brother, A.M., for providing essential data for this book and for his wonderful hospitality while I worked on his data. I am further grateful to my family for their encouragement and for contributing various details of this story.

There are no words, in any language, that are adequate to covey my gratitude and indebtedness to my husband, T.M.A, for inspiring me to achieve all my goals, for persistently pushing me to finish this work, and for surrounding me with love and kindness throughout not only the duration of this project, but also coincidentally an immensely difficult time in my life. I thank him for such an enduring love and to him I would like to say that it is your love and care that kept me alive over the past year.

Contents

Author's Note

This is a true story. It is very special to me and to my family. For the sake of clarity and organization and in order to respect the privacy and security of all the individuals mentioned, I have had to change names, dates and certain details of some events. It may be that other people who know this story have different details or perspectives. I have told the events as I experienced them.

Also, a note on language: Although this book was first written in English, most of the conversations took place in Arabic. I have tried my best to convey the meaning rather than give a word-by-word translation. Some expressions in Arabic, especially in the Iraqi dialect, are indeed difficult to translate into English.

Preface

I was fourteen years old when vice president Saddam Hussein became the president of Iraq in 1979. He gave a televised speech during which he announced his presidency and talked about various nationalistic issues. He concluded with a chilling, frightening statement: *"Anyone who attempts to take this government from our hands, shall receive Iraq as a land without people."* After the speech was over, I remember that my father was in a deep, somber mood. Things are headed for the worst, he said.

This book is about the atrocities of the Iraqi regime long before it invaded Kuwait, long before the Gulf War of 1991, and even long before the first Gulf War, the Iran-Iraq War. The events of this story took place in Baghdad in the early seventies. The ruthless Ba'ath regime* of Baghdad, like a savage animal, preyed on innocent citizens and inflicted pain and suffering on the people of Iraq. It committed atrocious abuses of human rights for many years during which Iraq was an ally and a friend of the Western world and the rest of the world community.

The pain told in this real story does not necessarily exceed that of others. There are many real stories of pain and horror inflicted by the Ba'ath regime on the people of Iraq and on other people outside of Iraq. However, this true tale is of events that *preceded* most of the others. During the early and mid 1970s the majority of the population in Iraq was

---

The term Ba'ath is used throughout the book to refer to the Iraqi branch of the Ba'ath party, originally a national socialist political organization. Those who controlled the government in Iraq in the mid sixties were a fascist faction of the Ba'ath party made up of closely linked gangs and militias who spread terror among the people. Saddam Hussein headed this fascist gang and he rose to power through controlling the entire apparatus of the party. Although Saddam Hussein was vice president initially, he was nevertheless Iraq's ruthless strongman from the late sixties.

content and enjoying some economic benefits from the Ba'ath government. If they knew of atrocities, they chose to look the other way, as did many Western and regional governments. They benefited from the Ba'ath regime and so chose to ignore the human rights abuses that were going on in Iraq. The pain and suffering told here was uncommon at the time. There may be a handful of stories like it, but not many. The severity of the injustice was then unheard of in Iraq. These events marked the beginning of an era of ruthless government, unsurpassed by any other regime in the Arab world. It is because the regime got away with its initial few crimes and abuses that it was able to grow more vicious and expand its crimes to the rest of Iraq and even abroad.

The Ba'ath regime began its atrocities on a small scale in Baghdad starting with a few people whom they terrorized and oppressed. Afterwards, in the late 1970s and throughout the 1980s, their terror spread to more people and even outside the borders of Iraq. Moreover, after the Gulf War II in the early 1990s and until today, the Ba'ath regime has perpetrated an injustice on the people of Iraq that is truly tantamount to genocide. The genocide was, and still is as this book is being written, widespread and systematic. The horrific abuses of human rights are the most outrageous act of the Iraqi government. There will come a day when these crimes and abuses will be judged as genocide and the people responsible will be tried for crimes against humanity. I hope this day will be in my lifetime.

The Iraqi regime has been outlawed not because it was involved in the attacks of September 11, 2001, in New York and Washington. There is no evidence of such involvement. It has not been outlawed because it now possesses, and may use in the future, weapons of mass destruction. It has been outlawed because it is evil and has committed atrocious abuses of human rights against the Iraqi population since 1970. This regime was evil when it possessed and used chemical weapons on Iraqi citizens while the rest of the world looked the other way. It was evil long before the U.S. Congress passed the "Iraq Liberation Act" in 1998. The Iraqi government was evil while it was our ally and friend and a member of the civilized world.

I have two reasons for writing this book. First, I lived through the traumatic events described here, and these events shaped my life and my personality, as I was seven years old at their onset. For the regime, these events were just a few among many crimes and atrocities that they committed. Perhaps the events meant nothing to them. Perhaps they do not even remember any of these events. For me, however, these events stripped from me my happiness and displaced me from my family for many years and permanently affected my life, and it is time that these crimes of the Iraqi regime are exposed. Second, I made a promise to my parents that I would tell their story. It was their wish and dream that this story be told. This book is a humble depiction of what they endured. I have finally fulfilled my promise.

Introduction

It had only been a few years since the Ba'ath party took power, but already life in Iraq was taking a different turn. The Ba'athists, members of the Ba'ath regime, dominated all aspects of life from the highest-ranking offices in the government to the local supermarket or kindergarten. Their policies and regulations affected ordinary citizens in the most basic aspects of their daily lives and in most intellectual aspects too.

The Ba'athists controlled newspapers, television, sports and schools. Television and the media became strictly state-controlled. All you saw on television were speeches and news about the revolution* and its accomplishments. Many books and magazines became banned or censored. Having become aware of the world during the Ba'ath years, it has been ingrained in my mind that certain books are banned and censored. Magazines would arrive at bookstores with many pages physically removed. Private schools and institutions were gradually being closed or becoming nationalized. These early steps of control were the foundations of the modern Iraq which has no free press, no independent academic freedom of research and no independent justice system.

During the early years under the Ba'ath rule, shortages of food and basic commodities became the norm in Iraq. People had to stand in excessively long lines to buy basic food and home items such as bread, eggs and Kleenex. This, in a country which had sustained its inhabitants since the dawn of civilization. This, in a country rich with oil wealth, with so much agriculture, and with two luscious rivers: the Tigris and the Euphrates. The Ba'athists also banned or restricted the import of many

*The coup d'état, which took place in July 1968, is referred to as a popular revolution. This was when the Ba'ath party seized power.

essential items such as spare parts for cars or film for cameras. Fine soaps and chocolates became items of luxury not to be found.

Any resident of or even visitor to Baghdad in the early seventies would have noticed that in every office, hospital, classroom, bus stop or any other public place, there were the twin pictures of then president Ahmed Hassan Albaker and then vice president Saddam Hussein. These pictures were even displayed in private retail stores and even some homes. Many shopkeepers and ordinary people put these pictures on their walls just to avoid being questioned about their loyalty to the Ba'ath regime. One would be exposed to these pictures daily from the moment he left his home to the end of the day when he returned.

The Ba'ath regime indoctrinated the masses with its ideology. The regime exerted tremendous effort in formulating methods of brainwashing the population and then implementing those methods. A combination of socialism and nationalism comprised the essence of Ba'ath ideology. Thus, many of their brutal methods and tactics in spreading their ideas and exercising control were reminiscent of those of Nazi Germany. And although the Ba'athists opposed Communism ideologically, they adopted many aspects of socialism. Thus, life in Iraq was also reminiscent of that in East European Communist countries.

Revolutionary ideology dominated all sectors of life from art and sports to health care and education. For example, as children in primary school, we were taught Ba'ath ideology and had to memorize quotes from the president and the vice president. We also had to memorize the accomplishments of the revolution of the 17th of July 1968, which is when the Ba'ath party took power. I still remember the white and blue "list of accomplishments of the revolution" which was framed and posted in every classroom in my school and even in the school hallways and the school entrance.

In Arabic and English composition classes we had to write essays about the Ba'ath party and the revolution and how blessed we were in having the party and the president and the vice president watching over our lives. Similarly, in art class we had to paint and draw various revolutionary themes. If you painted the most striking work of art that was not about the revolution and the party, it would not get noticed and you would get some mediocre mark.

Teachers in schools and professors in universities were promoted or demoted based on their devotion to the Ba'ath party or lack thereof, and not their performance or qualifications. In fact teachers and professors had to join the party to keep their jobs. They had to incorporate in the classroom work all kinds of slogans about the Ba'ath ideology. Textbooks of the arts and humanities and languages were all changed in new editions which incorporated Ba'ath ideology, while the classical content of the former textbooks was deleted. After an important speech by the president or the vice president, we were quizzed the next day on what he said. And God help anyone who did not know the correct answer. Not only would he or she receive poor grades, but also become suspected of being an antirevolutionary and reactionary.

Mass indoctrination took other forms too. Every day at school right when the bell rang, we (children of all ages) had to line up and sing some pro-Ba'ath songs praising the revolution, the president and the vice president. There were supervisors and decoy supervisors who would be watching and taking note of who was not singing. If you did not sing and participate, it meant your family was against the country and Ba'ath party and it brought trouble to your family.

Also, massive numbers of children from various schools were pooled together and kept in the public arenas in the heat of the sun to be trained to perform on-the-ground displays of various nationalistic themes such as the Iraqi flag or some artistic human representation of the Arab land or some Ba'athist concept. All the kids would be wearing special uniforms with colors to match their parts of the display. These displays were frequent and especially performed for occasions such as the birthday of the Ba'ath party or the anniversary of the revolution or when there were foreign dignitaries visiting Iraq. You had to participate in these events otherwise you would be bringing doubt on your sincerity and devotion to the party even though you were only a kid. Days of school were missed because of this training and performance. Children whose fathers, uncles or parents were part of the previous regimes were ridiculed and harassed as belonging to the former era, or the dark ages, referring mainly to the days of the monarchy, or they were accused of being reactionary and so on.

The Ba'ath menace caught you wherever you were: in kindergarten, high school, university, work, in the market and even on the bus where there were slogans and revolutionary literature. Whatever you did for a living, you had to prove that you were a passionate supporter of the revolution and join one of the Ba'ath organizations such as the party itself or affiliated unions like the union for women, the union for students and the union for youth. This affiliation gave you power against the highest authority at your school or job. Being a senior Ba'athist or even a normal level Ba'athist gave you authority over your teacher, boss and elders. For example, if you wanted to leave you job for a Ba'ath party meeting, then you could go out when you wanted for as long as you wanted; it did not matter whether this affected your work or the work of others. Your boss or supervisor had to approve that or else you, as a Ba'athist, could punish him and even get him fired.

Even worse, from their early days, the Ba'athists conducted a brutal campaign to eliminate their opponents and would-be opponents. Initially, their targets were mostly members of the former governments and some ex-members of the Ba'ath party or its earlier factions. However, what started as a small-scale campaign of eliminating opponents escalated into a systematic campaign of terror. The Ba'athists terrorized anyone who did not directly and overtly support their agenda, even people who simply did not want to involve themselves in politics. Within a few years, no one in Iraq could claim that he or she was politically "independent" or simply had no political affiliation. You either supported the regime openly and overtly or they branded you as an anti-revolutionary and punished you. If Aristotle described virtue as doing the common good, the Ba'ath regime defined it as serving them without any question or objection and your denying of all your principles for their purposes. Even ordinary people with no political aspirations soon learned to fear this new type of control, which Iraqis had not been used to.

Soon, the Ba'ath regime made and eradicated laws as they wished. Government became a tool for the Ba'ath party to pursue their repressive goals and control every soul and every breath in Iraq. Every week or so some bizarre law or new regulation took effect that further restricted our lives. It did not matter in Iraq what education and expertise one had to serve his country. Support of the regime and the revolution always overrode all other considerations. One had to join and support the Ba'ath party or face being fought and punished in every way imaginable. At that time, nearly every institution in Iraq became "nationalized" or was in the process of being nationalized. This meant it came under the control of the party. The private sector was severely diminished but still existed in these early days of Ba'ath rule.

Ba'ath rule disrupted the foundations of society and changed many norms and traditions. Their methods of dealing with people created an atmosphere of suspicion among ordinary citizens. Everyone thought that others were Ba'ath agents and were spying on them. Everyone was afraid to voice even the smallest criticism of the government. Also, senior people and people of good name were being ridiculed and disrespected by young Ba'athist gangs who were in charge of various offices. Moreover, the Ba'athists fought religious practices and made it impossible for people to worship their God. They banned many normal religious traditions. It became taboo and brought suspicion upon you to go to the mosque or to dress in religious attire or to even think about religion or discuss it.

Instead, the regime promoted their Ba'ath ideology and taught it as a supreme set of values.

The party and the revolution became more important than your dreams, your family, your country, and your religion and even more important than God. Moreover, if you needed to get anything done, you had to win the favor of some Ba'athist in the relevant office or administration. That was the best way and sometimes the only way to get your documents processed and things done. Otherwise, if you went by the rules, it would take weeks and months. In contrast, if you had a Ba'athist friend do it, it would be done in one day.

Additionally, there was an official party representative in every school, residential district, mosque, and club and even in the markets. These officials had so much authority and power to the point that some kids or even adults would revere these people more than their parents, their teachers and their elders. These officials used to spy on people and train others to spy; they observed all the activities of the population and reported them to the Ba'ath party. Ba'ath corruption and power abuse was widespread. For example, a decent man or woman would go to some office to conduct some business such as acquiring a birth certificate or a passport for their child. They would get mistreated and disrespected by some armed militia or they would be turned back because some Ba'athist took the day off for party obligations. And the process would take some three or four days of going and coming and being ridiculed and harassed. There was so much of this inefficiency and negativity.

In order to be impartial, however, one must say that the Ba'ath regime brought some advances in education and health care and made Iraq a modern state, especially in the late seventies and eighties. For example, the government instituted mandatory education for adults who had never gone to school. Thus, they made a serious effort to eradicate illiteracy. Also, they advanced the science curriculum and established several controlled-price clinics and hospitals for those who could not afford private health care. Moreover, they established free immunizations for all children. Education from kindergarten stage to university was free of charge, and when you finished university you were guaranteed employment, even though it may not have been your first choice in location or job type. They did other good things such as regulating bus fares and taxi fares, paving the main roads in Baghdad and things like that. Indeed they did a few good things and these are important contributions to the modernization of the country, and for that they deserve acknowledgement.

The majority of the Ba'ath members were from poor backgrounds and some like Saddam Hussein were actual murderers. It is well known

among Iraqis that President Saddam Hussein killed a family relative during a dispute a long time ago. Also, the Ba'ath party used him as a hit
man in the 1950s, and he participated in the assassination plot against the
prime minister. Poor and uneducated people were lured in with money
and power. They joined the Ba'ath party and they performed their dirty
work for them such as harassing and terrorizing decent families and killing
others in cold blood. Important offices in the government were being run
by gangs of young Ba'athists who knew nothing professionally and had
no respect for the law or due process. A few Ba'athists were indeed educated and dedicated to the cause of the party, but even they were being
slowly eliminated; many of them fled to Arab countries or Europe while
they could.

A few people joined the Ba'ath party because they sincerely believed
in its original nationalist ideology. But even they were disappointed by
the corruption and the anarchy that was taking place in the name of the
party. The Ba'ath party in its early years was a true representation of Ara-
bism and nationalism and there were many people who supported these
beautiful sentiments with passion not only in Iraq but also in other Arab
states. However, the Iraqi version of the Ba'ath was something else and
had deviated dramatically from its original aspirations and became cor-
rupted.

On the other hand, many simple people, especially in poverty-
stricken areas, were lured into joining the Ba'ath party by money, status,
and materialistic gains. Such people, who were without hope or any bright
prospect for their future, found refuge in the mass Ba'ath slogans. They
believed that the Ba'ath was going to be their savior, and indeed they
benefited from all the public programs that gave them access to education and healthcare and transportation, things which they did not have
before. However, in return the Ba'ath in effect took the souls of these
people and made them submit, through their allegiance, to all its devi-
ous demands. These people were recruited to the popular army and other
Ba'ath organizations and used for various revolutionary tasks the party
needed done.

Prominent Iraqi families did not join the party initially. Many of
them resisted and gave all sorts of excuses to the Ba'ath officials as to why
they could not join. But even some of them had to join eventually, because
of force or fear. If the party approached you to join and you refused, that
was considered an overt attack on the revolution and the party and auto-
matically made you a reactionary force, a traitor. Some people resisted
joining the party, but they suffered dearly. The Ba'ath was like a big wave
and it hit everyone and swept them away. Some people were able to cling

to their values and principles and refused to join the Ba‘ath; nevertheless, the wave hit them and damaged their lives somehow.

Thugs and criminals were running the country. The wealth from the oil industry was being diverted into private bank accounts for senior Ba‘athists in Western countries. Yet there were poor families and even some beggars in certain sectors of Baghdad. The Ba‘ath members and their families drove the latest model cars, American and German made. They had their designer clothes delivered from Paris and New York. Their women had special hairdressers come from Italy and France to be at their service. They had access to the best medical care anywhere in the world. They even had special chefs from famous places come to cater for them. The Ba‘athists thought of themselves as royalty or super human beings and the rest of the population as commoners, and they made themselves quite an elite materialistically even though they were nobody in the social stratum of the country.

To anyone who lived in Iraq in the 1970s and the 1980s, the word Ba‘athist is associated with greed, control, power without limits, being nobody, being above the law and being above everyone else. The party interests were always supreme. From my early childhood when I could first see, I knew Ba‘athists and their family members to be the ones who got preferential treatment in nearly everything in life. They never had to stand in line; they could just cut anyone off. They never needed to wait for any documentation or bureaucratic procedures. All their documents, be they school papers, university diplomas, travel documents and the like, were ready and done for them without any effort on their part. On many occasions, various streets of Baghdad would be closed for hours because some senior Ba‘athist was passing by or visiting someone in that area. There was no regard for the rest of the people who had to drive through these areas and conduct their daily business.

The Ba‘ath regime launched a war against the people of Iraq, which lasted throughout the 1970s and which the rest of the world community was silent about, long before they committed any international atrocities. The Ba‘athists were on a mission to strip Iraqi citizens of their humanity and their basic rights of peace, dignity and respect for human beings. They put people in prison without formal charges. They tortured and executed people on a massive scale. They suppressed all freedoms. They controlled what books and magazines people read. They controlled what people watched and listened to on television and radio. They banned short-wave radio. They restricted travel severely so that they could further control the exposure of their citizens to the outside world. I remember when there were blocks of time where no one was allowed to travel unless they were in the Ba'athist circle of influence. When travel was allowed at other times, certain individuals were banned from obtaining an exit visa which was necessary for any travel. Also, certain countries were off-limits, and travel was forbidden for certain classes of the population such as young college-aged men.

The Ba'athists particularly envied and hated people of status, wealth and education; they considered such people their enemies and a threat to their own rise and fake prestige and wanted to finish them. In addition to eliminating people with political aspirations, the Ba'athists also wanted to neutralize those of great accomplishments, whether intellectual or financial, or those who just had a good name, even when such people had no political goals. The Ba'athists were like savages who had come across a beautiful oasis. They destroyed so many things, and they ruined so many lives.

People were paralyzed and shocked by those thugs who were controlling their lives and introducing many restrictions on them and denying them the most basic freedoms. Iraq became a country where owning an old-fashioned typewriter was grounds for detention and perhaps execution. Iraq became a country where you were afraid to speak in front of your neighbors because they may be spying on you, or even in front of your own children because they may be questioned by the authorities without your knowledge. Iraq became the only country in the world where using your surname (family name) was illegal! All of Iraq became dissolute in Ba'ath ideology and slogans. All of Iraq was quickly turning into a machine to enslave and terrorize people and deny them the most basic dignity and human rights. It was in such an Iraq that this story took place: the story of Makki and Lydia, my parents.

CHAPTER 1

Baghdad 1971

Makki and Lydia, my parents, were the epitome of sincerity and honesty. They were lawful and sincere citizens who served their society and country. In any country in the world, they would have had a happy life. They would have been appreciated for their character, for their knowledge, and for all the services they provided their society. They would have been respected and cherished anywhere else, but not in Ba'athist Iraq where morality and principles were left behind for the sake of the party and the revolution.

My parents refused to support the Ba'ath corruption. They were among the first families in Iraq to be fought and terrorized by the Ba'ath regime. They fought the cruelty and the ruthlessness of the regime not with weapons, but with values and sincerity. They struggled to survive through the terrorizing events without bending to the Ba'ath. They stood by their principles. They were like diamonds, which fell into the hands of savages who did not know their value. They struggled to rise above the tide of the Ba'ath regime. They fought all the way. In the end, they were crushed by the wave of revolutionary madness.

My memories of Iraq today take me back to the early 1970s when I remember a happy, harmonious life. I remember my childhood days in my parents' house in an upscale neighborhood of Baghdad. In spite of the rapidly changing political atmosphere, Baghdad was a beautiful city. It was fun and cosmopolitan. The city lights were exhilarating and the crowds were exciting. Baghdad had many historic and modern attributes. There were traditional shops and markets as well as modern shopping centers. A trip to the shopping area Shari al Nahar was very exciting. Some of the independent merchants and owners of those stores had not yet been

13

hit by the nationalization frenzy. This old-fashioned shopping strip had so many narrow alleys lined with shops and small boutiques filled with all kinds of exciting goods.

As you walked and drove along the various boulevards and alleys, a great sense of history and heritage would strike you and capture your imagination. The elegant shrine of Algailani, the glittering shrines of Alkadimain, the Almustansirya University, and many ruins and archeological sites on the outskirts of Baghdad were only a few of the historic wonders of the city. It was a place that spoke of history and centuries of civilization.

In Baghdad, you could have traditional specialty food such as the instantly grilled fish *masgoof*, especially as you walked along Abu Nuas Boulevard, which overlooks the beautiful river Tigris. Alternatively, you could go for an elegant meal at five star restaurants and hotels. You could walk, ride a bus, take a taxi or drive your own car and visit many wonderful parks and arenas. People walked around seemingly happy. Going out for a walk in the early evening was especially popular for young people. We would stop to get ice cream and buy little things from the stores that still carried some imported chocolates. Such shop owners sold imported "most likely smuggled" English chocolates at very high prices. We used to pay approximately $1.50 for such a small luxury like a chocolate bar, three times what we pay in the U.S. thirty years later.

Baghdad also had the most enchanting summer nights. There is nothing in the world that compares to a summer evening in Baghdad. It was like a romantic dream. As the high daytime temperatures dropped, there would be a nice cool breeze in the outdoors especially in spots where there were many trees around. Many people enjoyed such evenings visiting and chatting with others in the gardens of their homes, drinking tea throughout the evening or having watermelon and grape and other summer fruits while surrounded by the beautiful scent of the *razqi* flowers. These small starry white flowers may be a member of the *Gardenia augusta* family but they are somewhat distinguished from other gardenias by their small size and sweeter fragrance. The *razqi* also was a lot more common in Baghdad than other gardenias.

In addition, Baghdad had several upscale neighborhoods with beautiful exquisite homes. People in Iraq enjoyed having beautiful homes. Unlike homes in Western countries where function and efficiency dictate the design, many homes in Iraq were pieces of art. People spent lots of money on making their homes unique and even extravagant. It was like a trustworthy investment because they did not invest their money in the government institutions for their lack of trust in the system.

Government offices such as ministries and official buildings were rather mighty with shining marbles and striking designs. These were modern buildings with many guards and checkpoints and monitoring cameras surrounding them. And the streets near them were polished and spotless. Similarly, residences of government officials were fantasy-like homes. They were something from another world. Even though many homes in Baghdad were beautiful, including my parents' home where I grew up, these governmental residences were very distinguished by their lavish ornaments and marbles from Italy and flowers from Paris and so on. They had special lighting effects and unique flowers normally not found in Iraq. Such flowers required a certain modified humidity and temperature and the equipment to ensure these special conditions was provided in the officials' homes. These homes were extravagant and too ornamented. They resembled a woman wearing too much make-up and too many pieces of fine jewelry. The roads leading to such homes were also exclusive and you could not drive by there, unless you lived nearby. There were guards who would stop you and ask what you were doing there. And God forbid if you did not stop or you failed to follow their commands; you would be shot.

Most homes in Iraq were custom built. Homes even of ordinary citizens were custom built and designed and there were a few "projects" where several homes looked alike. But for most well to do people, their homes were custom designed. At least that's what I saw. I must admit, I did not see the ugly neighborhoods of Baghdad, the slums. I am sure they existed then, and they do now. But I did not see them. My memory of Baghdad is of a beautiful city with lots of excitement.

*   *   *

Our house was beautiful and I had a happy life there, if only for a few years. The house was huge, at least from the viewpoint of a child. A tall fence surrounded the house. This was typical in Baghdad and in general in the Middle East. It was both for privacy and security. The fence itself was surrounded outside by trees and shrubs to create a prettier image and also for even more privacy. Inside, there were two big gardens and patios. I remember the gardens well as we used to play soccer there with my brothers and my cousins. We used to team up girls against boys. We also used to have water fights there during the brutal mid-day summer heat in Baghdad. We would be soaking wet in the heat. It was fun.

There was a narrow pathway that went around the house. It further separated the house from the street and created more peace and seclusion and calming shades. It was almost like a virtual fence inside the house. I think it was what I loved most about the design of the house. I used to walk with my dad along this narrow pathway which was filled with exquisite rocks and trees and flowers of many kinds. It was like having your own botanical garden at home.

Dad was a man of impeccable taste and he enjoyed these peaceful walks around the house admiring the trees and flowers and checking which ones needed care. He even took some of our visitors and relatives who were interested in gardening out to the walkway to show them these beautiful arrangements. Even though we had a gardener who took care of all those plants, Dad liked to look after them himself. He often watered them himself and told the gardener which ones needed care. Along this secluded walkway, which surrounded the house, there were the big luscious roses known as new dawn, which were bushier and bigger than the normal roses. These were mostly pink and sometimes they came in red. There were also bougainvillea trees with their countless brilliantly colored flowers, and citrus trees with their white flowers that filled the walkway with their sweet "citrusy" scent.

In the patios at the front entrance there was a little oasis of plants and flowers. This one had different kinds of cacti with their densely packed spines and intriguing shapes. Also aligned along the patio were little clay pots, which contained individually planted cacti and some little red flowers, which I cannot remember the name of. In the gardens, there were many other kinds of flowers of astonishing shapes and colors. There were rows of roses on two opposite sides of the garden. I recall most unusual lavender- and orange-colored roses in addition to the more common white, pink and red roses. On the other two sides, there was a beautiful constellation of many other kinds of flowers such as sunflowers, daisies, and wild carnations which were typically astonishing shades of pink such as salmon pink, luscious pink, dark pink, and pink and white stripes, and also plain white. They were beautiful.

My favorite flowers in the garden when I was a kid were the violas. They captured my little mind so much. I was quite taken by their unusual bicolor and tricolor combinations and their velvet-like appearance. I was intrigued by how flowers could be brown and black and dark red and navy blue and brilliant blue, side by side with bright yellow. I admired those tiny flowers so much. They were little and so colorful.

Schoolgirls in Baghdad, including my sisters and I, developed a culture of taking three or four freshly cut roses and giving those to our one or two favorite teachers. This was mostly in the spring when all the flowers blossomed and the weather was so beautiful in Baghdad. So, every morning we would be in the garden collecting flowers. Then, at school we would be in search of our favorite teachers to give them the flowers. My sisters and I did that as well as many of our friends. The teachers would be carrying those flowers all day with them from one classroom to another. They looked cute that way. The teachers enjoyed this attention from their students and were happy to receive such tokens of affection. My mother, herself a teacher in high school, would often come home with similar flowers. The flowers obviously would not last more than a few hours because they would have been deprived of water all day. My mom would say the girls in class gave her those flowers that morning. Secondary or high schools were segregated according to gender. So mom taught in a girls-only school and we attended a girls-only school.

Teachers received perhaps the most and best flowers on one particular day of the year. The first of March in Iraq was typically celebrated as *teachers' day*. Teachers were very well respected in Iraq. We as students revered our teachers and did all kinds of things to win their approval and attention. So we celebrated teachers' day and wanted to show our teachers how much we liked them. That day, classes would be off for half a day or even the whole day but we still went to school. Also, we were allowed on this occasion to come to school without our normal daily uniform but in our dressy clothes. There would also be cake and sweets for everyone. We would honor our teachers by giving them bouquets of flowers. This time, however, the flowers would be professionally prepared by one of the few but prestigious flower shops in Baghdad.

Actually, such flower shops were beautifully decorated and typically staffed by charming young men or women. The stores carried flowers that were not normally grown in Iraq such as tulips and gladioli and blue irises and some really large carnations. They were mostly imported flowers. For teachers' day, students would typically collect money from their class and one or two of the students would go to these magnificent and highly expensive flower shops to buy the flowers and bring them to school the next day. Those flowers would typically be luscious red gladioli also known as "red majesty;" they would be wrapped in cellophane and looked so appealing. Again, on teachers' day Mom would come home with such bouquets. It was so exciting.

Our house had beautiful architecture and a unique design but it was not extravagant. It was unlike many of the lavish homes one would see in Baghdad in the sixties and seventies. It had special features and design. It had elegant arches inside and out. Dad loved the arches and idealized them. They reminded him of Andalusian times. There was also an inner patio with a small pool and some small shrubs and tall trees. This unique design of traditional Mediterranean homes was something that my dad loved. The inner patio was nice. It brought peaceful feelings, light and fresh air into all the rooms surrounding it. It was a semi-outdoor seclusion inside the house. There were patches of shade from the tall trees within this little oasis.

The carport was covered with a grapevine. This was rather common in Baghdad, and it brought a beautiful shade and lots of mixed color fruit. There were dark luscious grapes and pale-green sour grapes, and we indeed collected the fruit. In fact we did make some juice, which we drank immediately on the same day so that it did not ferment and become alcoholic. Between the carport and the patios, there were exquisite rocks and marbles, and the brilliantly colored bougainvillea trees climbed on these rocky walls. Theirs were indeed the most beautiful, luscious colors of any plants. I still love those trees today.

Inside, the house was rather spacious too. There was a section of the house for us girls, a section for my brothers, a section for my parents, a huge section for various guest functions. It included two guest sitting areas, dining room overlooking the beautiful narrow walkway surrounding the house, and of course a special guest entrance. There was even a little room with special Middle Eastern setting and sometimes we used it as a reading room.

There were corners and hideouts inside and outside for all kinds of moods. My sister and I used to play with our cousins on the outdoor patios for hours and hours. I also used to study outside in the garden or in the inner patio or audition on my own for all the poetry we had to memorize for school. Walking around the house and sitting under the arches or on the patios, you were surrounded by enigmatic beauty, which aroused the mind and pleased the senses. When you walked about these gardens and walkways, you were in solitude, you could reflect and lose track of time, you felt like you were in a fantasy. You could lose yourself and go on daydreaming that you were in some romantic paradise and forget for a while that you were in Iraq under the mercy of the Ba'ath regime.

*　*　*

My parents were idealists indeed. That was perhaps their great shortcoming. They went through life as if it were an island of romance and perfection. They got tremendous happiness from their family life, traveling, helping others and being surrounded by the ones they loved and having the opportunity to excel in and enjoy their lives. They were very principle-oriented and assumed that everyone else should be as such. Although they were not political and had no political goals, they had strong opinions about the new regime. They did not like Ba'ath corruption, mis-management, inefficiency and so on and sometimes they made their sentiments known. And in some instances, they took a stand against the regime such as refusing to join the Ba'ath institutions and not giving in to the Ba'ath demands. Moreover, they incorrectly assumed that everyone else was going to spell out their disgust of the Ba'ath. Their sincerity and kindness made them naïve and this combination was simply incompatible with the viciousness and the ruthlessness of the Ba'ath regime.

My parents' aspirations and lifestyle of pursuing dignified happiness and enjoying a beautiful life with their family and serving their country was reminiscent of the fantasy idealism depicted in the well-known poem by Gibran called *Almawakib,** a poem which my dad loved and read often:

> Have you taken the forest, as I have?
> A home
> but not the palaces
> So you followed the small rivers
> And you climbed (the mountainous) rocks
> Have you bathed
> with scent and perfume?
> And wrapped yourself with light
> And have you taken wine at dawn?
> In glasses of celestial delight
> Have you sat in the afternoon
> as I have?
> Under the leaves of the vine trees
> Grapes, dancingly leaning
> Just like golden chandeliers
> They are aliment for the hungry
> They are honey and perfume
> And eternity for whoever seeks it.

They were truly an enchanting couple. Both were educated and highly sophisticated. My father had received his education in the United Kingdom in the 1940s, during the Second World War, and spoke English fluently. In just a few years after his return to Iraq in the early fifties, he became chief director and later deputy minister at one of the major government agencies in the ministry of communications. So he was in an official government post. He brought his talent and knowledge into this agency. His talents and achievements made him quite a star. He represented Iraq in various international conferences and symposia all over the world.

*Personal translation from Almawakib

His study at home was full of pictures and awards from various conferences and assemblies. He enjoyed tremendous successes and recognition
in the fifties and sixties. Moreover, he also ran his own private consulting
business and enjoyed many successes there too.

He was kind and very well respected by everyone who knew him.
Many colleagues respected his talent and sincerity and liked his style. He
had a charming, likable personality, which attracted people around him
all the time. He also was social and amiable and enjoyed the company of
others. Kindness flowed out of his heart. He was handsome and had great
style.

After the Ba'ath party took over in 1968, things changed dramatically and almost all professions became "nationalized." However, this did
not mean nationalized for the interest of the country's economy as one
may infer. It meant politicization and total control by the Ba'ath officials
over every aspect of all professions; it meant Ba'athists in responsible positions even when they were unqualified. New rules and regulations came
into effect that limited the possibility of my dad keeping his private business, so he decided to close it to avoid hassle with the new government.
However, he kept his official government post then because the regime
had not yet infiltrated each and every office.

My father was honest and truthful. And this was a matter of black
and white to him. When he saw many aspects of the corruption that came
with the new regime, he took a firm stand against it. He was a man of
principles and he was tough with the new Ba'athist gangs; he did not give
in to their demands and punished their corruption. There was an incident where they forged his signature for some official government transactions in order to make some personal gain for themselves. My father
was so upright; he reprimanded those people and warned them that he
would take them to court for forging his signature, for the violation of
his office and tampering with various materials in it, and for acting in his
name without his knowledge.

In another incident, Dad was abroad for a few weeks for some conference or symposium. When he got back to work, he went to his office
as usual. He attempted to open the door but noticed that the lock had
been broken. It looked like it had been smashed with some heavy object,
and the door had been left open. Normally Dad and other senior personnel
locked their offices. This was normal practice because of the nature of
their work and to maintain confidentiality. Dad went in and saw that his
office had been ransacked. All the cabinets where he normally stored files
and other valuables looked like they had been opened and rifled. And it
appeared that some items and files had been removed.

Dad was shocked to see that mess. It was the first break-in at his office, ever. He called his assistants and the guard of the building to see if they had seen anything or if they knew about this. The building itself was secure and had several guards at the outside monitoring who entered and left; in addition, there was an attendant inside to oversee the general affairs of the offices. No outsiders were let in without permission. The guards reported no incident where any outsiders had broken in. It appeared to Dad and his assistant that this was the work of someone inside the office. Most likely, it was someone who had normal access to the building itself. He knew that this attack must have been led by the senior Ba'athists at the office. This was a serious violation and aggression because Dad was the head of his division, the second or third in command in the ministry. And not many outsiders had access to that area of the office headquarters except the Ba'ath party members—they had the power to override any regulation or authority which applied to ordinary people. Dad informed the building manager and his boss that he was starting an investigation into this attack on his office. He was speaking about fingerprints and wanted to question several people about their possible knowledge of or involvement in this incident. He spent the rest of the day cleaning up and putting things back in order. He also ordered the door to be repaired on the same day, and there was a new lock placed on the door. Ultimately, the investigation was not pursued and the events were covered up.

So from the beginning my father opposed the corruption of the regime; he did not accept any of it in his division. He was horrified by the turn the country was taking. Sometimes he spoke his mind about it, but often he was prudent. But he was not going to change his sincere and truthful style for the Ba'ath regime.

* * *

Though an engineer by profession, my father enjoyed art and poetry, classical Iraqi music and the traditional heritage of the older Baghdad. In fact he often took us children to the Baghdadi Museum to make us learn and appreciate this heritage. In the years that we traveled abroad, he took us to museums and showed us beautiful things. He would tell us stories about the old days in Baghdad and the neighborhood where he grew up. He would also tell us about living in the United Kingdom during the Second World War: about not having water, about the bombing raids, about how the war affected the people there, and about the homes and flats destroyed and turned to rubble.

He was a loving father. He encouraged us to appreciate our talents. For example, my sisters, Dalia and Zeena, were into art and painting. He praised them and took an interest in their budding talent. He bought them all their painting tools and supplies and admired their then amateur work. When my brothers were younger, they were into science. My dad arranged for one of the extra rooms upstairs in the roof to be their "laboratory" where they used to play and create all kinds of mess but away from the house. He had bought them all kinds of science play sets and kits from the United States and from Europe and even some tools and other materials to develop their creativity and talents. He ensured that each of us had a collection of books. My sister and I as children had so many stories and books for our age. And Dad himself had a library in his office at home; it was not huge but contained rather exquisite books on art and history, and some on poetry; and there were lots of engineering books and journals. I remember spending time with him in his study looking at magazines and books and an unusual collection of pens.

Although my dad was not into the house affairs at all and did not know how to cook or do anything in the kitchen, he took care of us and looked after our needs. I remember that my sister Dalia was always very skinny so she got much attention for that and my father worried about her all the time. He would sit daily with her and convince her to drink milk every night; he would give her all kinds or rewards for drinking the milk and checked with her daily as to whether she had drunk the milk. I did not get the same attention because I was not skinny.

Also, both my sister Dalia and I used to really like to go to the bookshops and stationery stores to buy little things such as pens and stationery and fancy paper. That was a favorite treat for us. My father was patient with us and used to take us to the bookshop, give us money and wait for us while we went in to buy our materials. In fact he knew how much my sister and I loved these colorful books and pictures and small items. He frequently brought us many of those things that we liked on his way back from work, and he would often surprise us with these little gifts. When I remember that, I think it was sweet and so kind of him to take all this time to satisfy our demands as kids. He also respected each of us and treated us kindly. In fact, I do not recall ever being yelled at by him. Maybe this is because I was such a good child, or that Dad was already in his mid forties when I was born. Or maybe it is just because I only spent a few years with him.

*　*　*

I should like to think that I take after my mother, not only in her looks but also in other attributes: her selfless caring, her unwavering resilience, and her tremendous hospitality. She was quite an extraordinary person. I have powerful images in my memory of her welcoming smile and resilient devotion to her family, not just to us her children but also to her sisters and brothers. She was like the epicenter of the family, our own and all the extended family. She was the oldest among her sisters and brothers and she was involved in all of their affairs and helped in some of their problems and missions. She was like their godmother even though her mother was still alive then. She had magical solutions to family problems and matters and she stepped ahead of others always to remedy a family crisis. She was very generous and ready to give and helped many poor families.

Her hospitality was overflowing. She was a shining hostess and threw the most exquisite dinner banquets. Even my Dad was surprised by the elegance and decorations she would put together for guests and family, some of whom were diplomats and former government officials. Those were evenings of glamour and style and most wonderful company. I remember the house with glittering lights all over. We would have beautiful clothes on and my mom would have prepared elegant dinners. I used to help her with decorating the dining table with lace and golden ribbons and colorful dinner napkins and beautiful silverware and china. We lit some candles. It was so exciting. At least that is how it felt for me as a child.

Mom had gathered an exquisite collection of artifacts and precious objects from all over the world as she traveled extensively with my father. These beautiful objects were displayed in many places in the house in special showcases and in various cabinets and corners of the house. The house was full of objects and artwork from so many countries, like precious crystals, dolls, small statues, fine fabrics and souvenirs from Japan, India, China, Sweden, Egypt, Australia, the United States and more. I was exposed to these impeccable things of exquisite colors and strange shapes from the moment I opened my eyes. There were also beautiful rugs, a golden engraved plate from the nineteenth century, coins from the days of the Ottoman empire, carved wood stands from India, traditional Iraqi pottery and so on. There was also a special copy of the Holy Quran, the Muslim holy book, handwritten in gold ink and covered with the most beautiful fabric. It was an exquisite manuscript and so strikingly handsome. It was an official gift that my father had received from the Shah of Iran who had hosted some international conference and given various gifts to the delegates from each country.

The collection of beautiful objects around the house gave you the feeling of living in a museum. And Mom remembered the story of each object, where she had bought it or who had given it to her or to my father as a gift. I remember standing in front of the displays for hours looking at these things, admiring their striking beauty and making up stories about each doll and each miniature house and each picture. It was so educational and intriguing to my little mind, and it was so enjoyable.

My mother studied history and social studies at Queen Alia University in Baghdad. So she understood and respected various cultures and she expected us to know the values of the things we had at home and the significance of many historical events. She was a school director and a high school teacher. She had a passion for history and Arab nationalist issues. She was outspoken and a fighter for her principles. In her college days, she led her fellow students in marches to protest the massacres of Palestinians in 1948 as well as the Portsmouth accord, a 1948 agreement between the British government, which maintained interests in and control over Iraq, and the Iraqi monarchy.

She was detained by the government for protesting and leading the students in these marches, which disrupted Baghdad and aroused nationalist sentiments in the city. The students then were passionate about Arab nationalism and often went on strike. When she was detained she was asked about her role in these protests. The university placed her on probation because of her political activities. And she was allowed to come back to the university only after her father was forced to sign an affidavit that she would not participate in political acts again and to pay a fine of 1000 Iraqi dinars. This was a big sum of money in 1948. Paying the money, he defended her saying that his daughter spoke against the foreign control over Iraq—she did not speak against her country.

My mother loved teaching and her students, and at some point she was promoted to school director. In the late 1960s as soon as the Ba'athists took power, my mother had firsthand experience of their corruption and abuse of power. As a school director of many years experience, she treated all the teachers in the same way, not giving preference to anyone for her Ba'athist affiliation. Mom had direct confrontations with senior Ba'athists at the school who wanted preferential treatment for themselves and their relatives because they were Ba'athists or they were related to senior government members. My mother, being feisty, outspoken and principled, did not give in to such demands. She was opposed to and appalled by the abuse that the Ba'athists had brought to all professions and institutions, even schools. As a result of her stance, she lost her position as a director; however, she remained a teacher and always loved her profession. Later in her teaching years she conducted various seminars to discuss the state of Arab nationalism; she gave talks and led various discussions. These meetings were attended by colleagues, students and various officials from the ministry of education. She inspired her students and taught them with sincerity and passion. Many of her students loved her and were inspired by what they learned.

Mom was happy to be a mother and a wife in addition to being a teacher. She was so devoted to her home and her children and her husband. She kept the house immaculate and welcoming. She made a beautiful environment for us. Her priority in life was to make a happy home and to give dad and us a feeling of well being. In fact, even if you did not know who lived there, when you walked around inside the house you would sense this love and devotion by looking around at her touches all over the house. She displayed family portraits: of my grandparents, of relatives in the old days of Baghdad, of Dad in his international conferences and at special functions, of my grandfathers, and of others. She also took meticulous care of us. She wanted to bring out the best in us. She wanted us to shine and expected us to excel.

When I was in kindergarten, there was a special event at our school one day. The minister of education and various officials and aides visited our school. I was chosen to greet the minister and his delegation by carrying a tray of sweets and offering the sweets to each of the guests. Mom made a beautiful red dress for me and I wore it on that occasion. There was a picture in our house, which Mom had displayed, of me in that dress carrying the tray of sweets as I was walking to greet the guests. I would not have remembered that event if it had not been for that 8 × 10 picture which was placed in a big frame and hung on the wall. Also, when I was in sixth grade, I participated in a play. And for the play, the teacher asked me to get a white dress for my role. I went home and told Mom about it. She made a flattering dress for me. It had lace and pearls and flowers. She even made a matching hair band for me. It was beautiful.

My parents' love and dedication to each other was unusual. It was like a romantic novel. It was like perfection. It was admirable even to their friends and colleagues. How they met was a beautiful love story in itself. It was rather enchanting and a little funny especially considering those were the early 1950s. In fact, they told us that story over and over and we were so excited to hear about it each time when we were kids. They met while Mom was in her third year in university and Dad had just gotten back home from England after completing his education there and been assigned to Queen Alia University as a junior professor.

There was typically a beginning-of-the-year banquet where the returning students and faculty met and the new students were introduced to the others. Many of the students were dancing and singing and having a great time. Mom was sitting charmingly with her friends. Dad noticed Mom at the party for her beauty and her reserved graceful personality, at the party and he was quite taken by her. He introduced himself and talked to the group and to her; he admired her a lot. It was love at first sight, for him at least. He was bold about it. He kept approaching her over the next few days to the point where she got annoyed and screamed at him to leave her alone.

Considering this was the early 1950s, his bold approach was a bit aggressive for a semiconservative society. But he was persistent and kept insisting on meeting her. He would go and sit in her classes, even though he was faculty. He got encouragement from the other professors; most of them were men and they would let him in their classes so that he could see her in support of his mission so that he could see her. Unlike some lectures here in the west that I have been to in school, university classes and lectures in those days, and even today, in Iraq were more structured and not open for attendance by anyone. So for Dad to go and sit in her classes was strange. He would go there to see her and maybe say a couple of words. He would go to the dormitories where she and all the women whose homes were far away or out of town would stay in during the school year. He would go there and wait for her to come and go, and finally on one of those days he proposed.

This was even more shocking to my Mom. In Iraq then, and even today, you did not propose to a girl directly. It was usually done through a third party like a friend or a family member. But the most common way to propose was for the parents of the man to pay a proposal visit to the parents of the woman. The girl herself would not be the first to receive the formal proposal. Dad was so innocent, and he had no clue what the norms of proposing were as he had lived abroad for most of his youth, not to mention the fact that he had practically raised himself. He was not exactly an expert on the protocol of proposing. His mother passed away shortly after he was born and his father passed away a few years later when Dad was six or seven. He lived with his grandmother for a few years; then she passed away too, and he lived with his older brother until he was seventeen or eighteen and then went abroad. So when he proposed to Mom directly, she was shocked. She yelled at him and told him how dare he propose to her directly and that he should go talk to her family and that he should know better.

Dad acted very quickly. He indeed went to her parents, who lived in northern Iraq then, and proposed formally. Her father in turn had to check out my Dad. So he, my grandfather, went to Baghdad to ask his friends and acquaints about my dad and his family. After several days they all agreed and there was an engagement party for my parents. This was during Mom's last year of university, they got married after her graduation. My parents said that their wedding party was rather simple. But I do remember their beautiful wedding portrait. They were so charming.

My father came from a prominent, well-known family in Baghdad with a legacy of holding political, diplomatic and other high-profile positions. His decision to marry a woman from outside the family and outside Baghdad provoked surprise and criticism from his extended family, his cousins and distant uncles and aunts. They were very protective of my father and they wanted him to marry with their guidance and approval. They really watched out for him and wanted him to make the right decision, especially because he grew up without his parents and in a way raised himself. They genuinely wanted to find a suitable choice for him. It was generally expected that he would marry within the family. This is a tradition in Iraq. Whom you marry should not really be based solely on love and admiration; you must also consider the social implications of your choice. In other words, there are certain "accepted" or "approved" families whom you can marry into. You don't just find a love and get married. Your love is accommodated as long as it is with someone from within these accepted families.

I really cannot say that in those days, the 1950s, there were "arranged marriages" in Iraq. It is a myth and a misconception here in the West that all marriages in the Middle East are arranged and somehow oppressive. In fact, arranged marriages, as depicted here in the West, are uncommon in the Middle East. They are practiced more in South and East Asian cultures. The overwhelming majority of marriage choices in Iraq were, and still are today, supervised by the parents of the bride and the groom.

Anyway, Dad was such a charmer; and he was rather successful and very much liked by his large extended family, so it was likely that some of his relatives wanted him to marry their daughters. Although marrying first and second cousins was common in those days in Iraq and throughout the Middle East, Dad was against it and would never have considered it. Still there were many other suitable women distantly related to him or from other prominent high-profile families in Baghdad, and he was expected to marry from these women.

My mother came from a simple, decent family from northern Iraq. Her family was much simpler and humbler than my Dad's and it was closely knit. Women in northern Iraq were known for their beauty; they had fair complexions, a feature that men in the Middle East like very much. It was the inter-ethnic marriages between Arabs, Kurds, Armenians, and Turks that produced these beautiful women. Although my Mom's family was well known for their good name and generosity locally in their small town, they were not well known in Baghdad. So my father's relatives were surprised by his marriage decision and kept asking him who this woman was whom he wanted to bring into the family and why he couldn't marry someone from Baghdad.

Actually, I must say that Baghdadis—the residents of Baghdad—in general, when I lived there, and even today, felt a sort of superiority over people from the rest of the towns in Iraq. Like residents of all big cities, they thought that they were better and more sophisticated because they lived in modern Baghdad. It was like a status symbol. Considering all these details, it was clear to my Dad that his marriage was not really welcomed by many of his relatives. But Dad was so innocent, and he was bewildered by all this fuss about his marriage. He persisted and told everyone, I love Lydia. She is my life. She is so beautiful. She is sweet and I am marrying her. I am not going to marry anyone else. That was considered bold action in those days. And indeed, initially Mom and Dad did not feel much enthusiasm about their marriage from the family; but then things changed quickly and everyone came to love my mother and admire her. They were impressed by her kindness, style, and etiquette.

Not only were my parents' backgrounds contrasting, their personalities were also contrasting. My mother was feisty, emotional, fiery, and impulsive. She absolutely could not hold back her anger and her opinion no matter who was there in front of her. If someone upset her or insulted her or was crude with her in any way, she would respond fervently, immediately and in the most forceful way. My father, on the other hand, was calm, solid, and conducted his matters with more wisdom and far-sightedness. He was analytical, he thoroughly thought through the consequences of his actions and planned things in the most organized way. He tried not to get upset about things in the first place. He would tell Mom, for example, Why do you care what so and so said about you and so on?

Mom was also extremely sentimental. She, for example, had saved and stored mementos from the birth of each of us. She had boxes and sacks filled with such things. For example, there was the blanket in which my first brother was received when he was born. Also, there was the towel that she used to wrap him with after first bathing him. There was a dress that I wore on my first birthday. She had recorded the dates on which we all spoke our first words, the days we walked for the first time, and so on. Mom loved these motherly things and she was so happy talking about them. It was rather funny how attached she was to them; Dad used to make fun of her sentimentality. Dad, on the other hand, was practical and saved all the vital house documents in the most organized and efficient manner.

Their contrasting personalities and styles complemented each other in the most beautiful way as they dealt with daily life matters so differently. I think they were funny and charming and really stunning especially when they dressed up to go to parties and banquets. I used to sit with my Mom as she put on her beautiful gowns and jewelry and admire her looks and style.

Both Mom and Dad enjoyed their travels and had loads of pictures and movies from those trips. In those days there were no home video cameras. Instead, we had some sort of movie camera that allowed you to record; then the film had to be sent abroad to the Kodak laboratory for developing and then sent back to us. We played the films in a special movie projector. We would sit together to watch them and look at the photographs and listen to stories about their travel adventures. Since my childhood, Mom and Dad have told us about beautiful places in the world that they visited: the Great Wall of China, Niagara Falls, the Taj Mahal, the Golden Gate Bridge, the Eiffel Tower, the Pyramids, Big Ben, Venice, and so on. I have seen pictures and postcards and some miniatures of these wonders of the world and longed to visit them myself.

My parents were also like eternal soul mates. They pleased each other in the most loving ways and were happy in the company of each other. They were truly enchanting. We celebrated the anniversaries of both their wedding and their engagement over the years. In fact, we had a party for their twenty-fifth wedding anniversary, when Dad bought Mom a silver plate engraved with their names. They had so many portraits taken at their anniversaries over the years.

While I am sure they had their arguments and disagreements like all couples and parents in the world, these must have been infrequent, or maybe they were simply conducted out of my sight. All in all, they always respected each other and cared for each other. I do not recall either of them insulting the other in public or private no matter what the circumstances were. Their love and devotion created a happy home for all of us children. Having first opened my eyes in such a loving and sophisticated environment, I have come to appreciate every moment in my life and know the importance of family integrity and marriage, and I think this is a major factor in the success of my personal life.

I enjoyed only a few years of this harmony and happiness with my parents and siblings. The idyll ended swiftly and abruptly over the period of a few years. Traumatic events took place one after another and displaced all this happiness. My innocent, dreamy childhood was shattered and smashed. Our family endured first grade terror and injustice at the hands of the Ba'ath regime in their first few but vicious attacks on prominent decent families. Life in Iraq turned into a horror which kept getting worse as the weeks went by.

CHAPTER 2

Enigma

My aunt Najia and her family had a serious car accident one night on their way back from the airport. The rain in winter was sometimes severe and the roads were slick. Not all the roads in Baghdad were well paved, and some roads were not even lit. Another car smashed into them, and theirs turned over. They all struggled to exit the car. My uncle and my cousin and others in the car were injured. Their injuries, however, were not too severe. But my aunt Najia got the worst of it. In those days no one wore seatbelts. I do not even know whether their Mercedes had seatbelts or not. My aunt was thrown out of the car and then struck by it. She was unconscious and it was a miracle from God that she did not die. She had several broken bones, she could not sit up or walk, and her neck was injured. She was hospitalized for many weeks in the Rahibat hospital. This was a private hospital staffed by Catholic nuns as nurses and was one of the best in Baghdad; it was perhaps one of the few institutions that escaped Ba'athist "nationalization." The hospital had an excellent reputation and it was rather nice inside.

We learned of the accident when my cousin called us. He was crying as he spoke to my Mom and told her what happened. The accident was a dramatic event for the family. We were all shaken by what happened to my aunt. There is a saying in Iraq that when such an event happens to you, where you are nearly dead but still alive, that God gives you a new life. We kept saying that to her family. We were glad that she was alive and we knew that her recovery was going to be long. My aunt Najia was good looking and elegant. She was stylish, followed the latest fashions and meticulously took care of her looks. It was sad to see what happened to her. She was bandaged and bed-ridden for weeks and weeks. She could barely sit up in the bed.

30

My Mom looked after her sister with love and compassion and she spent some days with her in the hospital. And in a way, we looked after our cousins and tried to cheer them up while their mom was in hospital. We did our best to make them feel okay. They used to come over to our house and have lunch or dinner and sometimes sleep over. And we did our homework together as they were the same age as my sister and I and we were in the same level in school. The whole extended family spent many evenings visiting my aunt at the hospital. We were glad that she was recovering, albeit slowly. We cheered her progress when she was able to sit in the bed on her own (that took a few weeks), and we were happy for each step towards recovery. We spent many such evenings in the hospital. And that made us all feel better, even aunt Najia herself; we brought her smiles and laughter and made her days in the hospital easier.

On one of those nights at the hospital visiting aunt Najia, we got ready to leave as visiting hours were over. We were all on our way out of the hospital when my Mom asked my older sister, Zeena, to ride with my other aunt, Mona, who was also visiting her sister, so that she would not have to drive alone. And my mother told Aunt Mona to drive close behind us so that the two vehicles would not be traveling alone. The hospital was quite far from where we lived; the roads were not well lit, and the way back home went through small streets, rather than highways. My Mom told Aunt Mona to drive to our house first, drop my sister off and meet us there, and then go to her house later, which was close to our house. My mother was so caring for everyone. She was like the godmother of all her family. She was being cautious and did not want my Aunt Mona to be driving alone at night. Those were days of fear in Baghdad because of the serial killer Abu Tubar. Just the mention of his name brings back feelings of fear and alarm.

Abu Tubar (literally, the "man with the ax" or the "one carrying an ax") was his title or the nickname that he was known by. He was the mysterious serial killer of Baghdad in the early seventies who murdered whole families together and marked the walls with their blood. He was vicious and savage like an animal. He chopped people up and beheaded them, dismembered them; he threw parts of their bodies all over the house. The crime scenes were ugly and bloody. Baghdadis, the citizens of Baghdad, had never seen such a savage series of crimes before, at least in the recent past. In fact, Baghdad used to be relatively safe; such things did not happen. There were some crimes motivated by robbery and there were some rape cases and some murders, but these were rare and very isolated events and they certainly were not of such a serious nature and systematic brutality. People were disgusted by this man, who demonstrated so much hate and sickness toward whole families, and who took out his rage and wrath even on women and children.

These Abu Tubar crimes were serious and everyone in the city was occupied with worry and fear. You never knew where or when he would strike. People were fearful and cautious and did not go out alone. The lively city of Baghdad was paralyzed. A sense of doom spread over all homes. Many homeowners trimmed bushes and trees around their houses to keep the area clear of hideouts and added more lights and left them on all night to feel safe. No one went out by himself or herself, no one stayed out late. People came home as soon as they could; they locked their doors and just wanted to be safe. The authorities were seemingly powerless in the face of this thug. Everyone was talking about Abu Tubar and the events that had rocked the city and brought it to such a fearful state.

The typical crime of Abu Tubar would start with a suspicious phone call by him or one of his "aides." He picked times when people were alone at home. The caller would engage the would-be victim in a useless conversation, threatening and cursing, and then there would be a knock on the door. The victim or their child might answer the door and Abu Tubar, masked and strong and carrying his bloody ax, would overpower the victim or her children and commence his bloodshed. The crime scenes were often marked with vengeful words or comments written on the walls in the blood of the victims. He also often killed people and dumped them in some remote area of Baghdad.

The time around these crimes was a terrorizing era. We were so scared of this killer and I had so many nightmares about him. I kept imagining him as a scary, violent man holding his ax and running after people. The city was in a state of alarm about him. The authorities searched homes and cars randomly to look for him. And on some occasions they announced a curfew for the city to prevent the spread of these murders and maintain control. People were even discussing the issue daily with their friends and neighbors and colleagues. He seemingly killed people with rage and vengeance. He was not a typical thief even. In most cases he did not steal anything, but he did wreck the places after killing his victims. So it was obvious that he did not kill people to steal.

There were all kinds of rumors about who he was, that he was a crazy man or that he was born retarded and was not treated well by his family. There were several television programs about him and his profile and even some featuring eyewitnesses who thought they might have seen him. There were reports on what he would look like with a beard or without a beard and in various costumes and clothes. There were shows giving out safety instructions to people and even call-in shows where people could phone in and ask the police about what to do if they saw him. Also, the police established hotlines to report anything suspicious. People were shaken by this monster and took all kinds of precautions such as not walking alone and not driving alone, which is what my Mom insisted my aunt do that night at the hospital.

* * *

The night that we were coming back home from the hospital, I was with my parents in the car. We drove through the back streets and it was frightening. I saw the silhouette of many big trees although the streets were dark. I kept imagining that Abu Tubar would all of a sudden emerge from behind a tree and butcher us with his ax. Then I felt better as we hit the main road leading away from the hospital because there were more lights and cars.

Initially my aunt was following us and I kept watching for them. But then my aunt sped up and we lost her about halfway to home; in the end, she arrived ahead of us. We got home about 8 P.M. or so. We saw a commotion at the house. We were alarmed. We thought something had happened to my aunt or my sister. Then, we saw that my Aunt Mona was angrily arguing with a man outside the house and there was a taxi parked at the driveway that led into the house. Officials taxis had a particular paint job in terms of design and color to indicate that they were licensed and would not overcharge. This was indeed a sign of the progress that the Ba'ath regime brought to Baghdad. So when we saw the car parked at the house it was obvious that it was a taxi. Our neighbors had been out too and had joined us, and some passersby had stopped also.

My parents jumped out of the car. They were afraid of what might have happened, that someone might have been hurt.

"Mona, Zeena, are you ok?" Mom asked. "What happened?"

"Makki, Lydia—look, this man is a taxi driver," my aunt said. "He is waiting here for someone named Hamid. He told me that Hamid was inside the house and that he has been waiting for Hamid for nearly an hour."

My parents were alarmed.

"What?" my Dad demanded. "What man? How did he get in?"

"I don't know," my aunt replied. "The Nasers' [our neighbors] were so kind they have already called the police and they waited here with us. Let's wait here and not enter the house."

Mr. Naser greeted my parents and told them that the police were on their way.

Dad turned to the taxi driver and said, "Who are you? What is your name?"

"Sir.... Mr.... I do not know anything," the man stammered. "I am only a driver, I do not know anything about it...."

Then he became nervous and afraid. "I picked up this man in the Alkarada district," he continued. "I do not know him. He first asked me to stop at a pharmacy. I waited for him there. I do not know what he did in the store. Then he came back and told me to drive to this house. He got in through the main gate. I saw him go through the main gate and I do not know whether he got in the house and I am just waiting for him here. It has been over an hour and he has not come back. I need to go home, I have been waiting for a long time. Please go find him. He has not paid me yet."

My parents were worried and stunned to hear this. They thought, What kind of a story was that? The house was secure and our neighborhood was safe and upper class. We had not had a break-in ever. They could not tell whether the man was being truthful or had just made up the story just to create a stir. But the outer gate was indeed open and gave the impression that someone had gotten in. Most homes in Iraq had an outer gate and a fence. It was for privacy and security. Typically you would walk a few steps, or in some homes longer, from the outer gate to the main entrance of the house. The gate was usually high but you could see through it because it was constructed as a decorative grille. Normally, we kids would play inside the gate and the fence and never on the street. This way we would be safe. That night we waited outside on the street until the police arrived shortly after.

The police questioned the taxi driver about his story. They detained him and took him to the local station. Our neighbor, Mr. Naser, told the police that earlier that evening some strange things had happened.

"I was sitting out on the porch," he told them and I saw a man standing near Mr. Makki's house. The man was there by the house for a long time, looking through the gate and over the fence intrusively. He was close to the gate but he did not open the gate. Mr. Naser further continued: I became suspicious of his behavior and I came over and asked him, 'Can I help you; what do you want? The family is not here at the moment.'

"The man was startled and said, 'No thank you, I think I have the wrong address,' and he walked away. But he did not go far. I saw him go to the guard of the next-door duplex homes. And he was talking to the guard."

Later, the police went to ask the guard next door about what happened. Adjacent to our house, there were two small homes or a duplex that my parents owned and were trying to rent to a couple of families. The duplex was brand new and had just been completed, and it was being shown to various people interested in renting it. It was small but rather cute, and although it was in the immediate vicinity of our house it was not attached to it. The two small homes had their own garage and entranceway and their own little garden. There was a guard who was contracted to live in the duplex until it was rented; he would show the homes to visitors and potential tenants.

The police asked the guard, Mr. Mahmood, if anyone had shown up to look at the homes that evening. Mr. Mahmood was worried when he saw the police.

"Oh God, what happened?" he immediately asked. "Did something happen to Mr. Makki's family?"

Mr. Mahmood actually liked us and he was a kind man. He looked after the homes well and he respected my parents. The police told him that they were investigating a possible break-in in our house.

"Yes indeed," he told the police, "a man came and said that he was interested in looking at the homes. So I let him in and showed him around both homes as I normally would."

"What did he look like?" a policeman asked.

The guard gave a similar description to Mr. Naser's.

"I showed him around," Mr. Mahmood continued. "We walked through the bedrooms and the living areas and then he told me he was just going to walk around and look some more on his own. So I said okay and I left him. I went downstairs to make some tea. A while later, I noticed that he was taking a long time. I went to look for him. I looked all over the home but could not find him. Then I went to look upstairs and saw the door to the roof was open."

Most homes in Iraq had a roof which was like another level of the house, almost like a patio on top of the house. This Mediterranean design was common in the Middle East, especially in Iraq, and had special use on summer nights: many people slept on their roof patios. They also had high fences and thus were semi-private locations. People typically slept there because the summer nights brought a lovely breeze, and it was much nicer than sleeping indoors. The roof also served other functions: people placed their laundry line there to get the clothes sun-dried, which was more a common way of drying clothes at that time than using electric dryers.

"I was surprised at where I found him," the guard further continued. "The man was on the roof level, but he was looking over at Mr. Makki's house, which was visible from the roof here—the roof overlooks the gardens and the whole west side of their home. I asked the man, 'What do you want? I thought you were looking at these homes?' He did not answer;

he just walked downstairs fast and went out. I followed him a few steps and I said, 'Hey … Mr., sir. Are you interested in renting or what?' But he was already outside. Then he disappeared into one of the shops on the main street. I am very worried now. I wish I had had a way of stopping him.'

The police also searched our house. It took a long time, as the house was big and had many hideouts, the gardens, the roofs and so on. Some police officers were actually disoriented in the house. Some rooms were connected and formed a circle and there was the inner patio around which a few rooms were situated. The upstairs of the house was connected via a smaller roof. It was confusing for these men who had not been there before. They would enter some place and leave it, only to go back to the spot where they began because of the circular design. So my Dad went with them to show them the way.

We all thought that the man could be hiding anywhere inside the house. There were some fourteen rooms with all kinds of closets and storage areas. We waited outside in the carport. It was a cold night but we had to stay outside. Our giant house seemed scary to me. I was very frightened. Someone strange might have broken into our home. He might still be there; perhaps he was going to harm us. Then, after a seemingly long wait, the police came out and said that there was no one in the house. They could not find this man named Hamid or anyone else. They stayed with us for a couple of hours and told us to look around and see if anything was stolen or damaged. We searched a lot. The house was big. And for me as a child it was huge. I was afraid to go places in the house alone. We searched more; it seemed that nothing valuable was stolen or damaged. My parents lit the whole house to make us feel safe and the police stayed overnight outside guarding us. The rest of the night seemed normal with no special events. The police rotated all night and then left in the morning.

The next day was Friday, the official weekend in Iraq as in most Muslim countries. So we were home on that day. We liked Friday mornings because we had no school. We could sleep in late and fool around all morning, watch some television and forget about school. But then in the afternoon and evening, reality hit and we had to think about school again and prepare our school bags for Saturday, which was a school day and a workday. That Friday, my Mom got up early to prepare breakfast and to do things as normally as possible, even though we were all shaken from the previous night.

During those months we did not have a maid. Before then, there was always a maid or a nanny at our house, a live-in usually. The only one I remember was an old lady who took care of me really well and whom I loved. Her name was Um Mustafa. She was like a friend to me, even though she was a few decades older than I. She had just passed away a few months earlier. She died abruptly. First she became ill, went home for a break and never came back. We learned of her death a couple of weeks after she had gone home. Her son called my parents and told them that she had passed away.

That was the first time I lost someone I loved and cared for. She was kind and loving and I still remember her today. Because I was young and she spent much time looking after me, I became attached to her and felt very sad at loosing her. I cried so much when I learned of her death. I was deeply hurt by it and had much sorrow and anguish for many days and weeks. I missed her so much. Her death was a sad time for the family and it coincidentally marked the beginning of all the turmoil that followed in our life. During this period my mom did all the housework by herself or with the help of my older sister, Zeena. It was hard because the house was so big and demanded lots of work.

So on that Friday morning Mom was preparing breakfast and we were still asleep or getting up. Mom heard the front door, which was near the kitchen, being opened and someone's steps. She thought it was one of us.

"Good morning," she said. 'Who is up? Is that you Amer?"

No one answered. Mom was surprised. Amer, my brother, was usually the first one up and came to greet her, to say good morning. She thought he had just opened the door to step out for a moment.

My mother went to see who had gone out. She saw a teenage or younger boy running towards the outer gate (the distance between this entrance to the house and the front gate was somewhat long, some twenty meters or so or 65 feet). Mom called on the boy to stop and come back but he just kept running. Mom could not run after him. She had arthritis and her knees were always painful. Mom came back inside quickly and met my brothers, Haider and Samir, who were just coming downstairs. She told them some kid just left the house. My brothers got in the car fast and tried to follow the boy. An elderly woman was passing by. They asked her whether she had seen anyone leaving the house.

"Yes," she replied. "I saw a young boy running out. He went that way."

She pointed in the direction the boy ran. My brothers drove through the crowded main street the way he was headed but he quickly got lost in the crowds. They came back home with no news.

My Dad called the police right away when he heard Mom talking about the boy. The police came quickly and looked around. They were dismayed at what had happened and looked all over the house again. It was obvious that the boy had spent the night in our home somewhere. They were very sorry that they had failed to locate him the night before when they had searched. The boy's wet footsteps were later traced to an old bathroom that was no longer in use in the house. This was an old style *traditional bath* in which the floors were heated; it contained its own heated water store. We did not use these old bathing facilities; they were sort of decorative or a luxury, like having your own old-fashioned Jacuzzi in the house. The room itself was used to house laundry stuff and the washing machine and such items. So the boy was hiding in the shallow water store all night; his feet and parts of his clothes were wet as there were water spots that traced back to the bathroom. He stayed overnight and escaped in the morning. The police were sorry and apologized again for having missed this spot and thought it was too small to accommodate a man, which indeed it was. But it could hide a boy.

The police met with my Dad and told him that they were still investigating the events. They had visited the pharmacy which the taxi driver had mentioned, the Almadina pharmacy, and asked the owner about the events of the previous night. The police related that the owner had said, "Yes, indeed. Such a man came last night, and he asked for some drug. But I told him we have no such thing, it was not normally sold, and it was rather a strange request. He sat for a few minutes and then he asked to use the phone. He made a phone call and I heard him say: the drug is not available. He then left." The storeowner had added that he was surprised at the man's request and that he found him to be unsettling.

All in all, it was a bizarre set of events: the break-in, the pharmacy, the boy. In addition to that, there were other traumatic events such as families vanishing or being slaughtered by Abu Tubar. We were all so frightened by this and so tired from it. My parents were discussing these events with the other adults such as my aunts and my uncles and Mr. Naser. We, the children, were scared and fearfully excited and wondered who this man of the previous night was and what he wanted from us. It became evident that he had attempted to enter the house. Maybe he wanted to poison or kill us or put some drug in our water or food. Maybe that's what the boy's mission was, we could not know. Obviously Hamid, the grown man who attempted to enter our house and may have succeeded was assisted by the young kid. Maybe they were related. We wondered if these two were working with Abu Tubar. Many bizarre thoughts came to mind. We just thanked God that no one was hurt and tried to have a normal time for the rest of the day.

*   *   *

The next day was Saturday, which was a workday, so we went to school and my parents went to work. A senior Ba'athist at my dad's work by the name Amjad Jibari stormed into my father's office and in a loud, crude tone said, "Mr. Makki, you have placed in detention a poor man, a helpless taxi driver. How could you?"

"I beg your pardon," Dad responded. "What? What do you mean?"

"The taxi driver who was detained Thursday night," Jibari continued. "You have placed him in detention. Do you know who we are? This man is one of us, he is one of our men, one of our own from Baquba [a small city north of Baghdad]. He is a poor helpless man and I am telling you ... you have to drop any charge against him. It will be bad for you otherwise."

Dad was stunned. Many thoughts raced in his mind. "What has Mr. Jabari got to do with it? What was he referring to?"

Dad said, "What do you mean? How do you know about this? It was only yesterday and the day before. It was a break-in at my house and the police are handling it."

Jibari just looked at Dad.

Then dad continued by asking him, "Mr. Amjad ... do you know anything about this break-in at my house? Please tell me because the police have not gotten anywhere with this case."

Jibari did not answer. He just looked at Dad and left.

At this stage, the Ba'ath party had only been in power for a few years. Although they could have released this man and done many other things without the consent of my Dad or anyone, in the early seventies they had not grown so vicious yet. It was just a matter of time, though. At that early stage, they used to try to cover up their corruption and interference in the normal affairs of the government. This incident at our house, for example, was in the hands of the local police force, which then came under the jurisdiction of the city of Baghdad's administrative affairs department. The Ba'ath regime still had not fully infiltrated all the department's offices. Perhaps the incident had not proceeded as anticipated and they were trying to extricate themselves from a mess.

My father came home and told Mom about the office event. My parents were very intrigued and worried by what was going on. They did not know whether Mr. Jibari was related to this man, the taxi driver, or just knew him. They had so many suspicions. It was confusing and worrisome, especially on top of the Abu Tubar crimes that had scared everyone and all the events of the previous few days. They did not know whom to turn to. They did not know whether to trust the police either. In fact they became suspicious of the police, especially over their failure to find the boy who was hiding in the bathroom. Maybe they had seen him and left him there on purpose. But then, we had lived in that neighborhood for years and the local police knew our family and the neighborhood. It was confusing.

My uncle Sadi (he was not really my uncle but was married to my aunt—the same word is used for a blood uncle and an uncle by marriage) had some influence with and connections among government officials and tried to find out about this whole thing. Uncle Sadi was so kind. He was tenacious and had so much intensity and energy and he loved us so much. He was very dynamic and rather charming. He always took the lead in various family matters and used his connections often to help us and the rest of the extended family. He had a high position in the army before the new regime came to power. As soon as he heard what happened he tried to help us through his connections. So, he spoke with a then high-ranking official, Hardan Tikriti, who had pull in the police service in Baghdad. He asked Tikriti to inquire about this case. Hardan Tikriti told my uncle to inform my parents to back off and forget about this event. He also said that the detained man would be released. Uncle Sadi could not get any further than that with Tikiti, even he was abruptly cut off from further information.

Uncle Sadi was himself disturbed and shocked that his contact was not more forthcoming and he could not probe any further. He was also disappointed because he could not help us, especially since he really liked to take the lead in family issues and wanted to be everyone's hero. He came and told my parents about his failure to get to the bottom of this matter. Both my parents were shocked and could not believe that such an obvious and simple matter was being covered up and being hidden away.

"Well, it is of no use to go any further," Uncle Sadi said. "Nothing was stolen from the house, no damage occurred. So do not ask me any more about this."

My mom was furious with him. She started yelling at him. "Sadi, what do you mean by that?"

"Look, Lydia," Uncle Sadi replied, "believe me, I cannot do anything about this. I myself am very upset that I did not get any further news on this."

"You've got to tell us," Mom fired back. "What did they tell you exactly…? Sadi … come on tell me. Are they plotting to kill us? What do you know that you are not telling us?"

He in turn got mad with my mother and said, "Lydia, you know that I would do anything for you and Makki but this is beyond me. Lydia, you know that I would die before I bring any harm to you. I am telling you the truth, that I cannot do anything." Then he turned to my father and said, "This case is finished. I do not have more; there is nothing more than what I am telling you. It is beyond me. It is much bigger than us.

"Makki, you know what I mean," he continued. "For the safety of the family it is better to drop this matter and forget it, especially since no one was hurt and nothing was stolen from the house. If we dig further, we shall just get more troubles."

After a lot of such talk, my Dad conceded. It was no use to object further. My parents were disheartened and disappointed. Uncle Sadi had powerful connections but even he could not help us. A few weeks went by.

*   *   *

After a long stay at the hospital my injured aunt went home. There was a big celebration for her. Uncle Sadi was delighted that his wife was finally coming home. As she took a few limping steps to enter the house, he had prepared bunches of cash, Iraqi notes of one, five and ten dinars, to be thrown all over her. During the seventies the Iraqi monetary unit, the dinar, was equal to U.S.$3.30. So for us kids that was lots of money to collect. He had also hired a popular band, somewhat equivalent to a DJ at parties here in the West. The band had several people and they just went around the house cheering and announcing the good news of her homecoming and singing songs in her honor. Also, her kids were throwing sweets and candy. In Iraq, all of these were common ways to celebrate when people came out of the hospital, got married, graduated and the like. We were happy and applauded and cheered for her as she walked in and took many gifts, although she had not yet recovered fully. But at least she was home, and had improved a lot and could walk a few steps. She still had many weeks of recovery and physical therapy. So even at home she needed to be looked after and she was attended by a visiting nurse who would come to see her every few days to attend to her needs and help her start walking. After the release of my aunt from the hospital, my Mom went every Friday morning thereafter and some evenings to be with her sister and see that the nurse was not ignoring her duties. My mother was so caring and radiated kindness and compassion. My aunt wanted her to be there; she felt safe that way.

One Friday morning, my mother was getting ready to leave to go to her sister's house. It was a beautiful crisp, cold morning, but it was bright and sunny. My Dad and my brother Amer were walking outside in the walkway, which ran around the house, looking at some of the trees and plants that were recently planted. They were enjoying and admiring the trees and the flowers in which Dad took tremendous joy and pride. He used to stop at each one and water it and see how well it had developed. There were many hideouts in this charming walkway around the house where you could see outside into the street but still had total privacy. My Dad and Amer heard the sound of the outer gate being opened. They were surprised since we were not expecting anyone. Then they saw a man attempting to open the gate, which is normally closed but not locked during the daytime hours. The gate could be opened with a simple manipulation of a lock. The man looked around him and opened the gate and was a few steps inside the port. He was looking around and through the windows. My Dad suddenly confronted him and shouted, 'Stop! Who are you? What are you doing?" The man looked at my Dad and Amer and was startled. He started running and was out of the gate quickly. At that moment, my other brothers were in the car getting ready to drive my mother to my aunt's house. My Dad screamed and told them to follow that man who had just run out of the house.

Meanwhile my Dad called the police and told them what had happened; then he and Amer got in the other car and went to the police station, which was not too far from our house. Police cars spread over the area quickly. Some went searching for the man in the same direction that he was going. Other cars went straight to the point where that road led but by a different route. In the area in which we lived, there were two main roads which crossed each other like the letter "T" and numerous smaller roads that connected the two main roads. So some police cars went on the main roads and others went along the smaller roads. They indeed caught the man.

My father and Amer identified him. He was detained. The police kept him all morning for questioning. They suspected that he was the same mysterious man of the past few weeks. The officers lined him up with other detainees at the station; they dressed them all up in the same way using a long white dress and a head cover traditionally worn by some men in Iraq. They went and summoned our neighbor, Mr. Naser, to the police station and asked him whether he recognized any of these men as the suspect of the past events. He identified the same man. Finally, "Hamid" was caught and detained. Hamid did not say much and refused to talk but he was in detention anyway. Back at home my Dad and my brothers sat down to rest from the day's events; my parents were worried by this persistent man who wanted to get in the house, even in broad daylight. Uncle Sadi came over. They were all talking about this event. I was very scared that day. The evening went by with considerable anticipation.

Next day at the office, an enraged Amjad Jibari stormed at my father again. This time he was with other armed Ba'athists. In the same threatening tone, he said, "Mr. Makki, there is a problem. You have detained one of us again. You don't get it, do you?"

Dad did not answer.

Jibari continued. "The man must be released. I am warning you to drop this case and to drop any charge against him."

My father was very angry and could not remain silent. "Mr. Amjad, what are you talking about? What does this have to do with you? You know these thieves who are breaking into my house? It's a local break-in, a crime, and the police are on this case according to the law of this country. There is still some law and order left in this country. The taxi driver was released because of your influence. Who is this man? Tell me why are you protecting him?"

Jabari shouted at my father. "Mr. Makki, you are an obstacle to the party and the revolution and I am telling you to drop this case or it will be bad for you."

The detained man, Hamid, was released whether we liked it or not. It was orders from high-ranking government officials that this should be done. Even the director of the local police was bewildered and dismayed. He told my Dad that it was orders from above. He could not supersede these orders. No one would tell us anything. Even my uncle Sadi who loved us so much and who had some top-ranking connections, could not get to the bottom of this. We were now on guard. We locked up all the gates even during the daytime. We left many lights on at night all around the house. We took these precautionary measures to ensure that any intruder would be seen. Moreover, my parents told our other neighbors about the repeated attempts to break in to our house. The neighbors were watchful too.

* * *

A few days went by. One afternoon, my brother Amer was walking back home from school. His path back home took him along the main road and the street which led to our house. He usually passed by the guest entrance and then turned and walked towards the main entrance of the house, or the one that we normally used daily. In Iraq, some homes had more than one entrance because they were big or because the homes had different sections or quarters. Our home had three entrances: one which we used on a daily basis, one used mostly by guests, and a third which was also used by guests and sometimes by us on special occasions. Because the house was relatively large, those three entrances were quite far from each other. During normal day hours the gates were closed but not locked. At night, my Dad went around and locked each of them. Amer saw a woman ringing the bell at our guest entrance; she opened the gate and entered. Amer thought she was a visitor or one of my Mom's friends. He himself entered through the other gate which we used daily. When he got in, he saw my Mom in the kitchen in her house clothes.

"Hi, Mom," he said. "How are you?"

"Hello, darling," my mother answered. "You want to get ready for lunch?"

"Mom, don't you have a guest? Why are you in your home clothes?"

"No," she said. "We have no guests."

"But I just saw a woman come in," Amer insisted. "She rang the bell and went in through the gate. I thought she was one of your friends. I thought you were having a visitor."

"What woman? No one came."

"But I just saw a woman come in through the gate."

Mom and Amer went out to look for the woman; there was no one outside. But it was obvious that the gate had been opened. They could not find anyone. They were intrigued by this guest. They came back in and thought maybe the woman would come back, but she did not.

A few days went by. One afternoon, my sister Zeena was walking home from the store. She saw a taxi drop off a woman at our house, and she saw the woman ring the bell and enter through the gate. Zeena thought we had guests that evening. Zeena continued to walk around to go through the other gate, the one which was used daily. When she got near the gate, she saw the same woman leaving the house. Zeena was surprised that this guest was leaving so quickly; she thought that the woman had just come to pick up something from my Mom or just to say hello as she was passing by the neighborhood. The pathway that went around the house connected all the gates, so the woman had entered through the guest gate, walked along the pathway until she had reached the other gate, and left. She got to the second gate faster than Zeena because she was walking inside the grounds; the distance between the two gates was shorter inside than out on the street. Zeena came in and wanted to ask Mom about this guest. But Mom was in her room resting and had her house clothes on. She was not dressed to receive guests.

"Mom, who is the woman I just saw come and leave?" Zeena asked.

Mom sat up in the bed and asked, "Whom did you see? What woman?"

Zeena told Mom what she saw. My Mom was now concerned. Dad came over and Zeena told him what she had seen.

"This is the second time this has happened," Mom said. "I do not know if it is the same woman that Amer saw. But this is the second time some woman has come to the house. We did not hear the bell ring. You know, maybe the bell is not working. Can you check it please."

Zeena and Dad went out and tested the bell. It was working fine and we would have heard it if the woman had really rung the bell. So it became apparent that she was just pretending to be ringing the bell so that it would not appear suspicious, her just entering a home without being let in. Mom and Dad were not sure whether to tell the police about this. They were becoming afraid that this may be a new set up for us.

A few days later, Amer was walking home again and as he was approaching the street that leads to our house—our house was at the end of that street—he saw that same woman leaving the house and walking away. So Amer turned around and followed her. She walked a few steps and took a taxi. He followed. As the road was crowded, he lost them in the crowd. Amer came home and told my parents that he had seen that woman again and that she had taken a taxi and disappeared. By then we were all worried and concerned. We could not make anything out of these events.

Finally, one morning a few days later, my mother and Zeena were at home by themselves. Zeena was helping Mom dust and clean the guestrooms. All the curtains in the guestrooms were open so there was a clear view of the gate and the pathway. A taxi stopped at the gate. A woman got out. She pretended to ring the bell at our house and then entered. Zeena saw all of this from her position inside the room with the curtains and windows open. Zeena instantly ran and got Mom. My Mom quickly opened the door and stepped out on the patio in front of the woman. She grabbed the woman forcefully and brought her up onto the doorstep. Zeena hid behind the door; she was shaking and afraid. The woman was wearing big dark sunglasses.

Mom said, "Remove your sunglasses!"

The woman took off her sunglasses. She appeared to be in her late twenties and had a sort of dark complexion. The woman did not say anything.

Mom yelled at the woman. "Who are you? What are you doing entering and leaving my house? Where does the taxi pick you up? Speak now or I will throw you out in the street, naked."

The woman started crying. She went down on her knees to kiss my mother's feet and begged to be let go.

"Get up and speak," Mom told her. "Tell me what you are doing here."

The woman said that she came to the area to visit her ex-husband because she still loved him. She was forced to leave him because of problems between her family and his family, and that she came to visit him. That was a bizarre story. Mom asked her for his name and where he lived; the woman gave her some name and described the place where he lived.

"Why do you use our house?" Mom asked her. "Why don't you go to his house?"

The woman just kept crying and did not answer. Mom was sentimental and soft-hearted. She let the woman go. She warned her not to come back to our house, ever.

What my mother did was dangerous, but that is how my mother was: impulsive and forceful. She just dealt with things immediately and instantly and with a lot of emotion. It was dangerous to let this woman in, especially as there was only Mom and Zeena at home. I think my mother scared the woman because we never saw her again. And that is not all—my Mom told the entire neighborhood to be cautious of this woman. Also, my parents tried to check out her story. They asked around in the neighborhood about the name of the family that the woman claimed to be going to. Usually, people knew who was living around them. No one in the neighborhood recognized the name or the story that the woman told. No one knew of a divorced man in the neighborhood by that name. This led us to be even more worried that this whole story was a big lie. Mom told our neighbors what happened. She asked them to be on guard both for our safety and theirs. Mom told them, "I do not know who this woman is. Maybe she comes and goes to bad neighborhoods. Maybe she comes and goes to a brothel or the like and it is a plot to ruin our family's reputation and good name." The neighbors were surprised to know about this woman and everyone was on guard. Thank God we never saw her again.

*   *   *

These unexplained events tired us out, but we were intrigued for days and weeks about what had happened—the enigma was never resolved. Who was this mysterious woman? Why did she make up this whole story? Who was Hamid? Why was he attempting to enter our house? Who was the teenage kid? How did the young boy enter the house, without breaking the door locks or the windows? What was the drug story? Were they trying to poison us all? Were they trying to put this drug in the water or food? What was the plot against us? Were the police really being truthful? We had so many questions and no answers. This story obviously involved the government. It appeared to us that there was some plot to attack us or to tarnish our reputation. My father thought that the Ba'athists in his office were planning to trap him somehow. But so far none of their plots were successful. We were still safe and unharmed. We had to be careful and watchful all the time. No one could answer any of our questions about these incidents. Fear of Abu Tubar and all these attempts to break in to our house and the obvious involvement of some Ba'ath members in this matter made us all worried and anxious. There was no way to seek justice or even a mere investigation. These events were covered up and made to disappear.

*   *   *

During the few following days, a couple came to visit us as potential tenants for one of the small homes. The young couple had two children and they seemed nice. The man said he was a teacher of physical education, and the woman said she was a nurse. So they rented one of the homes and moved in quickly. Rental agreements were mostly done verbally and documented via a sort of paralegal office, which was like a notary public/attorney's office which made various transactions among people official. So there were no special forms and credit checks and formal procedures as there were in many Western countries. So my parents and this couple agreed on the rental duties and rental fees, and they documented all this at the paralegal office.

The rental laws in Iraq, then, fully protected the tenant: they gave them an advantage over the owners and made it impossible to evict someone who was renting a home once they had moved in. This was based on the fact that the renters did not own a home and the owners did. Anyway, a few days later, we shockingly learned, through a friend of ours, that our new tenant, Mr. Kader, was holding a special post in our district: He was the representative of the *Secret Police* (Alamin) in our district. Every district or neighborhood had someone assigned by the Ba'ath party as the representative of the secret police. Their job was to keep an eye on any and all of the activities of the families in that area, to spy on people, to see who was going where and who was visiting whom, and of course to generate reports to the party about all these activities.

This was quite a blow to us, to know this about our tenant. So, Mr. Kader had lied about his abhorred profession. Or worse, he had deleted an important part of his career. Although he was indeed a teacher, he did not mention that he had a significant post at the Ba'ath party. Of course, we could not evict him based on his affiliation with the secret police. We could not say that he had lied and not told us that he was working with the secret police. And more importantly, like any tenant, he had the rental law on his side. So evicting him was a battle that my parents attempted but lost. They did not want this man near our house and they felt so betrayed by the fact that he had boldly lied about his profession, but now we were stuck with these people. We had to live with the reality; basically, we were stuck with these people next to us. We tried our best to minimize our contact with them and not to provoke any conflict with them.

One night the doorbell rang and my brother Amer went to answer it. Normally we expected guests to come through this particular doorway. Amer went to answer the guest door. Because of the recent crimes in the city, we never opened the door right away. We first opened the window to ask the visitor to identify himself or herself. We did not open the door unless we were expecting someone whom we knew at that moment. It was not uncommon in Iraq for guests to show up anytime, even without calling. This was different from traditions in Western cultures where you must call before you visit anybody. The fact that most homes in Iraq had a special entrance for the guests and an especially designated guestroom and area of the house reflected this culture of random visiting. You must receive your guests anytime they showed up. It would be very rude to tell them that you were busy or that you had other plans. If you were not home then whoever was at home, for example your grown up children, would be expected to receive the guests and tell them that you were not there. Normally the guests would leave under such circumstances. Also, your guest areas and room must be immaculate and ready to receive people all the time; this room was typically situated away from the normal living area and the kitchen and the TV and the kids.

So on that night, Amer opened the window and asked who it was. There was no answer. He asked again. There was still no answer. Then, he heard a sound near the window, and suddenly he was splashed with something. Amer was startled and jumped away from the window. He started screaming, "Help! It's Abu Tubar," and fell down. Our minds had been set to alarm; after all that had happened we lived with tension and apprehension every day. We anticipated that whoever it was that got in our house before, a few weeks earlier, would try again. So Amer was yelling and screaming and he thought that he was hit with some poisonous substance. My mother heard that, and she saw Amer lying on the floor screaming, "My eyes, my eyes, I can't see anything, I have been hit by poisons." Meanwhile the bell continued to ring incessantly. She was in a panic. She went to attend to Amer and then ran to the phone. She called Uncle Sadi and she herself was screaming on the phone, "Sadi, help, help!"

Uncle Sadi did not understand what had happened. Mom was not explaining the situation. He just realized it was her and that she was screaming for help on the phone. He jumped in his car and drove to our home like a madman. His home was not too far from us; maybe it took fifteen or so minutes to get there under normal circumstances. He arrived near our street and took out his gun and started shooting rounds in the air from his car as he approached our house.

Near our house was the home of a high-ranking Ba'ath official. It was only some four blocks or so away from us. The place had armed guards and security. These guards heard the gunshots and thought there was an attack taking place on the home of the official. They came over to our house where the shots were heard, and they had their weapons drawn and ready. It was such a drama. Uncle Sadi was so impulsive and emotional. He got out of the car not realizing he was only in his boxer shorts and undershirt. My father was the only calm person in this frantic scene. He was trying to talk to Uncle Sadi, who was running all over the house, and the guards, who were at the door. He said, "Sadi, Sadi, stop! It's not Abu Tubar. It is my son Samir. Sadi, stop! Everyone is okay."

In the midst of all the frenzy, my father heard my bother Samir who was yelling from the window, "It's me, it's only me…. Open the door…! Stop screaming! It's me, it's Samir." My father opened the door and let my brother Samir in. Samir was just being mischievous and playing a trick on Amer. He had gotten in through the outer gate. Between the outer gate and the entrance door, there was a small garden and patio. Samir had tuned on the water faucet and was splashing water from the hose on Amer through the window. Dad was trying to calm everyone down. He said it was all a silly joke and thank God no one was hurt. The guards who came over went back to their location. We all burst out laughing. Mom, however, was mad with Samir for this childish trick. She yelled at him for causing such a scene and he apologized. Amer sat up and realized it was only water from the hose that was splashed on him, not some deadly poison as he thought, and he realized that his eyesight was fine. It was a silly and funny affair that happened because my teenage brothers were both acting silly. We all sat down to calm ourselves. It was a funny and bizarre incident.

The Abu Tubar scare continued for many months. During that time people were still afraid and the thought of Abu Tubar still haunted them.

CHAPTER 3

My Father Is Detained

The summer that followed the car accident of aunt Najia and the troubling events at our house, we went on a family trip to Beirut. It was my first time on an airplane. It was, then, the most exciting feeling in the world, to be in an airplane. We had gone before on many trips by car such as to Syria and Kuwait and to the beautiful resorts in the north of Iraq, but that was by car and it was not the same feeling as being in an airplane.

The trip was fun. We bought chocolates and new clothes and we visited so many exciting places. One memorable place was Alhambra Boulevard with its exhilarating lights and shops. It was the equivalent of the Champs Élysées in Paris. It was so exciting to walk along by the cafes and bookshops and cinemas especially at night when there would be a cool breeze. And there were so many people walking in the streets. It was even more exciting than the crowds in Baghdad. Another amazing place was the cave of Gaita with its extraordinary calcified walls. It was breathtaking for me as a child to see these beautiful things from nature. It was like magic for me. Because the cave was so cold and wet and kind of dark, except for a few light bulbs over a pathway that went through the cave, it felt dramatic and intriguing to be there. In all, the trip was fun. We spent a couple of exciting weeks there. That was also my first time seeing the Mediterranean Sea; I even went swimming in it. It was breathtaking.

During one of these touristy adventures we were at a café in the mountains overlooking the city. It was a rather beautiful afternoon. The sun was mild and there was a nice breeze. The city view from the mountains was so breathtaking. However, I was not having a good time because of motion sickness. The place was on top of the mountain and we drove on a curved road to get there. I was dizzy and nauseated and felt miserable. So, when we got to the café, I was leaning on my mother's lap and was rather pale, and I could not stand the smell of food. A few minutes after resting on solid ground and whining and getting all the attention from everyone, I felt better and sat up quietly.

Throughout this period there was a woman looking at us with particular curiosity; she was especially looking at me, and with affection. She kept sending flirty smiles to us and then she walked over to introduce herself. She was very charming and looked very well dressed. She was totally infatuated with me, or at least she pretended to be. Her name was Samar and she was beautiful and rather elegant. She kept saying, "Oh, what a cute child, what a lovely girl." My parents were amused by her compliments about me, and of course they too thought that I was rather cute. The woman spoke Arabic well and she claimed to be an actress. My sisters and I were elated that we were looking at an actress. She was beautiful and dressed up really nicely and had professional makeup. We were just looking at her and were impressed by her charms and clothes; we did not recognize who she was.

We had afternoon lunch with her and talked about different things and she kept complimenting my parents on what a beautiful family they had. Later she said, "I am coming over to Baghdad soon in the next few weeks and I would like to visit you." My parents, being very social and outgoing, said of course, they would be delighted to see her, and gave her all our contact information. We left the café where we met her and were intrigued by the coincidence that led us to meet this actress. None of us recognized her, and we thought she must be a budding star and that we would see her in future films. We went back to our hotel, and a few days later our trip ended. We were happy to go home and had great memories from our time in Beirut.

One night after our return, maybe a couple of weeks after, Samar called and said that she was in Baghdad and that she wanted to visit us at home right away. It was not so strange how she insisted on coming over. That was typical in Iraqi and Arab culture. Guests simply showed up at your door. At least in her case she called. She just called and said I am coming over.

My brother Haider was very religious and was not fond of cinema celebrities and movie stars. He overheard my parents talking about Samar visiting. He was mad and threw a major fit. He did not like the story of that woman from the start. "Mom, you are not letting this woman into the house," he told my mother. "What do you know about her?"

"Haider, come on," mom replied. "She will just be here for an hour or so. She is a guest."

"But you only met her by coincidence. You do not know her. I will not let her come in. You know I am not fond of actresses and their 'high' moral content. I shall stand at the door and not let her in."

"Haider, do not be silly," Dad said. "You do not to have to see her. No one is forcing you to entertain her. You mother and I will talk to her awhile and then she will leave."

Haider was so dogmatic. He made a big fuss to my parents and said that she should not come to this house, she was probably an alcoholic, we did not know anything about her background, and thus we must not let her in.

Actually, Haider's sentiments were a reflection of the conservative nature of society and a taboo view of actresses. In Iraq in those days, it was not considered a big deal to be an actor or an actress as it is in the West. It usually indicated that you had failed in traditional schooling and that you had no real education and no business expertise. In addition, the acting profession was associated with promiscuity and lax morals, perhaps incorrectly. Some of these taboos and sentiments may have been justified, but clearly they should not have been applied to all. During the Ba'ath days, the government actually improved the nature of the acting profession by instituting a real school of theater and drama, and they gave the profession a slightly better name. However, the sentiments of the general population towards the profession remained the same.

My parents finally conceded to my brother. My Mom called Samar back and told her there were some circumstances that prevented them meeting her at home and asked her if they could come over to her hotel and take her out to see Baghdad instead. Mom also said that she could bring the girls too. Samar accepted this arrangement and thus we went to the Abu Nuas hotel where she was staying.

The Abu Nuas hotel was a fancy five star hotel. It was luxurious and had all kinds of beautiful ornaments and décor. The carpets were spotlessly clean. The windows were sparkling. The staff members were well dressed and groomed and looked immaculate. We arrived at the hotel and waited for her. The servant told us that she was in the bar area waiting for us. We went there looking for her. In contrast to the hotel lobby, that corner was dark and secluded and did not feel pleasant to us. We did not like to be in the bar; it was awfully dark and barely lit. The place was not appropriate for children at all.

Samar was in the bar area with a few men drinking. The men did not appear Iraqis although they spoke Arabic. Their dress and dialect indicated that they were Kuwaitis and Jordanians. We were surprised to see all these people for our social visit with her. Mom whispered to Dad that this might be a trap. In Iraq in those days, having any contact with foreign nationals was grounds for suspicion and would immediately open you to accusations of conspiring against the government and the Ba'ath party. Indeed, even if the contact was social and personal in nature, it still brought immediate suspicion and accusations upon the Iraqi national who was meeting with the foreigners. My parents were afraid of this being such a setup, and they also saw that this was not a place for us children to be. They decided not to stay long.

We only stayed for a little while, said a few words to her and then got ready to leave. Samar said that she was engaged to one of these men and that she would be married soon. She added that she still wanted to come and visit us. She was acting in a different way than when we first saw her. It was like she was another person. She was somewhat drunk though. We left and were puzzled by what we had seen. A few days went by but my parents were still unsettled by her and began to have suspicions about her friendship. These suspicions were a normal way to react in Iraq those days but especially after what we had just been through. The break-in at our house, and the repeated attempts to break in, the mysterious woman who came and went and now this woman, Samar.

* * *

It was a busy evening at our house. The late-autumn nights of Baghdad were brutally cold and the fearful conditions of the country made these cold nights seem vicious. But these conditions brought people together. Most people spent time at home with their families or went visiting with their relatives and did not venture out in public places in the city at night. This was true in our family too. It brought everyone together. My aunts and my grandmother were visiting us at home, and all of us and some of our cousins were crowded in the living room trying to stay warm. We were having tea after dinner and talking. It was also common in Baghdad on such cold nights to eat warmly cooked chestnuts. This was quite a treat.

Chestnuts are not very common in Baghdad. They were brought in from northern Iraq in the cold season. They were so luscious and they had a rich dark brown color. We would typically cook them over the traditional kerosene heaters. These were specially designed heaters which must be filled with kerosene oil; they were lit with matches, like you would light a gas stove. The heaters were very suitable for the huge rooms in Iraqi homes. There was no central heating in those days; and really, central heating would have been impractical because the Iraqi homes were not compact like American homes and were typically more dispersed and much bigger. So each room had its own heating device, either the kerosene or alternatively a small electric heater. We would place a metal tray over the heater and put the fresh chestnuts on it and flip them a couple of times until they cracked. The cooked nuts had a distinct aroma that filled the room. Once they cracked, we would peel them and eat the nut. They were delicious and they kept us warm. My cousins, my sister and I were playing. We were all crowded in the living room and the adjacent room. Many lively and loud conversations were going on and we were having a nice evening.

The phone rang. My mother answered it. She told my father that the call was for him and that the caller sounded disturbed and said it was an urgent matter and apologized for calling at home so late. My mother was concerned as the man sounded really in a panic. Dad was indeed surprised that someone from work would call him at this late hour on a Friday night. He went into the other room to take the call.

The caller was frantic, his voice was shaking and he pleaded for help. "Mr. Makki, Mr. Makki … please, for God's sake … help us…. I beg you, please help us, and please save us. Mr. Makki, please…."

"What?", my father responded. "Who is this? What's wrong?"

The man said in a shaking voice, "Mr. Makki, I am Kamil, from the Almamun office. Mr. Makki please, please … we are going to die…. We are finished."

The caller was an employee of the telephone security service working with the anti-crime unit; he was based at the Almamun (it is a neighborhood of Baghdad) district switchboard. This official government facility controlled the major telephone services to the city of Baghdad and it was under the auspices of the agency that my Dad headed. They operated a special service that traced threatening phone calls to people in the midst of the Abu Tubar crime affair that rocked Baghdad. Their job was to trace the call, identify the caller and, depending on the situation, disable that phone line or hold the line for investigation or something like that.

"What happened?" Dad asked. "Please … I am listening … please calm down … tell me what happened?"

"We received a complaint call from a woman telling us that she had been getting threats from Abu Tubar and harassing calls so her phone line was being monitored and then…. Oh, God…. Oh, my God…. This evening … this evening, there was a threatening call to her house and we traced the call and we put a hold on the line. Oh God.... Oh God.... I can't believe...."

Kamil stopped talking for a few seconds. He sounded like he was gasping for air and losing his breath.

"Son. Son please ... calm down.... Don't be afraid."

"We identified the line and we put a hold on it, but we did not then know that the call had originated from the presidential palace. Oh God.... Mr. Makki ... I swear we did not know.... A while later, a car came from the presidential palace, they stormed in. They came with weapons ... the security guard tried to stop them. Oh my God, the poor man, he did not know at first who they were. One of them pushed him to the ground and hit him with the edge of a gun on his head. They got in and took the tape where we recorded the call, and they ripped it and threw it all over. They said how dare we interrupt a call from the presidential palace. They threatened us further. They called us names.... Oh, God, Mr. Makki, you would not believe it. It was such a rampage here, you would not believe it."

Kamil stopped again to catch his breath and then continued. "Oh, God. We are dead scared and the guard is injured on his head and we are taking him to the doctor. Please tell me what we should do. We are going to die. Oh, God, what shall we do?"

My father was shocked to hear this and was visibly angry. His face was turning pale as he listened on the phone. He seemed very alarmed but he told the man to calm down and then said, "Okay, Kamil.... Listen to me ... calm down.... Listen to me. What about the second copy? The back-up copy of the tape? Did they take it too?"

"No. No. They did not, it is safe, they did not know about it."

"Thank God," Dad said. "Thank God. Oh, God thank you."

Dad stopped talking for a few seconds and then firmly told Kamil, "Okay, okay, good. Listen, son! You did your job as you were told. You have done nothing wrong. Just remember you were trying to save that poor family. Don't be scared. Listen, don't be afraid."

Dad continued in a confident voice. "Listen to me well. I want you to come to my office tomorrow first thing in the morning, and bring the second copy of the tape and all the men who witnessed what happened. I shall conduct an investigation into this matter. We are a civilized society. We are not living in a jungle."

Dad put down the phone. He was shocked and angry. He whispered to my Mom quietly what had happened. The man who had called was afraid for his life, not at the hands of the serial killer Abu Tubar, but the authorities. The anguish with which he reacted to the event was indicative of how much fear the regime had planted in people's lives. These innocent workers at the Almamun switchboard office had every reason to be afraid as no one challenged Ba'ath officials in those days. If they had known initially that they were dealing with the presidential palace, they would not have dared to intervene. The Ba'ath was above all. No one could stand in their way or tell them no.

My dad was distressed. These thoughts raced in his head. That the government may be involved in the Abu Tubar crime string was shocking and bewildering. Abu Tubar may be a creation of the Ba'ath government. Maybe they were killing people whom they wanted to eliminate in the name of this monster. But Dad wanted to be sure about this. Maybe it was just a group pretending to be from the government. But then, who else would dare to ransack a high security government building? The telephone service belonged entirely to the government; there were no private companies providing such services. And who else possessed guns and weapons other than the Ba'athists? He was disturbed by that event. The frightening revelation kept him awake all night. What was to come of the country now if the government was leading this crime spree? He could not sleep, he kept thinking all night. The night's incident indicated that Abu Tubar might be the creation of the Ba'ath party. Maybe there was no mysterious killer. Maybe it was all just a big scheme to scare people, to provide justification for all the random searching of cars and homes that they were doing and, most importantly, to get rid of political enemies. No wonder all the victims were somehow against the Ba'ath party or had some grievance with this new government or were families of prominent political figures; no wonder he did not hit just ordinary citizens or steal. It was all beginning to add up now.

My father knew that he himself would become a target now that he knew about the government's involvement in these horrible crimes, which had shaken the sense of security of Baghdadis for months. It was like a Pandora's box had been opened and now all kinds of revelations were going to appear. Dad had an eerie feeling that this was only the beginning. My father was distraught; although he promised the young man he would investigate the matter, whom was he going to tell? And what could he alone do in the face of this monstrous government. The revelation that kept him awake was disturbing and it engendered the feeling that the days ahead were not going to be easy. That was only the beginning.

His conscience would not let him ignore the cry of help that he had just received. He was determined to conduct the investigation as he had promised, knowing he was entering a danger zone. Throughout the Abu Tubar affair in Baghdad, some people could not help but notice that many of his victims had some quarrel with the regime, or were political opponents of the government such as ex-government families, or members of another faction of the Ba'ath party which was based in Syria, or were merely obstacles. Sometimes they were not high-profile people, just ordinary families, but one never knew what argument they had with the government. There was the family who lived in the Almansour district by the renowned club Nadi al Said, which was known to be a center of Ba'ath activities including their indecent entertainment. There was the Armenian family who lived too close to the presidential palace and who did not want to move out of their home (which they had owned for generations) as required by the government. They were slaughtered too, and so were many others. My parents, like everybody else, would whisper about these things, but no one could say anything in public.

The next morning, Dad went to work with a thick feeling in his chest. He knew that standing up in the face of the government was not going to be a breeze. But his conscience was his guide and his strength at that moment. The men from the telephone security station came to his office. There were four of them. He greeted them and congratulated them on their sincerity and honesty. He ordered tea for them and asked about each of them. He asked about the guard who could not join them because of his injuries. He started preparing a report on what had happened. He had the second copy of the tape as evidence of the conversation. He listened to the tape. It was awful. It was exactly what people reported the threatening phone calls to be like. It was full of threats and swearing and cursing at those poor would-be victims. The men were overwhelmed; they were shaken as they told Dad again what had happened the previous night. He took down the account of each of the men who were involved in the incident. He was absorbed in this matter all morning and in the midst of that, he got a note that there was an urgent phone call for him.

He went to another room to pick up the phone. It was a call from the presidential palace. It was Munther Almutlig, the son-in-law of then president Ahmed Hasan Albakr. More importantly, he was a powerful thug of the government and perhaps the third or fourth most powerful man in the country at that time, in his control and influence. He spoke in a loud voice but in a laid back tone. "Mr. Makki, I hear that you are investigating an incident that happened yesterday at Almamun station."

"Yes, of course," my father said. "How did you know? I am not even done with that. I am right in the middle of that."

Almutlig did not answer. Apparently he had gotten instant word of the investigation from other Ba'athists at the office where my Dad worked, people such as Mr. Jibari or others. Finally he continued and directly threatened my father in the then typical Ba'ath language of intimidation and accusation.

"You must cancel this investigation," he told my father. "It is not necessary to document this event. You must stop any further investigation of this matter and you must forget about it. Do not take any action in this matter."

My father did not concede to these orders. He said in a confident tone, "Mr. Munther, what do you mean? This is my job, you know, to investigate this event. You know I am in charge of that office and I must investigate. These are serious crimes. People's lives are at stake. We are following the law of this country. As you know, we live in a civil society. The government wants us to find Abu Tubar and prosecute him. Is that not our duty?"

"Mr. Makki, I just told you that this matter must be closed. Did you hear what I said?"

Dad was getting angry. "Mr. Munther.... Are you stopping me from doing my duty? Are you telling me to ignore my duties? We have lawfulness left in this country, you know. A man was injured yesterday and he is in the hospital, government property was damaged.... How can I not investigate?"

Almutlig crudely interrupted my Dad and said, "Mr. Makki, do you know who I am? Close the investigation." He repeated his threats and hung up.

My father put down the phone. He was angry. He could not move or talk for a few minutes. He was disturbed by this telephone confrontation. Dad was methodical and a man of principles. He had always been respected by his staff and colleagues. He had never had such a crude encounter. He was disgusted by the deception and the blatant threats and tone that he had just heard from this powerful man, Munther Almutlig. He recalled every word of his conversation with Almutlig. The voice and the threats were resonating in his head. He was angry and distraught. Dad remembered what happened during the break-in-events at our home and he realized that this was like trying to bring down a big wall with your bear hands. He sat alone thinking about all that. Then, he went back to his meeting with the crew from yesterday's events. He told them, "Gentlemen, I am sorry. Orders came from the presidential palace that I must cancel this investigation. It is against my will. They would not let me do my job. Let me see what can be done still, if anything."

Dad was too methodical, however. He documented in his report that he was closing this investigation per this phone call from the presidential palace. This file was now an official document and the matter was indeed closed. He told the men, "I am so sorry. This is beyond us; it is bigger than what I can do." The telephone technicians were disappointed and left. Dad was upset and disappointed for the rest of the day.

* * *

A few daunting days went by, and one afternoon the phone rang at about 2:30. Mom answered. It was Mr. Abdul Fattah, the director of the Baghdad police anti-crime task force requesting to speak to my father urgently. But Dad had not yet arrived home from work; Mom told him that Dad should be home any minute. Mr. Abdul Fattah told my mom, "Please, madam, as soon as Mr. Makki gets home he should proceed to the Ministry of Interior. We have an urgent matter ... we need him here right away.... Please tell him that we need him urgently." My mother assured Mr. Abdul Fattah that she would do so. Then she told the maid to wait outside and inform Dad that there was a message for him at home and not to send the driver back. As soon as Dad arrived, Mom told him about that message and he went straight to the Ministry of Interior headquarters.

He was gone all afternoon and into the evening, he came back around 6 P.M. or so and he was exhausted. It was already dark by then. Mom had been worried about him. She sat down with him to have dinner and looked after him well.

"Darling!" Mom said. "Are you ok? You look exhausted.... Please have something to eat."

"Thank you," he replied. "Yes, definitely ... the food smells great. Have you had dinner yet?"

"No. I wanted to wait for you."

She was helping him rest and feel better as he seemed concerned and worried. She was pouring some water for him and they sat to eat quietly.

When they were done, Mom asked him, "Makki, is everything okay? What kept you so long? I was worried about you. You poor thing, you look so tired."

"Lydia, you are not going to believe this." Then he whispered quietly, "There was a complaint from the anti-crime unit. Their headquarters is located within the Ministry of Interior." Dad stopped for a second and then continued. "You know, the anti-crime unit? That special task force trying to hunt the serial killer Abu Tubar. Well, they themselves had a problem. There is a serious security breach at this agency. The emergency hotline that they established was no longer receiving frantic calls from people. Mr. Abdul Fattah is running this program; surely you must have seen him on television?"

"Yes, I think so," Mom said. "What happened to him? He is the one who called this afternoon for you?"

"Yes, that's him. He is a kind man and he does his job very well. He is competent and I trust him too, and he sincerely wants to protect the citizens of Baghdad from these crimes. He and his staff are doing the best they can."

"Is he all right? He said there was trouble when he called."

"Yes," Dad responded. "He was frustrated at the lack of success that the police have had so far. People complained and cursed at the police because when people call and report suspicious persons and unusual events, the police never show up. Abdul Fattah told me that the police never get these calls. He wanted me to find out why they were not receiving the calls."

"What?" Mom gasped. "Oh, my God! What do you mean?"

"Lydia, you are not going to believe this. I examined their emergency calls system at their headquarters at the Ministry of Interior and I found that the calls were being diverted to the intelligence office [Almukhabarat]. When people call the police, the police never get these calls. Instead, someone at Almukhabarat answers these calls and they pretend to be the police. They tell people things like, okay, we are on our way, or something like that. And that's why the police never show up as people are complaining. The police are sincere and they do want to catch this killer. Both Mr. Abdul Fattah and I could not believe it. We were in shock. Abdul Fattah was pale and scared. We looked at each other silently. I ordered that this problem be fixed, but I think the lines will be tampered with again. This is real bad news Lydia; remember the last story with Almutlig? It's them, the Ba'athists, it's their entire creation. I now have firsthand information on this. If I had any doubts before, they are now dispelled. It is unequivocal now.... There is no serial killer ... it is a creation of the Ba'ath government.... Abu Tubar is the Ba'ath government. They killed innocent families. They are terrorizing people. They are making a mockery out of our lives and our emotions. The police do not even know about this connection. It is top secret. The whole city is wrecked with this affair and it is all a plot. It's a game for them; they are playing with our lives, and they are ruining this beautiful country. Oh, God where are we heading ... if this government is in charge of our lives? I fear that things are only headed for the worse."

My mother heard these remarks and she felt a tingling all over her body. She did not say anything. She looked at Dad with shock and worry. She feared what was to come now from the Ba'ath regime. A sense of doom draped them. They sat alone all evening. Mom had a gloomy sensation about this revelation. She stared at Dad. She dreaded what was going to happen to her husband now that he had uncovered the first evidence of the corruption of the Ba'ath government and its involvement in terrorizing the whole city and killing innocent families and people whom it did not like. My parents were now certain that all the atrocities they had been hearing about were true and that the Ba'ath government was the orchestrator of the serial crimes of Abu Tubar.

The night went by with fear and anticipation. This was like a nightmare that was creeping in to replace a happy dream. Mom sensed that Dad was in danger, imminent danger. But she had no way of protecting him. It was like he was being hunted and cornered gradually by vicious enemies. Mom sat later by herself for a long time. She remembered so many happy moments in their life: the family, her children growing up, the house, the travels, and all the dreams they had ahead. Suddenly she woke up from daydreaming and began to realize that their idyllic, happy life was in jeopardy and was crumbling and that there would be difficult days ahead. It was no longer the same Iraq that they had once lived in. There was constant worry and fear of what the government would do next. Life in Iraq was becoming so difficult as the days went by and it was going from bad to worse. And the worst had not yet come.

Mom kept praying and although she was worried, she also felt empowered and inspired by her faith. My mother was not really that religious on the outside. But she had the most unwavering faith and confidence that God Almighty would see her through the difficulties ahead. Her attachment to religion was not ritualistic; it was more like she had a core of inner faith and a complete trust in God Almighty. She relied on her prayers and on the mercy and care that she believed God always gives us. She prayed and hoped for the best.

I think both Dad and Mom were nervous and anxious about this latest development. But they were not scared of the Ba'ath. They were confident. Their idealism shaded their vision of reality. They were empowered by the truth. They feared nothing. They probably looked at the principles involved, stuck to the principles and perhaps just thought and said to themselves, We have not done anything wrong. Why should we be afraid? It is the government that is corrupt and that someone needs to do something about it.

My parents assumed that the truth could stand alone against the Ba'ath. They did not realize the extent of the Ba'ath's vicious greed for power and control. They did not realize that it meant nothing for this regime to kill a few people or many or to terrorize the whole country. They did not realize that for the Ba'ath, the truth meant nothing. If the truth stood in their way, they just crushed it. And even better, the Ba'athists twisted the truth, changed it, and gave it many shapes and colors to serve their goals. They even fabricated many "truths."

A few days went by full of anxiety and worry.

*   *   *

The day was December 15, 1973. It was a dark cold afternoon. The dull color of the cloudy sky losing sunlight exasperated the already tense atmosphere at home. This is fear that I have not yet forgotten, some twenty-eight years later. I shall never forget that afternoon. It may have been a normal winter afternoon for many people in Baghdad, but for us it was horrible. The sense of doom and despair of that afternoon was reminiscent, perhaps, only of the feelings you have when someone you love is no more. It was even worse. It was like when you are about to pass out or when you are choking and cannot breath. The weakness and lack of stamina I felt was awful. Every minute that passed was agonizing. That slow evening, it felt like time had stopped, that there was no motion in my world. It felt like every minute of those few hours was taking forever. It was like being lost in a desert with nowhere to turn. I remember the panic and the worried demeanor of my mother. I remember my brothers, Haider and Samir, talking with my mother and sitting by her trying to keep her calm, but they themselves were worried. They were on the phone on and off. I remember my brother Amer was in and out. Everyone at home was agitated and uneasy but they did not admit to it. Even as an eight-year-old child, I knew something was terribly wrong.

It was nearly six in the evening but my father had not come home yet. This was unusual because normally he would come home about two thirty or quarter to three or so. Normal working hours in Iraq, then, for official business were from 8 A.M. until 2 P.M. six days a week, Saturday through Thursday; the one-day weekend was on Friday. So normally, Dad was back about 2:30 or 2:40 P.M. unless he had other engagements and plans. That day, he did not call to inform us that he might be late. He had no other known commitments for that day, so he was expected to be home as usual. We called at his office; he was not there; there was no one there. The office had closed. In those days there were no mobile phones or pagers so we could not contact him.

Panic fell on the family, especially my mother. She told my older brothers Haider and Samir, "I feel something went wrong. I know something is wrong. Your father is always prompt and exact. If he were all right, he would have called to let us know." My brothers and others at home tried to ease her fears by saying things like, Oh, he will show up any minute, or perhaps he stopped at some shops or the post office. When I think about it now I believe those initial feelings of impending disaster one has are usually accurate and most of us deny in order to cope. It is like we do not want to believe that something is wrong. It is denial. I think we all have this way of coping. But I think my mother vocalized her fears and emotions right from the start; she was impatient and her emotions were more overt. In this and other cases she was right and her fears were well placed. In less than an hour or so everyone was feeling the serious fear she had had earlier. Those few hours taught me about the fragility of our human emotions and how unpredictable life is; in that short time period everything seemed to be falling apart. We all think of ourselves as strong and invincible, and especially as children we all thought of our parents as symbols of strength and reassurance. All children feel that way. We like to think that our parents are eternal and will endure everything and that they will always be there. But in this case, with the seeming absence of my father and the obvious worry and panic of my mother, I was feeling stripped, naked. It was like my source of strength was not there anymore.

There was escalating tension and fear at home. In those days, if someone did not show up, it meant Abu Tubar had gotten them or they had become one of those who "disappeared" for days and days only later to be found dead and chopped into pieces and dumped somewhere. The Ba‘ath government was sweeping out anyone whom they disliked, or anyone whom they saw as their potential enemy. Many prominent and decent people vanished this way. It was a time of fear and anguish in Baghdad.

My brother Amer went out to look at the main street to see if there was any sign of Dad's car. Dad had a government driver from his office pick him up and return him home and drive him between meetings and things that he had to do. Amer noticed some unusual cars and movements around the house. And he saw some men standing near our house. Amer came in and told my mother that there were three men out by the house, one looking at each of the three gates of our house. They looked like members of Almukhabarat, the secret intelligence service.

These people had a typical profile. They wore dark sunglasses. They wore normal civil suits but they were armed. And they had some type of wireless communication devices on them. In those days such devices were rare and only found in the possession of government officers. They were out of the reach of ordinary citizens. These people were near our house and we were scared of them. The presence of these men disturbed us, as they did not normally bring good news. But we were overwhelmed by worry at that point because Dad still had not come home. And anyway, we were afraid of those people and could not really go to ask them what they wanted. Normally, one would avoid any confrontation or provocation with those people. However, it was abnormal in the culture of the city for men to be just hanging out near people's homes. Normally people respected the privacy of others and no one would just hang out near someone's home; it was perceived as an intrusion. A while later, Amer went out to see if the men were still there. He saw them walking to Mr. Kader's home, the small home which he was renting from us. It was not a good feeling to know that Mr. Kader, who was a first grade Ba'athist was so near to our house and was perhaps collaborating in these events we were going through. The tension continued all evening.

My mother told my brothers Haider and Samir to go to my father's office to see if there was any indication as to what might have happened— a break-in, a murder, or merely perhaps his passing out in his office. She told them, "We have to know … whatever it is…. Maybe Abu Tubar attacked him. You have to be prepared for anything. Just go and search for your father. And call me right away if you find anything."

My brothers went to the office. When they got there, the building was closed, as business hours were over. There was a guard there. They explained to the guard who they were and why they had come. The guard knew my Dad well because he saw him daily. The guard let them in and unlocked the office. There was nothing unusual in the office. There was no sign that anything abnormal had taken place. The office was neat and looked like Dad had left it under usual circumstances. All the furniture was in its normal position; there was no indication of any violence or disturbance. My brothers left; later they decided to go to the driver's home. The guard at the office building informed them how to get there. The driver was so surprised to see them after he learned who they were, and he asked, "Oh, God, what happened? Is Mr. Makki okay?"

My brother told him what was happening, that Dad had never come home and seemed to be missing. They were hoping that the driver would know what had happened because he would have been the last person to see him.

"Well, today in the afternoon," the man said, "I was relieved from my duties. I was told there would be another driver for Mr. Makki. They did not tell me why they changed drivers…. Oh, God…. Oh, God, I wish I had stayed with him; this would not have happened. It is my fault…. Oh, God, I shall pray that he is all right and he will be safe."

My brothers thanked the driver for his kindness and left. At home we were hoping and waiting for any news from them; they came home a couple of hours later and told my Mom there was no news. They also told us about the driver switch. They were exhausted.

The eerie feelings kept getting worse. It was like the more time that passed, the more it became obvious that something terrible had happened. My mother was drained of energy and she was overwhelmed with worry and tension. She quickly deteriorated. She could not move, as if she were incapacitated temporarily. She did not know where to turn or what to do. These few hours were so grueling and intense. My grandmother came over to our house as soon as she heard the news; my aunt had called her and told her about my father. She was able to calm my mother down for a while, and she reminded her of her faith and that God Almighty was watching over us all and that she should not despair. They sat for a while and Mom was feeling slightly better.

After resting a bit and feeling reassured by her mother, my mother got a hold of herself a little. She decided to call Mr. Rashid Rifai at his house. He was a high-ranking government official and my Dad's boss. She told Mr. Rifai that Makki had not come home and asked whether Mr. Rifai knew of anything that was keeping Dad so late—a meeting, a conference.

Mr. Rifai was surprised and sorry to hear this news. "Oh, Madam Lydia," he said. "I am sorry. I do not know of anything out of the ordinary. There are no meetings or other commitments for the evening. I saw him today; he was fine. There were no problems whatsoever; in fact, this morning I just presented him with an acknowledgment award for his outstanding efforts and service. I do not understand why he would stay late at work. Whatever is keeping him late it is not work-related."

"Mr. Rifai," Mom responded, "my sons went to the office and to the driver's home but they had no news. I thought maybe something had happened there. They said that the office looked normal and there were no signs of any incidents. Oh, God? I can't bear to think about what might have happened."

"You know," Rifai said, "he must have gotten in a car accident and been injured. That is the only thing I can think of. Oh, my God, you should check the hospitals. God forbid, I mean I hope he is okay. And please, do let me know when you have some news. Let me see what I can find out too."

My mom was in panic and distressed by the thought of a car accident. She thanked Mr. Rifai and told him we would check the hospitals. Although a Ba'athist himself, Mr. Rifai was actually nice to my father, and he respected his talents and knowledge, which were rare in Iraq at that time. He enjoyed interacting with Dad on a professional level. Dad worked very sincerely in his job and brought great success and advancement to the agency where he worked.

Having listened to this conversation between Mom and Mr. Rifai, my brothers left the house and frantically went to the trauma hospitals in Baghdad to search for Dad in case he had gotten into some car accident. They went from one hospital to another like madmen. They looked at dead bodies and injured people in the emergency rooms. There was no sign of my father. A few hours later, they came home traumatized by what they had seen, with no news. They were exhausted.

By this time my aunts and my uncles had all come and they congregated in the house not knowing what had happened. Everyone was tense. No one could eat. The atmosphere was one of despair. I could not talk to Mom; I was afraid that I may upset her and she would yell at me. I just wanted her to be calm and fine. The house had eerie feelings. We were in and out just to see if Dad would suddenly show up. Inside, the phone rang all the time. My grandmother and my aunt Weda stayed at our house overnight. I stayed close to my grandmother. She was reassuring and loving. She held me and kissed me and said to pray to God that Dad would be back. Her presence made me feel a little safe. I think I went to sleep much later. My Mom and brothers stayed up all night with my aunt and grandmother.

Finally came the verdict. Mr. Rifai called about four in the morning the next day. He spoke to my mother and told her that Dad had been detained by the secret police, the Almukhabarat. My mother was shocked to hear that.

"What?" she said. "What…? Makki? Detained? Are you sure, Mr. Rifai? Oh, my God. Oh, God. No. No."

She started crying, then said, "Mr. Rifai, please. What do you mean? For what? How can this happen?"

"I am sorry," Mr. Rifai said.

"How could this happen?" Mom asked. "Did you know about it?"

"No! No! Nothing of it. I do not have more details than what I told you. I just learned about it myself now. And I called you right away."

Rifai said he would call if he got more news.

The phone fell from Mom's hands and she collapsed on the floor. Her legs were numb. Her mother and sister were by her side as they were with her during the phone call. They embraced her and kissed her. She was in immense anguish. She was lamenting incessantly and uncontrollably. Her speech was frightening in tone and in content. She was saying things like, I don't want to live. God, please take me. He is probably dead already. Oh, God…. Makki is gone, in their hands, they will kill him.

It was a horrible scene. My brothers and my older sister, Zeena, came running to her. They sat by her. They kissed her hands.

Haider said, "Mom, mom, you can't despair. Mom, you must have faith. God will save him. Mom, please; you can't collapse like this."

Amer, my other brother, started crying and he embraced Mom and my grandmother. Mom was in trauma all morning. She knew that once the Ba'ath got you they did not let you out.

Almukhabarat was the most feared institution that the Ba'ath invented. It was their ugliest institution, a secret place with secret operations. People who were taken by Almukhabarat usually did not come back. Its people were notorious for their cruelty, for torturing people, raping women, fabricating evidence, and spying. The institution was staffed by actual murderers. They were like the children of Satan himself. They were trained professionally in terror and torture. They enjoyed the screams of their victims, the terror they saw in their eyes when they were at their mercy. They were thugs and killers and it was common knowledge among Iraqis that these people were trained in Germany and that their spying equipment came from many Western countries. It was obvious. Such people would suddenly have trips abroad to some western country or East European country. These were not personal pleasure trips. In those days, personal travel was banned. It was amazing how some of them rose in a matter of weeks and months to become rich and powerful when they had been nobody before their affiliation with this institution. They were the reason why so many people in Iraq vanished into thin air. They were truly the Ba'ath regime at its worst. Almukhabarat people had so much power initially and their level of authority kept escalating. They could bypass anyone and everyone. Their orders superseded those of all other agencies and authorities. For example, although Mr. Rifai was my Dad's boss and he himself was a senior Ba'athist, he did not know about my father's detention and it was carried out without his knowledge.

My mother knew in her heart that they had detained my father because of what he had uncovered about the regime—that *they* had created the Abu Tubar crime string—and also because of his firm stance against their corruption and embezzlement. He did not allow them leeway as many other directors did to win favors from them. He did not want their favors. He reprimanded a couple of Ba'athists because they forged his signature to get some deals passed of which he did not approve. He did not do them any favors; he was like a big wall in their way and they had to crush it. Not many people knew about the Abu Tubar matter. Only Dad and the people working on the crime hotlines such as Mr. Abdul Fattah and a few others perhaps. Mom feared now that they had Dad, they would finish him off to cover this matter up. It would have been easy to finish off the few people who knew about this. She was crying and overcome by emotions. My aunt and my grandmother sat beside her and put their arms around her and tried to comfort her, although they themselves were worried and overcome by fear too.

My mother and father were like the center of the family emotionally. Our home housed all kinds of extended family celebrations and events, happy and sad. This stemmed from the fact that my mother was the oldest among her family and also the first one among her brothers and sisters to get married and have a family. Also my mother's family was closely knit. They did all kinds of things together. We saw them every other day or so. We were always visiting each other. This was also more of a social norm: family relations in Mediterranean cultures are much stronger than they are in Western cultures.

We were all overcome by the sad news and we were praying. My grandmother was religious. She was saying prayers all day. She made a "holy vow" to visit the holy site of the Prophet Jonah. Such a promise or vow was made when you had an urgent problem and you prayed to God to help you. You would go to some holy shrine (there are several such shrines in Iraq) and ask God to bless you and answer your prayers. The shrine was just a place of worship, a place to feel blessed. It is believed that in northern Iraq, in the city of Mosul, there is a shrine which is respected and loved by Muslims and Christians alike. It is thought to be the site where the Prophet Jonah was buried. It is said to bring you blessings when you visit and pray there. People would go there from Baghdad and from all over Iraq. Some visitors would even come from Lebanon and Syria to visit this site and to pray and ask God to help them in their problems.

The bad news was a shock to all of us. It was like a powerful strike on the head. We were in disbelief. But slowly, the fear and tension of the previous night was now becoming like a chronic nauseating feeling. For me, that morning was like the end of the world. I was feeling sick, distraught, shattered. There was nothing worse that I had felt in my life prior to that day. From my viewpoint as a child, my parents were dearer than my own life. Prior to these events, I always asked God to make my parents live long, live forever. Like all children, I felt that the most awful thing that could happen to me was losing my parents. It was the worst state of being that I had endured. It was like the end of the world. That these monstrous people had detained my Dad and that my Mom was collapsing crushed my happiness and my dreamy life of leisure and luxuries. Our fortress of happiness had been broken and Dad was gone for now, maybe he was already dead. From that time I knew and understood that the Ba'ath regime was an evil and a menace and that they had the power to inflict so much pain on us.

I felt like death had already conquered me. When I think about my life, that awful day scarred me with a deep permanent wound, it was a turning point in my life and literally the end of our happy days in Baghdad. On that day, I took a big leap from being a child into being an adult. I had to be responsible and I often hid my emotions; I developed a strong will and determination and it made me close to God. I tried to help my mother by being grown up and responsible and not just a whiny child. I don't know really whether I was of any help. I do not remember much from that time in my life other than this episode. I do not remember school, I do not remember my birthday, or anything else in life other than pain and frustration, my Dad being gone, my Mom in bad shape, my aunts being with us, and lots of people coming in and out.

The anguish continued over the next few days. My Mom collapsed emotionally and physically; she could not go to her job. She stayed home mourning and crying most of the days. She could not do anything. My brother Haider would give her Valium by force just to keep her quiet. My aunts were in and out all the time. They never left her alone. Although I always thought of my mother as strong, I think that even strong people are not invincible; they must have some vulnerable point. From my own life experience, I think this is true. Certainly, fear of government wrath and retaliation was the most awful thing that existed in Iraq, and I know it affected her. I also think that no matter how strong you are in the face of certain problems, there are probably other traumas that will get you. For my mother, it seems part of her strength was the confidence she had from my Dad being there and being her own fortress and source of secret strength. It is hard to understand this emotional dynamic which exists between true lovers and between couples who have been together for such a long time and have endured good and bad times together.

My aunt Weda knew the family of a high-ranking official of Almukhabarat, Sadun Shakir. They were friends of hers at her job. She arranged for my Mom to meet with him. Both my mother and my aunt were not exactly happy that they had to go and seek help from this senior official. But they had to. This was the only way to get information. During the Ba'ath era, this was the best if not the only way to get anything done, that is, to use the influence of any Ba'athists whom you knew. It was more effective than any other means, and actually it was the only means sometimes, as in this case, to get answers and find out what had happened to someone. The next day, my Mom went to meet with him. She had to pass through so many security gates and armed guards just to get to the house, but they let her in because there was notice of her visit. Mom met with Mr. Shakir and his wife.

"Mr. Shakir," she told him, "my husband is a sincere man, all of Baghdad would vouch for him. He has served this country for decades, he loves this country. He is innocent.... You know. He was trying to protect people from the crimes.... Is that not what the government wants? Do they not want to catch Abu Tubar?"

Mr. Shakir looked at her with intrigue and said, "Of course we want to catch Abu Tubar."

Mom was not sure whether Mr. Shakir knew of the details that my Dad had uncovered. "Please tell me what they have fabricated against him." she continued. "Do you know?"

And she kept on and on. Shakir was stunned by her direct remarks about the government and her eloquence. He was not used to having ordinary citizens visit him and speak to him directly and request his help. "I do not know yet about this case," he told her. "I was away for a while. I did not know about his arrest. I shall see what I can do."

Gloomy days went by. There was no way to know what had happened, or why. There was no way to check exactly where my father was. The intelligence and the secret police operated from so many places and owned so many buildings and houses. They were known to be reckless and brutal. They tortured and killed people and it meant nothing to them. They were the poor and hopeless people of no education and no status but they were trained to be thugs and killers. They had control over people's lives with their means of terror and weapons. Western and East European countries happily provided their training and equipment.*

Uncle Sadi, who was a high-ranking army officer before the Ba'ath thugs came to power, used all his pull and connections in the government. But he could not shed a light on where Dad was exactly. Was he still alive? My Mom only wanted to be sure that he was alive. She kept saying, oh, my God, they've killed him, otherwise why is there no word? She was very worried. She survived those days one hour at a time. Thirty-four days went by with agony and anguish. It was a nightmare, but a living nightmare.

During those days, my mother, even with all her resilience, collapsed emotionally and physically. She missed many days of work and became incapacitated. These were long and sad days for all of us. There was so much

*That the Western and other governments supported this regime is evident from numerous documented accounts of people and transactions. However, it is not within the scope of this book to discuss these facts.

tension at home. In a way, our family was falling apart. The emotional trauma was severe on all of us. I became ill during those days and had various medical checkups and minor procedures. This lasted several weeks. My mother had to take me to the hospital several times. Sometimes I went with my uncle. My sister Zeena used to go upstairs all the way to the roof on the third floor to sit and cry alone there. My older brothers left the house a lot. I do not know where they went. My brother Amer decided that he wanted to share the suffering of my Dad wherever my Dad was. So he never changed into his house clothes during all the time that Dad was away. Typically in Baghdad we put on our house clothes when we were at home. They were just casual and comfortable clothes that normally were not worn outside the house. Our life was not normal. We just passed the time. It was a horrible time. We were all shattered. Also, my mother had to borrow money to keep the big house running. My aunts stayed with us and took care of the cooking and daily affairs of the house like the shopping.

Relatives and friends poured in to visit daily. They were shocked at the news of my father's disappearance. Hundreds of people came over to our house over the weeks. They did not know what to say. They did not know if Dad was alive or dead. They would sit and cry with us; sometimes they were just in disbelief at what had happened. They all asked and wondered, How can this happen? Makki, this honorable man whom all of Baghdad know as kind and honest … who has devoted all his life to serving his country and helping people … and has contributed so much, how can he be detained by these thugs and street killers? It sounded impossible.

Everyone was distraught at what had happened to this country, that is, its being run by criminal gangs. People were bewildered by it. They kept whispering about how bad things had gotten in Iraq. They could not believe what had happened to Dad. They did not know what to say. So many people came over; it was like having a funeral or a wedding. I never knew that Dad was such a popular man. People came from his office, from my Mom's school, her old college friends came, university students whom my Dad had taught in the past, our relatives and they were so many I did not even know some of them. Even people from outside Baghdad came to ask about what had happened to Dad. We had visitors daily; it was like having an open house every day. It was strange because this type of extensive visitation occurred only when someone in the family died or there was a wedding. But for us it was neither.

* * *

The agony continued and got worse by the day. The cold winter days, the mood of despair. These were days void of meaning and happiness. I do not remember much of our daily life then, other than this episode. I just remember a block of time with fear and tears and the absence of laughter. Some days we just thought it would be over and Dad would knock on the door. But this never happened. Over a month went by and we still had no word.

One day, Uncle Sadi came and told my mother that he had some news. Uncle Sadi, through his connections as an army officer, was able to get word that Dad was still alive and that he was indeed detained by the Almukhabarat. More importantly, he told my mother that he was finally able to arrange for her to see Dad in the intelligence detention center where he was being held. It had taken many heroic efforts from Uncle Sadi and his contacts to get this meeting arranged. He whispered this news to my Mom and he told her not to say anything about it. She could not take anyone or anything with her. She could only see him, she could not discuss anything with him. And it would only be for a few minutes. Uncle Sadi told Mom that he had done his best to get this arranged. It was through the favor of one high-ranking army officer who had personal influence with the director of the Almukhabarat, a thug by the name of Fadil Albarrak. Mom was relieved just to know that Dad was alive. She thanked Uncle Sadi and was crying out of gratitude to him. She could barely wait for the visit.

It was a miracle, the visit that is, because normally they do not allow visitors there under any circumstances. It is a top-secret place where they torture and kill people and no one can go there. The next day, Uncle Sadi came over and took Mom into some neighborhood in Baghdad. Mom had not been there before. It looked like residential homes for the most part. It was plain from the outside; it did not look like a detention center. The area was surrounded by shops and small offices. Mom thought that all the shops and offices belonged to them anyway.

Uncle Sadi escorted Mom in and then had to wait outside. She went in a few steps and was stopped. First, she was searched all over, her clothes, her purse, her shoes. There were security cameras in the lobby. Then, she was guided to another building through an underground tunnel. She walked for a short period behind the guard. Then they stopped at a door and another guard he told her to wait. That place was weird. It was kind of clean and well kept but it was lifeless. The place was big inside unlike the impression you got when you saw it from the outside. Mom knew that they went underground, but she did not realize the place was so big. As she was walking, she heard a few sounds of people talking and some laughter. Mom waited by the door. Another guard came to talk to the first guard then told her to follow him through the small door. Mom was scared. Her mouth was dry as if she could not talk. She was afraid that she would be kidnapped and harmed. They went into a room and she was told to wait. The room had another door and it must have led elsewhere.

It was cold in that room. There was one chair and a table. She sat and waited. The room was quiet. Her heart was racing. For a moment she forgot where she was. It was an overwhelming few minutes. She was anxious to see Dad. She just wanted to touch him to believe that he was still alive. Those tense moments were so long. She was afraid of disappointment, that he would not come or that he would not be there, that he may have been moved elsewhere or that they may have changed their minds about allowing the visit. She was afraid that they had already killed him and that they would just give her the body or that he was dead already and they had forgotten that detail. All those thoughts were firing in her head. It seemed to her that she waited so long.

Then all of a sudden, that other door opened and Dad walked in with a guard. Dad did not know where he was going. They did not inform him that he had a visitor. Mom got up from the chair; she looked at him. She was shocked. He did not look the same. He looked distraught. He looked some twenty years older and drained of life. He had a bent back. He had not shaved for days and days. He was barefoot. He was bruised and wounded. His feet were blue. His left eye was dripping incessantly. His body was cold.

Mom held his hands not believing this was reality or a dream. She embraced him and started crying. She held his hands and was kissing them and warming them with her tears. Moments went by where they could not talk. They were both crying. Mom could not believe this was the same man she knew. She was shaking and crying.

"Lydia, how are you?" he simply said. "How are the children? I am all right, I am all right. Don't worry about me."

"Oh, God," she cried. "Oh my God, Makki."

Mom could not speak. She could not say one sentence. She was overcome by emotions. Neither could say much, they were both overwhelmed by the pain and the emotion. They were both crying.

The visit lasted ten or so minutes. The guard interrupted them and told her, "That's enough; get out now." Mom had to leave as she was told. And Dad was escorted out of the room. Their eyes said a lot to each other, but they could not say good-bye. Mom was now afraid of what they might do to Dad because of this emotional outburst of hers. She walked out. She was shattered. She was in immense anguish. She followed the guard but she could not feel or see anything. She was escorted to another exit, which led to the car where Uncle Sadi was waiting for her. She could barely walk the few steps to the car. She leaned on it. She was crying in agony. Uncle Sadi got out of the car and helped her into it. "Sadi," she pleaded, "please, for God's sake … please do something. I am going to die…. Please … oh, my God."

Uncle Sadi held her. "Lydia," he said, "I swear to God, I shall do everything I can. But it is not in my hands. I will keep trying. I promise. It kills me to see you like this. Oh, God. What is happening to us?"

Mom did not say anything. She cried all the way home. She could not believe what had happened to her husband. She had always known him to be strong like a castle, like a mountain, like a giant ship on the ocean. He rocked the floor when he walked; he was respected, bold and wonderful. He drew attention wherever he went. He was so charming and good-looking. During the entire drive home she was struck by the contrasting images of what she had seen that day and what she had always known Dad to look like. She felt like someone who was falling off a cliff or someone who had been hit by a truck. She was quite devastated when she got home and told us what she had seen. My aunts sat around her and embraced her and they told her that she must persevere and have patience. We were around her. Everyone was crying but we all thanked God that at least my father was alive.

Many sad days went by. They were all the same: sad, long and empty. Several weeks later, we learned that Dad had been transferred to another detention center known as Alfidailia. This horrible detention place was slightly less notorious than Almukhabarat center. At least this was a publicly known detention place, not secret as the former. Here at Alfidailia, people were kept for the longer term. It was more like a jail. Here, they allowed visitors. One day Mom came and told us that Uncle Sadi had made some contacts and that we could all go to see Dad. All of us. It was a miracle that we were going to go and see him. It was just around the time of Eid Al Adha, the Muslim holiday of the pilgrimage, which is when people go to visit the holy land in Mecca. This is a major religious holiday in Iraq. Of course we did not really plan any celebrations that year. We were in the midst of the crisis and no one was in the mood to celebrate. This was in striking contrast to what we had normally done for the Eid celebrations in other years and in good times.

Under normal circumstances, the Eid Al Adha was a joyous, exciting time. It was just like the holiday season here in the West. The typical Eid preparations and celebrations were exciting and full of anticipation. We would clean the house and decorate the living and dining rooms. Mom would make tons and tons of pastries and cookies. The baking smell was so good. Some of these cookies were for us and all the guests whom we were expecting. And some were for the neighbors and some were given to the poor. In fact Mom prepared special things for some poor families whom we knew and would take those goodies to in the Eid.

We kids would have spent the preceding few weeks preparing our Eid wardrobe. This was so exciting. Kids got new clothes for the Eid. I mean new everything. New outfits: at least one but sometimes more than one. New shoes, new hair bands and ribbons if you had long hair, even new socks and underwear. This wardrobe was very special and we took care of it and did not use it until the Eid morning. We would take pictures and show off our new clothes. Not only did we get new clothes, we also got cash. That was even better.

Typically, the adults in the family would give the children cash for the Eid. We usually got money from our parents and our uncles and aunts. And the older you were, the more money you got. I, being the youngest of my brothers and sisters, always got the least. So did my cousin who was also the youngest in her family. But that was okay—we were still happy with what we got.

During the Eid days, there would be visitors every day as the holiday was four days long. But most of the visiting was done over the first two days. It was like open house; there would be visitors and relatives and sweets and gifts. It was so exciting. That year however, we had none of that because of the events in our family. We were sad, and the Eid days just went by. We missed Dad very much. So instead, Mom thought she could take all of us to see Dad after a few months of the arrest. It would be good for us and Dad and her to be together, even just for a little while.

The holidays had just finished and we were back at school. We had to take a day off from school in order to go on the visit. I was in fourth grade. My Mom had prepared a note to the school principal to let us out, myself and my sister who was in fifth grade. My brother Samir came to the school. He met with the principal and gave her the note. The principal knew both my parents well. She had heard what had happened from other people. She told my brother that she could not believe what had happened to my Dad. She was sad about it. She knew him well because of all his contributions to the school—he was a leading member of the parents' council, as all of us went to that school, even my brothers long before my sister and I, so the principal knew the family for many years. An attendant came to my class. He gave my teacher the note, which was approved by the principal. The note said to give me permission to be off the rest of the day to go visit my father. The teacher read the note and asked me in front of my classmates, "So, where is your father? Is he in hospital? Or in prison." I was traumatized by the question and could not answer her for a few seconds. Ultimately, I said in a shaking voice, that my Dad was detained. I left the classroom and followed my brother to the car.

The day was rainy and cold. But I was happy that we were going to see Dad finally. So we went to Alfidailia. It was quite a long way to get there. We parked the car in some courtyard near the entrance, but it was just an unpaved area, all mud, with little ponds of mud water. We stood in the courtyard waiting. We waited a long time until we were let in. This was not a normal visitation like you might see in any prison; it was a rather disorganized place. There were many people trying to get in to visit detainees. All these people were crammed together at a small window where a couple of attendants were taking names of the detainees and names of the visitors. I do not remember seeing many children my age. We were not treated in a civilized way. You had to plead with these attendants to take down your name and to go inside to see whether the detainees were there. It was sad to see some people being turned down and told that their son or family member whom they had come to visit was no longer there. It usually meant that they had been executed or sent back to Almukhabarat center. At least we knew that my Dad was there for sure. The guards questioned us and after their long deliberations and our waiting outside in the cold, they let us into some large room. It was the most shocking place I had seen.

It was a dark cold dungeon. There were only a couple of light bulbs hanging from the ceiling. People were standing there because there was nowhere to sit. The floor was wet and slippery from the rain, which was leaking in from the roof. There were a few windows in the room, but they were either open or the glass was broken because freezing wind was coming in. The prisoners were on one side of the room behind a dividing rope or low fence. It was not really a barrier as people were able to talk and embrace each other. Embracing and weeping filled the room as many other families had come to see someone at this horrible place. Armed guards were dispersed among the detainees and the families. They mocked us and did not respect our privacy or the pain we were all enduring. It was a humiliating scene. The room was somewhat crowded and people were crying and embracing each other and there was a lot of talking and chatter.

Being small in the crowd, I could not see well and could not find Dad initially. I was disappointed because I thought they had lied to us, that Dad was not there. I was distraught. Perhaps more so because I was in shock as I had not seen such a filthy place before with so many people crying and weeping. Then a few minutes later I saw my father; he had the most loving gentle smile on his face. But I was shocked to see him because he looked different. He was frail and shaken. He was wearing a ripped coat and slippers. He was coughing and had some kind of bronchitis. The place was filthy and unhygienic. I was scared, shocked, traumatized. I had never seen Dad in such a poor condition before. I was used to his charming, sophisticated look. Throughout the few minutes since we arrived I had been holding back my tears and was pretending to be okay. But then when I saw Dad in this shape, I started crying as I said hello to him and we embraced. Then I pulled away and went to my Mom and stuck myself to her coat. I was crying incessantly. I remember a young man in that room who was also detained and who was being visited by an older woman, perhaps his mother. They looked at me as I was hiding my face from my Dad behind my Mom's coat, crying. They smiled at me gently. Dad looked old and frail. He held us and embraced us. My sisters and I were crying. Mom was holding her tears in check. It was a traumatic experience. It was devastating and so painful to see my graceful, dignified father in this shambles.

The visit was brief, maybe a half-hour to forty minutes or so, but it was the most traumatizing experience of my life up to then. At the end, Dad embraced Mom and told her, "Lydia, this is a paradise compared to where I was before in Almukhabarat. I was in a grave. I did not see light for days and days. I thought I would never see you and the children again. At least there is light in here." Then he whispered to my Mom to be cautious at home because our house was bugged. He said that they made him listen to tapes of our conversations at home and that we should not talk freely inside the house. He said they analyzed every voice and knew who was saying what. He told Mom not to say anything about this case at home. He thought the bug was some recording instrument attached to the telephones perhaps. He said he knew of such devices used by intelligence. They got them from some Western countries. They were very small, no one could see them.

The dreadful visit ended. We were in tears. We said good-bye to Dad and told him we wished we could see him again soon. We went out to the car. My sister Dalia and I kept crying and the others were quiet. There was only the sound of my sister and me crying, the sound of the raindrops on the windshield, and the sound of the windshield wipers running. My brother Haider was driving. My heart was torn and my soul was in pain over the sight of my father. I could not understand why my father, this wonderful, loving, intelligent man was in that horrible place. With the simple logic I had at the age of eight, I could not accept what was happening. I understood later that it was wrong and unfair and that many things that the Ba'ath regime was doing were bad and evil. They ruined my life at that time and I did not understand why they were doing this to us.

My mother was torn up about what had happened to us at Alfidailia. She had thought it would be good for us to go and see Dad. She did not know that the place would be that bad and the experience would be so traumatic. At home, my aunts told Mom that she should not take us again to this place, especially me and my sister, as we were too young to see that environment—we were only eight and nine. It was a painful experience. Mom was so upset about what had happened to us. She felt guilty about taking us there. She tried to cheer us a little. She kept talking to us and telling us some happy stories all day.

Later, Mom told us all about the house being bugged. She also told my aunts what Dad had said. My uncle, my Mom's brother, Uncle Raid, who was trained in electronics went about the house to figure out where the bugs were. He and my brother looked at the phones in the house. They were not able to find anything. Therefore, we developed a family rule that we could not talk about the case or about Dad or the government inside the house.

Mom visited Dad in this detention center every day that visits were allowed—I think it was twice a week. During her visits Dad told her what had happened to him. He was arrested from his office on December 15th. He said it was a sudden attack by a bunch of armed men, a couple of them were from his office and he knew them as they were among his staff. One of them was Adib Mufti, a senior Ba'athist at the office where my Dad worked. Dad said that he was leaving to come home as usual and he went out expecting to see the driver waiting for him. Instead, those men were waiting for him.

They said, "Mr. Makki, you need to come with us for a few minutes."

"Where to?" he demanded. "What is it about?"

"Just come with us, Mr. Makki," one of the men said.

"But, I am leaving to go home. Can it wait until tomorrow? Let me find the driver."

"I am telling you that you must come with us … now…. There is no driver."

"What? Is this a joke? Are you playing some joke on me?"

My father had such a good heart that he did not want to believe that these men who worked with him had conspired against him and that they had come to harm him. The men did not answer. Instead, they held a gun at his head and pushed him into the car that was waiting nearby. There were other men whom he did not know in the car. They tied a blindfold over his eyes and the car left.

"Who are you?" Dad asked them. "And what do you want from me?" The men did not answer.

They drove at length. Dad did not know where they were going. He tried to focus on the direction, but the drive did not last too long. They stopped, someone opened the car door, and they forced him out. The grim group walked to some building and went in.

At that moment, the men untied his blindfold and began screaming, "You are a spy and we shall kill you."

"What?" my father exclaimed. "What? What do you mean? What? I am not a spy."

"You are against the revolution," one of the men said. "You are a spy."

"Are you crazy?" Dad threw back. "What are you talking about? You've got the wrong man. I assure you ... you've got the wrong man."

They were questioning him about his loyalty to the Ba'ath party and why he did not join.

"Look, I am an old man," Dad said. "I never joined any party. I am serving the country with my knowledge ... so leave me alone."

They were yelling and screaming at him and asking why he opposed the party, why he did not cover up what he knew about Abu Tubar and why he investigated the matter, and why he did not let them do what they wanted at the office. Dad tried to talk sense into them. He told them of his many years of service to the country and of all his accomplishments for Iraq and that they were mistaken about him, but it was no use.

The government agency which my father headed was in charge of major contracts with foreign companies. Dad approved or rejected these contracts objectively based on their validity and use and the benefits to the programs they served. The Ba'athists in his office wanted to reap personal financial benefits by awarding these contracts to foreign companies they had corrupt ties with. In addition, they manipulated transactions under these contracts to their advantage. They even forged Dad's signature for some of these deals. He confronted them and reprimanded them. He also warned them that he would take them to court for this fraud. Dad was so principled and upright. The Ba'athists took offense and considered him an enemy of the revolution. They thought that because they were Ba'athists, they could do as they pleased and for them it was a case of, Who are you to stop us? Dad opposed their corruption and made it known to all that he would never tolerate such wrongdoing. One of his abductors that cold December day told my father, "Listen, Makki, you are going to pay for this."

A few hours after this first encounter with them, they took him and shoved him into a small room. It was more like a box than a room, approximately one meter (3ft 3in) in all directions. He could not stand in that room or lie down extending his legs, and he was somewhat tall. So it was very confining. Also, the room was cold and had no light. Dad was a great man to have endured this. I do not know how he could breathe because I think that one would feel suffocated under such conditions. I am so sad and so sorry that he had to go through this frightening experience.

Once in a while, the door was opened and he was given bread and water. Dad still had his watch on him. This was the only thing he could see because it had fluorescent material on the arms and the numbers. So he could tell the time of the day even though he was in the dark and in isolation. His watch also displayed the date, so he knew that he was there for thirty-four days. The watch was his only companion.

I cannot even imagine how my father felt being locked up in the dark with no way out and being there for many hours during a day and many days at a time. I feel a choking sensation just thinking about that and writing these words. Just how did those awful hours and minutes pass for him? I just know from my own life experiences how impatient we human beings are about simple and silly things. For example, we do not like waiting in line for something or we get upset if we have to wait for something to arrive or anything like that. But being in this confinement in the dark and amongst enemies and killers is beyond my imagination. I do not know how my father went through this. He was a great man and he had a strong soul. His body was in pain and agony and discomfort, but I think his mind was in command all the time.

Dad was resilient and he had a strong will and iron nerves. I do not know what kept him alive. It is amazing how he survived. It was a horrible fate. As much as he wanted to get out of this confining place, he did not want to leave it because that inevitably meant the interrogation and torture sessions. It was a losing battle on both ends. When I think about what my father had to endure, I realize how strong and determined he was. I wonder what it was that kept him alive and kept him from losing his mind. Perhaps it was hope of going back home, or maybe it was all the warm and happy memories of his life, or maybe it was faith. I do not really know. But I do wonder what he thought about each of those horrible moments in the small boxy room where he was kept. Most people would respond to such severe trauma by becoming hysterical or suicidal. Dad maintained a strong grip on his thoughts and emotions throughout this horrible time.

During subsequent interrogations, they beat him and insulted him. They were exceptionally violent—they strapped him to a chair and beat him until he passed out. They made him stand barefoot on the freezing cold concrete floor for hours and hours. The interrogation sessions lasted many days and took some hours of each day, but there were days when they just left him in that room. That was how he spent those thirty-four days in which we knew nothing of his fate. They also tortured him with electric shocks. Dad had iron nerves, and he maintained a grip on his thoughts and sanity. He was strong like the trunk of a giant tree. Although they kept hammering away at him, they could not crush him with their lies and accusations.

Dad began to wear down when they told him about their "evidence" against him. They told him that he had told a joke about the Ba'ath party and its leadership. Dad was shaken by this revelation because he was so careful about what he said in public. He might have told such a joke only to my mother in their bedroom. Indeed, they made him listen to a tape of their private conversations in their bedroom. In the tape, he laughed at the joke that he and my Mom were repeating and had heard from someone earlier. Dad was stunned when he listened to the "incriminating" evidence—a joke that he and my Mom were sharing and laughing at in the privacy of their bed. Getting into people's beds was then the latest Ba'ath tactic. Not only did they kill and kidnap people, they also intruded on their privacy in their homes and in their beds. Dad was amazed by how advanced their tactics were, that they were able to get some recording device into his bed; and the tape he had just listened to was from over a year before.

Torture in Almukhabarat center was not only physical but also psychological. They threatened him and told him that they were going to bring his wife and children to join him there. This threat, of harming the family, the women and the children, is a weapon that tyrants and dictators all over the world have used against men since the dawn of humanity. Such a threat is used as a weapon to make men of resistance crumble and to get anything they want from them. No man in the world wants his family harmed. All men have this natural weakness. My Dad was no exception. He wanted his family, us and my mother, to be safe. He himself had endured tremendous pain and physical torture but he collapsed emotionally once he heard that. He was pleading with them.

"Leave my family alone," he adjured them. "I beg you. Do whatever you want to me.... It is I whom you are after.... Kill me. Go ahead finish me now or leave me here as long as you want, but don't touch my family. I will do anything you want."

Having identified this vulnerability in him, they forced him to obey all their commands. They made him sign blank documents, which would probably be used later to incriminate him, although their exact use was unclear. Dad asked them whether he could see what he was signing. In response to this question, he was hit severely on the head. His left eye was badly injured and dripped all the time thereafter. Mom later learned from him that for all the period that he was there, he slept on the floor; they gave him no more than a few crusts of bread and a little water. He had no clothes except for his undershirt and shorts, and he became ill and weak. He was hit severely and repeatedly on the head, and after a few days at Almukhabarat center, he passed out for a few hours. Later we learned that he had had a stroke. He said some doctor from the military came to look at him briefly.

Dad also told Mom stories of what he saw both at Almukhabarat center and at Alfidailia—so much horror and injustice. It was unbelievable. He saw a man at Almukhabarat center, all of whose bones had been broken in torture. The man could not sit or stand. Dad was frightened by what he saw. He briefly saw some men who were blindfolded and being dragged to some interrogation. Most of his time at Almukhabarat center was spent between solitary confinement and torture sessions. At Alfidailia, which was more like a conventional jail, there was no torture. But the place was awful and ugly. Dad said many men were kept in medium size rooms. There was no air, no sun, and no hygiene. In that awful place, Dad met another prominent man, a doctor and a graduate of Harvard University, who had also taken a stance against the Ba'ath regime and they wanted to finish him off too.

This agony continued. There was no hope of any progress. There was no timeline. The government could hold people in detention for no reason for months, years, forever. People were lucky to stay alive. A few more months went by and Dad remained away from us. It was a horrible time, a time that we do not like to remember, because it was so painful. It is a pain that one keeps inside. In Iraq in those days, and even more so nowadays, you could not petition or inquire about such cases. The government was a power without check. It was made up of thugs and criminals. Corruption was ubiquitous. Such a system was best exemplified by the Khmer Rouge and their atrocities in Cambodia. The Ba'athists had the authority to arrest, kill, detain, and torture anyone. They raped women in the presence of their fathers or husbands. This was a standard method of terrorizing and humiliating people. The Ba'ath was a Stalinist-Nazi–like regime at its worst. There are many untold stories of atrocities as severe as those of even the holocaust.

After weeks of waiting, my father's case was given to a "revolutionary judge." This judge was a member of the Ba'ath party, a thug and a criminal himself. His name was Jarala Allaf. He was responsible for sentencing to death so many innocent and decent people including Mr. Aref Albasri. Mr. Aref Albasri was a prominent religious scholar and one of the five prominent clerics and teachers whom the government executed and who were known later as "the five martyrs." These men were arrested and murdered just for providing religious education to the youth. Accusations were fabricated against them: they were accused of being against the Ba'ath and being loyal to "reactionary forces." In fact, the government fabricated stories about many people to legitimize their killings and detentions. During these early years of Ba'ath rule, there still were some agencies of the government which had not been fully penetrated by the Ba'ath, although it was only a matter of time before they established full control. So in these earlier cases of detentions and arrests, especially against prominent or well known people—people whom the whole city of Baghdad knew to be kind and sincere, such as my Dad or the five martyrs—the Ba'ath regime needed to justify their actions. They were overturning deeply ingrained social norms in attacking and arresting the pillars of Iraqi society just because they refused to support the Ba'ath, and so had to mount at least the semblance of a legal case against these respected people in the early days.

The government also accused many of being Freemasons. Whenever they wanted to finish someone off, they labeled him as such, especially if he had any kind of contact with foreign nationals, even if it was a simple personal friendship. Thus, they arrested numerous individuals with such a blanket charge, that they were members of the Freemasons, and exterminated them. In fact, because of such accusations, ordinary people thought of anyone who was detained in those days as Freemasons, even though this organization did not really have widespread representation in Iraq and most Iraqis did not know anything about it.

They fabricated similar accusations against my Dad. There was actually nothing against him. On the contrary, he was a prominent man of integrity and honor. All of Baghdad knew him as such and that he had been wrongfully accused and detained. Some of our relatives were well known attorneys in Baghdad and had some connections, and they forced their way into Dad's case. In Iraq in those days, you could not have an attorney defend you and you could not even ask what the charges were against you. The government was like a monster you could not argue with or question. However, through some contacts and because of my Dad's pristine reputation in town, these attorneys were able to influence his case. They used what was left of the judicial system—after the Ba'ath had taken over—and managed to be present in the hearings to know what the formal charges for holding him were.

The day of the sentencing came after many delays and cancellations. A date was often set by the revolutionary court but later changed. This happened countless times. Mom and my brothers would go to the court and be turned back. They would be disappointed; they just wanted it to be over. Finally we heard that sentencing was going to take place the next day. Mom and everyone got ready to go. Uncle Sadi knew a high-ranking attorney in Baghdad, who also had connections in the government. The attorney, Mr. Hazem, came over to visit us the night before the sentencing. He delivered some bad news. He said that through his contacts he had learned that my father was going to be sentenced to one year in prison. It had already been decided. The court hearing was meaningless. It was just a show. Mom and Uncle Sadi were so shocked and dismayed.

"How can this be?" Mom asked Mr. Hazem. "What country in the world allows this kind of insult to people's rights? It has already been decided?"

Mr. Hazem did not say much.

"And they call it a court hearing?" Mom continued. "They have already decided...?"

"That's the way it is," Mr. Hazem responded. "No matter what is said tomorrow, there will be a sentencing of one year. They've already decided."

"Will you be there?" Mom asked the attorney. "Will you speak to defend Makki? Maybe if you speak, things will change. I mean ... maybe if they hear the facts...."

"Yes, they will let me in. I will also do my best to allow Makki to speak in his own defense. I think it is more powerful that way. I think they will let me do that at least. But I do not think it will change the outcome. I am telling you now because I think you have to be ready for that. They have already decided. I am so sorry to bring you this news."

Mom was in grief all night. She was suffering and felt awful because of this news of the impending development. This was so much injustice and abuse, and it was unbearable and unbelievable. She was angry and dismayed. She wanted to call Amnesty International or the United Nations, someone. She wanted to go out in the street and scream to protest this injustice, that a sentencing had taken place before they even looked at the case. My aunt Weda and my brother Haider forced her to stay home and told her that such actions would make things worse for Dad. She kept thinking and sighing, What kind of a mockery is this of human life? They reach a verdict that is convenient for them. Without even looking at facts. She could not sleep all night. It was a horrible night.

The next day Mom and my brothers went to the court. They were later met by Uncle Sadi and Uncle Mizhar. It was raining heavily that day. Mom, my brothers, Uncle Sadi, Uncle Mizhar and others were told that they had to wait outside the court. It was called the "court of the revolution." It was a small white building, just one story; it almost looked like a house rather than an official building. They were not allowed in and had to stand outside in the cold. They waited a few hours by the door. It was an agonizing wait. Nobody would tell them what was going on. They knew there was nothing they could do to stop this injustice. Then suddenly the door opened and they caught a glimpse of Dad inside. An attendant from the revolutionary court read a statement that Dad was sentenced to prison for one year, just as Mr. Hazem had said. This decision by the revolutionary judge was final; there was no mechanism to reverse it or even to know how this decision had been reached. They further announced that he would be taken to "Abu Graib Prison."

There was no way to appeal this decision, to protest it, to review evidence, to question it. The case had been decided by Allaf and his gang of thugs. There was no system of justice. It was a mockery of justice. It was sheer lawlessness in a land governed by criminals who maintained a strong grip on every breath we took. That the case of my father was given to this thug, Allaf, to decide was one of many evils. It could have been worse. At least my father was alive and had not been killed. And there was hope that he would remain alive. It was otherwise a hopeless episode. One could not object or appeal. Dad was escorted out like a criminal and put in a car that was waiting.

My mother and brothers were standing outside in the rain. My Dad was in the car which was getting ready to be driven away. It was a heart-rending scene. This was unadulterated injustice and it felt like the end of the world. They were not allowed to see him or discuss what had happened inside or even to say hello or good-bye. Dad saw them; he attempted to say something, but he was being pushed into the car. He pulled down the window of the car to try to see my Mom. My brother Amer saw Dad and waved at him the V (victory) signal, trying to give him some encouragement. Amer was a teenager then. My mother was so disheartened, seeing him like this. Out of her desperation, she screamed from afar, with all the power of her voice, as the car was pulling in front of them and she saw Dad for a few seconds through the window of the car: *"Makki, never mind these thugs."* Then she recited a powerful, well-known verse from Arabic poetry by the tenth century poet Almutanabi: *"That I should be condemned by inferiors is indeed a testimony to my perfection."* This verse is used as a proverb in Arabic and has a clear and beautiful meaning: when a person of honor and grace and with a long history of fame and sincerity and accomplishment, like my father, is condemned by such as the Ba'athists, who are criminals and thugs and gangsters, it is a testimony to the true character of that person. It is hard to translate this proverb into English.

My mother made this statement out of anger and frustration and also because of her fiery nature. She had to make a point. It did not help my father in any way that she said that, but it may well have helped her. She always had to say what was on her mind. However, this was an obvious protest against the cruel treatment of my father. Speaking your mind in Iraq then, and even more so today, was a crime and an attack on the party and the revolution. The guards looked at Mom, thinking this woman was crazy for speaking out and protesting a government decision. She could have been detained herself. Uncle Mizhar pushed my Mom into the car yelling at her, "Are you crazy? Shut up and stop this nonsense." Mom got in the car. "We shall all be harmed because of what you said," he continued.

Everyone got in the car to go home. They were angry and disheartened. The rain kept pouring and the sound of the raindrops on the car windshield exacerbated the feelings of despair. My mother and my brothers were crying. Uncle Sadi was sad. He thought that he could help somehow. This was so unfair. There was no justice and no one to complain to. While in the car, Mom slipped into a daydream about the past happy days and the hopes and aspirations that she and my Dad had for their lives and their children. It was all being shattered by the withering away of her man right in front of her eyes. Yet she was powerless to stop it or to save him. She was afraid of the days ahead. How would she manage on her own without my Dad? She kept thanking God that Dad was alive.

Later Mr. Hazem came round. He was sad and disappointed too and told my Mom and the others about the events inside the courtroom. During a pre-sentencing hearing, some fabrications were presented against my father that he was in contact with foreigners. Dad had written a letter of recommendation to a former student of his who also worked at his office. The student, Isam Izat, was applying for admission for a graduate degree in England. At least that is what he told my father, and my father believed that. He needed a letter of recommendation and Dad wrote him one. That same letter was used against Dad during his interrogation and sentencing as evidence that he was conspiring against the party and the revolution because he was contacting people abroad! My father, and our relatives the attorneys could not believe how ridiculous this was. Dad was even shown a picture of himself holding the letter in his hands. It was amazing for him to see that picture. It was indeed the same letter that he had written for his student Isam Izat.

The picture was strange. It was a photograph of the letter in Dad's hands. He noted that the background of the picture was a pattern of the carpet in our house. Dad realized immediately that Isam Izat, his student, had been working for intelligence. It was a setup of Dad. Isam had pretended that he wanted this letter and came to our house to request it. And my father wholeheartedly wrote the letter; he truly wanted to help his student. He was sincere and naïve, and while he was discussing the letter with Isam, Isam was taking pictures of the whole visit. It was amazing to my father how advanced the intelligence system was during those days and what high tech methods they used to spy on people and fabricate evidence. The picture was shot very close to the letter, and Dad thought it must have been taken by a miniature camera, which may have been worn by Isam as a watch or carried by him as a pen. Dad knew of the existence of such devices from hi tech foreign companies, but he did not realize that the Ba'ath government had already acquired them from Western countries. They were so advanced.

The picture of that letter was used as evidence against my father that he was contacting foreign nationals and was conspiring against the party and the revolution. Dad responded to this bizarre story and tried to defend himself by explaining the purpose of the letter. But of course no one would listen. They twisted facts and fabricated stories against people.

They also asked him about Samar, the woman whom we accidentally met during our trip to Beirut, and who came later to Baghdad. In fact, Samar was sent by the regime to trap my Dad so that they could accuse him of contacting foreigners, of conspiring against the party. It was all so bizarre. Dad tried hard to speak. He told the judge that he was tortured. He showed the judge his bruised back, and he took off his shoes and showed the judge that his toenails had been pulled out and that his feet were blue and purple from bruises and infections. No matter what Dad said or showed them, they took no notice.

* * *

Mom and the others got home. They told us the bad news: Dad would be in prison for one year. My mother was angry and very sad. She was in despair. This was so unfair. My sister and I started crying. We could not understand why Dad was in prison. Being children of eight and nine, we had thought or hoped that this whole thing of Dad being detained would be temporary and that it was just a mistake or an accident. We had hoped that after they examined the facts they would release him and he would be back. But now it was worse, now he was sentenced to prison. We were very upset; no one could eat or sleep. My aunt sat with us, she put her arms around us to comfort us. Everyone was quiet. It was a sad day.

Mom told us that in a few weeks we could see Dad on the weekend. He was being moved to another place that she thought should be better than the awful place we had seen him in before. We started preparing some things to take to our father: stuff from school to show him and things like that. We were looking forward to seeing him.

Then came the time when my father was moved to Abu Graib prison, which was a main prison located on the outskirts of Baghdad. It was far from our house. When you arrived you saw that it was a huge complex. We walked and walked until we reached the entrance. We were searched and our hands were stamped with a visitor mark when we got in. That was to distinguish the visitors from the prisoners. We were led to a big room and were told that Dad would be there. We looked for Dad and saw him sitting on a mattress on the floor. We went to greet him. I remember that his hands were cold and that he was not happy.

Although to us the place looked much better than the detention center we had gone to before, our first visit to Dad in this new place was very upsetting because he himself was depressed. For the first time in weeks we were able to speak to him without immediate surveillance and without guards watching directly over us. This was mostly because the room was big and many families were crowded in together, visiting their imprisoned relatives.

My father was upset and angry. He talked about this whole ordeal being a setup and a plan to remove him, to get rid of him. He was upset that the judge did not listen to his argument. He wanted to be heard. They set him up and now there was no chance of him getting out. His story was buried; no one was going to look into it anymore. The Ba'athists did not want him there at his office. He represented truth and honesty. He had evidence of the corruption of the regime. They wanted to get rid of him, so they set him up the way they did. Many people in his office conspired against him. He spoke in disbelief about what Isam Izat and the others had done to him; he was shocked and so disappointed.

Moreover, the prospect of his being unjustly in prison for one year was too much for him and he could not accept it. He had already endured tremendous pain and torture, but he was able to keep his hope alive that this agony was temporary and that there must be some mistake. He had thought that once they examined his pristine, faultless record they would release him. He had truly thought that once the judge heard his argument and saw the evidence that he would rule in his favor. I think that he had had his hopes really high that somehow justice would prevail. He was very disappointed.

I also think that when you are in a desperate situation and put all your hope in some prospect to get you out of your troubles and that prospect does not materialize, you become even more upset than you were originally. At least previously you had some hope. And hope is what keeps us alive in agonizing situations. It can calm us down. It can bring a thought of bright days ahead. But when that hope also collapses, the situation seems to become even worse. Despair follows, a sense of loss, darkness, pain. It is a horrible feeling when you are waiting anxiously for something to bring you relief from a problem or a situation but it never materializes. I think that is what happened with my father after the court hearing. My father had underestimated the viciousness of the regime; this type of setup and abuse had never happened much in Iraq before. This cruelty was something new. In later years it became normal and many times more severe. Dad was depressed indeed.

In addition, the place was terrible for him. Dad was in a large room, a huge room that housed over one hundred people. He was sleeping on a filthy mattress on the floor. All the prisoners had such mattresses lined up on the floor. There was no hygiene, no comfort, and no privacy. The lights were always on and there was talk and chatter all the time. He was ill and weak from all the previous torture, the lack of normal food, the lack of sleep, the cold. Dad was depressed about having to be there for a year. I think the prospect of the continuation of this agony really hurt him. This time, he himself was in tears from all this suffering and the realization that it was going to last a whole year. It seemed to him that it would never end.

Mom was just relieved that he was alive, that they had not killed him in Almukhabarat center, and that he was sitting with her and she could see him. But her heart was torn and she was worried about his lack of hope and his depression. She had not seen him like that before. And even during the detention, his spirits seemed stronger, at least to her. But now, her soul was reading his pain and her soul was aching because of it. Mom put all that was left of her confidence together into words of encouragement. She wanted to empower my father and give him new hope. She kept saying, "Thank God you are alive. That is all I want.... Remember, you are out of that grave.... It's okay. We shall endure this together.... I shall never leave you.... I shall be here every day that they allow visits ... and when I am not here, my heart and soul will be here with you." She kept trying to ignite some fires of life and hope by her loving and inspiring words. She kept encouraging him and tried to bring him inspiration, but he was too depressed. He was already counting the days to when this agony would be over even before he got to Abu Graib. And the count was so long and so daunting.

A few weeks later, Dad was moved into another section of the prison. It was a relief for him after all the other places he had been in. Although still part of the prison, this place was not as traumatizing as Alfidailia or the other part of the prison. This one had open spaces, there was some fresh air and sun, and it was kind of clean. We walked a long way from the entrance to reach a big courtyard where some of the prisoners were kept inside a barbed wire fence in a compound they could walk about in. Luckily, that was not where my Dad was being kept. Instead, he was sharing a semi-private room with two other prisoners. They could move about as they wished. All the men received their guests inside the room. They could walk out a few steps, but not far. The room was not like a prison cell; it was more like a normal room with a normal door and a couple of windows. It was clean, and Dad and the two other men were allowed to wear their own clothes inside. We went as a family every Friday. Friday was the weekend.

In this prison, family visits were allowed, and we were also allowed to take some baked food and simple items to share, so Mom and my aunt prepared some of Dad's favorite food. Week upon week we went there. Every Friday, we did the same thing: we prepared some stuff for Dad, and went to Abu Graib prison. Mom brought him fresh clothes and towels every week. We would spend a few hours there—I think maybe three or four hours.

It was good to see Dad; he was so concerned about each of us. He would ask about school, about our exams and talk to each of us. Some days I would bring my school report to show him my good grades. Then visiting time would be over by 4 P.M. or so and it would be announced that visitors must leave. So we collected our things, kissed Dad good-bye and then left. He anxiously awaited us until the next visit. Week upon week we did the same thing. We went to the prison, we visited with Dad, and we left.

Memories, spanning many months, of the Abu Graib prison are part of my life and my childhood. We went there for many weeks and months in winter, spring and summer so Abu Graib prison is ingrained in my mind. Today when I hear the name of Abu Graib, I have instant images of our long walk from the prison gate to the entrance, my sister and I strolling behind my mother. I also have instant images of my father anxiously waiting to see us in that room with gray bricks, and all of us gathering around Dad, talking to him, and him being happy to see us in spite of his pain and agony.

I have opposing and contrasting feelings about Abu Graib. One can indeed love and hate something at the same time. I hated the place because it was a prison and it was unjust and unfair that they put my father there. But I also liked the place because that is where my father was. It is ironic how I feel about that place because on the one hand I was happy to go there to see my father and he was happy to see all of us during those visits; however, we were meeting in a prison and I hated that place. I never liked the fact that my father was there. I knew that he was there unjustly. But as much as I hated the place, I did have happy moments there because it was the only place where I could see my father and talk to him. It was the only place where we could gather as a family. Indeed, we had some happy moments where we all laughed. And when we left for the day, we felt sad because Dad had to stay there. And now I think it must have felt so lonely for my father after we left. How did he spend the days Saturday through Friday until we visited him again and cheered him up a bit?

Small, colorful beads also remind me instantly of my father and the Abu Graib prison. This is because sometimes during our visits, my father gave us various items made of beads. These included necklaces, chains and little bracelets. He bought these things in the prison. Some of the men in the prison worked on making these items and selling them. I am not sure whether this was to get some income while they were in prison or just to pass the time. The bead items were of many assorted colors and shapes. They took meticulous patience to make because they had unique patterns and designs. They were not really fancy, or fashionable, but we wore them anyway. I think they reminded us that Dad was alive. It was typical of him to think to give us those simple gifts even while he was in prison. Every time I see beads, I remember these little prison gifts, which we got at Abu Graib.

During one of our regular visits on Fridays, we got in to greet my father and the two men who were with him in the prison room. We greeted my father and his companions but they were all sad and their faces were pale. All three men were in a gloomy mood. They hardly smiled. We were surprised because normally they were all happy to see us. The other two men had become friends with us. And sometimes we met their families as they also came to visit. But that day they were all upset.

We asked Dad and his mates what was wrong? They told us that something terrible had happened in the morning of that day, and that they had seen it with their own eyes. We all sat around them listening as they told us that several men had just been executed by shooting a few hours earlier, just like that. They were all young Kurdish men who appeared to be fifteen to twenty years of age. They were shot and left lying in the open for a while until their bodies were collected in bags and taken somewhere. It was a horrible scene with so much cruelty, such a waste of young lives.

On that day, Dad was very upset after what he had seen earlier. He was feeling sick and nauseated by it. He told my mother, "Lydia, I saw these young men being taken to their death.... Oh, God.... They were lined up and then a few minutes later they were lying on the floor motionless. It was devastating. I could not believe what I was seeing. It is painful to see a young life wasted like that. Those boys were in the prime of their youth, they should be enjoying life, they had their whole lives ahead of them.... They were only kids.... Oh, God.... God forbid, they are the same age as our sons.... The future of this country is grim with these Ba'athist thugs in power running our lives.... I may not make it out of here Lydia, and if I do not make it out of here, then you must find a way to send our children abroad. They should not stay here. Their lives will be ruined in this country. By God, if I make it out of here I want my children out of Iraq. I shall do everything possible to get my sons out." We were all sad after having heard about the death of these men and the way they were left in the prison's arena. I was very scared to listen to the whole story and to see both my parents so worried about my brothers.

*   *   *

Winter was over and spring had come and gone and summer started. So many weeks and months went by. School days, birthdays, and all other family events went by week after week. Our beautiful life was withering away. Mom and Dad looked tense and so much older. My father, this great man of knowledge, sophistication, and kindness, was left to wither away in a prison room because of his stance on the Ba'ath regime, because he did not accept their corruption and crimes and because he knew the ugly truth about them. My father was suffering and our family was devastated and we went through grueling pain, while outside the Ba'ath members and their followers were enjoying their time abusing innocent people slowly but steadily. They did not care about us, about the pain they inflicted on us. These were hard times. We survived but I do not know how other than by the grace of God. It was sad but it became mundane. It became something that we all had to adapt to. To be sad for such a long time is horrible. It is demoralizing.

All the days of the whole ordeal of my father's detention and imprisonment are imprinted in my mind like a carving in stone. I have a strikingly clear memory of all these events. I shall never forget that afternoon in December when my father was arrested, my mother was in panic, and my grandmother held me. I still remember the rainy day the teacher asked me where my father was in front of the classroom and that dreadful visit to the Alfidailia detention center. And I still remember hiding my face behind my mother's coat after being shocked to see my father in that place. I remember those days and events very well. Yet, I do not remember much of the following months, other than our visits to the prison: the gates of the Abu Graib complex, the long walk between the gate and the entrance, my hands and arms being stamped as we entered the prison, the gray brick walls of the room in which my Dad was held. It is like this is the only thing that happened in my life.

Many weeks and months went by like that. While we thought that we had already gotten through the worst of it with Dad being away, there were more shocking events coming our way.

CHAPTER 4

Jasmine

Several months or so before these events, my parents had hired a new maid in the house, a live-in. Her name was Jasmine. She was from Egypt. A tall dark woman of intermediate build, she was perhaps in her mid thirties. Jasmine had her own room and bathroom in the house. She helped Mom with the cleaning and cooking and all kinds of household duties. In the past, Mom had always had a maid or a nanny in the house, the last of whom was the elderly woman, Um Mustafa, who had passed away. We had remained without a maid for maybe less than a year, and then we hired this woman from Egypt.

During the early seventies a number of people from Egypt sought work in Iraq. Jasmine was one of them. After she started working in our house, we soon got used to her. We tried our best to make her feel happy because she was away from her family and her children. In fact, every Eid (a religious holiday), Mom gave her additional money to send to her family and children. She adapted well to living with us. She seemed happy and so were we. We children in particular talked to her a lot about all the movie stars from Egypt. Movies from Egypt were very popular in Iraq. So we kept asking Jasmine, Have you ever seen so and so [various movie stars]? or have you met so and so? Have you been to the pyramids? And so on. Mom was happy with her work as she helped her with managing the big house and running its affairs. Jasmine also made some new and interesting foods for us from Egyptian recipes. One memorable dish was sautéed eggplant garnished with salt and vinegar. It tasted really good. Anyway, we liked Jasmine and she was a great help to my mother, and some time seemingly went by without problems.

One morning several weeks prior to Dad's arrest, my parents were having a casual breakfast together in the kitchen. They seemed happy.

There is nothing more charming than a couple who are in love and happy. They looked enchanting, and it was a beautiful morning, sunny but cool, with a cold breeze coming through the window. Jasmine was pouring tea for them.

During breakfast, Dad asked, "Lydia, did you hear some voice in the garden last night?"

"No," Mom answered.

"I thought I heard some steps all along the garage and they stopped kind of near Jasmine's room. There was also some chatter and talk. Did you hear any of it?"

"No," my mother replied. "You must have been dreaming, dear. Anyway, I was so tired I just went to sleep."

"No, I am sure that I heard something. I am just worried that maybe some thieves were trying to break in. Although I looked around in the patio and walked along that path, nothing seemed unusual. I mean the gate was locked as I left it last night."

"How could anyone get in?" Mom responded. "Don't worry too much. All the gates are locked. You said there were no broken locks today. And the fence is two meters high—who is going to jump over that at night? I think you were dreaming."

Dad laughed and said, "No, I was awake."

Later on that day, Jasmine was talking to my Mom and she said, "Well, madam, I have to tell you something. Can you please come to my room? But don't be scared.... Just listen to what I shall tell you."

Mom walked with Jasmine to her room and asked, "What's wrong?"

"Last night," Jasmine said, "I saw a snake here on my window. And it was really long...."

Mom was in a panic right away. She looked at Jasmine and said, "What? A snake? No.... No. There are no snakes in this house. Are you sure?"

Mom was in panic because she disliked insects and snakes and she could not bare the thought that there was a snake in the house. In fact, all her years in that house had been pleasant; it was a clean and immaculate place. She had never seen any snake before in the house.

"Oh, no madam, do not worry, don't worry please," Jasmine returned. "I did not mean for you to worry. I assure you that the snake will never come back."

"What do you mean?"

"I said a prayer over it and it will not come back. I do that all the time back home. We have them there too. Don't worry, it will not come back."

But Mom was worried. She was scared of snakes and was disgusted by the idea that there might be one in the house. But she was more surprised by what Jasmine had said about the prayer. It sounded like superstition. Mom remained nervous about this whole episode. A couple of days went by.

Jasmine started having a regular visitor; her name was Zainab. She was also from Egypt. The first time she came by, she just showed up. We did not know who she was and Jasmine said that this woman was a friend. We were a bit surprised that she knew where Jasmine was and that she just came without prior arrangement. This was mostly because she could not just bring anyone over to the house. This was the case for all the foreign workers. And in general, contact with foreigners was very much frowned upon by the Ba'ath regime. Zainab came over to the house a few times and asked Jasmine if she wanted to send any gifts or money home as she (Zainab) was going back and forth to Egypt. They became close pals because they both had family back home and they were both maids. I was happy that Jasmine had found a friend from home. Zainab came a few times. She delivered gifts and other items between Jasmine and her family.

However, my mother, and even we girls, were surprised by how well off Zainab looked. She was indeed very well dressed and did not look like a maid. She had full makeup, wore high heels, and her figure was good. She seemed well looked-after. Generally the maids did not dress up in any extravagant way, and also they could not afford that for the most part. And Mom wondered why Zainab was going to Egypt so frequently. Zainab, however, was a very funny lady; she had a charming personality and was rather talkative and very upbeat, unlike Jasmine who was very quiet and shy. We always supposed Jasmine was homesick and missed her family, so we tried to make her happy by not discouraging Zainab from coming every once in a while.

* * *

During the time that Dad was away in detention, our house was full of visitors; also my aunts and uncles were there daily, and sometimes they stayed over and practically camped at the house. People were in and out all the time. The house was never quiet. It was a good thing for all of us and especially for my mother. Her sisters did not want to leave her alone. My aunts helped my mother a lot during this ordeal. They took care of the house affairs and they kept us company.

My aunt Kamila was cooking for us daily. She was actually my Mom's cousin but we called her aunt. She was so kind and wonderful. She came over every day and brought some goodies and food and also spent the whole day cooking for everyone. She cooked so much food because there were so many people. It was indeed like having an open house. And we would not have survived without the wonderful food of aunt Kamila. There were people there all the time and there was nice food. However, there was also a strange set of events.

Uncle Mizhar, who was married to aunt Kamila, would come to the house sometimes with her. He behaved rather strangely. He would say hello to everyone, then, "Where is Mizhar? I do not see him here? Has he called?" and such like. This happened many times.

No one understood why he was saying this. We thought it was some joke—the first time. But he kept doing it every time he came over. We thought that he was still playing some game and we did not get it. Mom, however, would look at him with surprise, and later she became suspicious that he knew for sure that the house was bugged. But she kept wondering why he was saying this. She told everyone including him that Dad had said to be careful and not to talk in the house. She wondered if he may be in with the government against my Dad and her? Was that really possible? Or did he just want to distance himself from them? It was then a typical Ba'ath strategy to have one distant or even close family relative to spy on someone. That would be easy, they would not arouse any suspicions and they would have access to the family and the house. Mom knew that he was newly a Ba'athist. He was one of those people who had to join the party to keep his prestigious university position. All university faculty had to be Ba'athists. It seemed to her that he was saying that on purpose, that he was not there in the house even though it was his own voice. It was strange behavior.

My mother was in a dilemma. She had all these thoughts in her mind. Her kindness and warm heart were conflicting with these thoughts. And sometimes she regretted having such thoughts and just realized that she was tired and confused because of all the events. She did not want to even think that Mizhar was involved with the government against us. But his actions were strange. Mom did not say anything. She pretended that she did not notice anything, but in her heart she became fearful, and sick. Why was he saying that he was not at the house; whom was he trying to tell? It seemed like a coded message. Mom became very suspicious; she was afraid for us children, for our safety. Although Dad told her to be careful about speaking in the house and that he was sure that the house was bugged, we never found any unusual objects and we could not tell who would be placing the devices. We remained careful, nevertheless. She was distraught, not only because she was alone without Dad, but because

she believed that there was a traitor in the house, someone who was coop-
erating with Almukhabarat from inside the house, someone who could
hear us and see us all the time. She became suspicious of Uncle Mizhar.
But she could not tell anyone. Mom had thought that the worst was over
with what happened to Dad. But if her suspicions were founded, then
things were going to get even worse.

We kept searching in the house for those devices which were recording our lives and our private conversations. This was such an invasion of
privacy, and it was not a common thing in Iraq to have such an experience. We always thought about the house being bugged and we always
had to remember not to speak against the government or about the case
of my Dad inside the house. We had to be very disciplined in what we
said. And sometimes we used coded words and signals. It was hard having to be on guard all the time even in your own house. Moreover, when
close relatives of my Dad came to visit, Mom took them outside to the
garden and talked to them freely there and told them not to say anything
about Makki's case or about the government, because the house was
bugged and they would be incriminating themselves. Sometimes she wrote
down a couple of lines to tell them the same. People were shocked to hear
that, and they thanked my mother for warning them. Spying on people
in their homes was a new Ba'ath invention that Iraqis had to endure.

One night, my aunt Weda and my mother were sitting alone and talking to each other in the garden. They often sat in the garden so that they
could talk freely. We could not imagine that the garden would be bugged
too. The garden was a safe place where we could talk without restrictions.
Aunt Weda loved us so much and cared for us and she was living with us
most of the time during this ordeal. She and my mother trusted each
other and they were confidantes. Aunt Weda was sincere with us and she
was heartbroken at what was happening to us. She tried her best to be
with Mom all the time during this ordeal.

As they were talking, she suddenly told my Mom, "Lydia, listen, it's
got to be Jasmine, the maid."

"What?" Mom stammered. "What about her?"

"It's her..., the tapes, you know..., it's got to be her. She is around
us all the time, she has access to the entire house twenty-four hours a day
and ... but then...."

Aunt Weda stopped for a minute and said, "No, wait ... but whom
does she see? She is in the house all day. She does not go out of the house
except with us. She does not know anybody here in Baghdad, except
Zainab, and neither knows her way around Baghdad."

Indeed, Jasmine was going out only with us and could not roam about in the city by herself. This was both because our family was responsible for her safety as she was a foreign worker inside Iraq and we had to gain all kinds of permission from the government to bring her over, and also because she herself was not really outgoing and did not know her way around Baghdad.

My aunt was still talking to my Mom about that and wondering who else could be the villain. Then mom said, "You know, I do not know what to say about her. I mean she is so quiet and she seems kind and innocent. And this week you know she saved my daughters from the kerosene poisoning. I mean I am grateful to her for that."

My mother was referring to an event in which my sister and I went to sleep without turning off the kerosene heater in our room. Those kerosene heaters are not safe when they run out of fuel. They produce carbon monoxide, a deadly poison. My sister and I had left the heater on all night and it ran out of fuel. To make matters worse, we had the door to our room closed. So we nearly died from this poison. In the morning, Jasmine came over and upstairs to our room to see why we had not gotten up yet because we were getting late for school. When she opened the door, she saw that we were still in bed and the heater had run out of kerosene. She thought we were dead. She started screaming. She opened the windows immediately and dragged us out of the room. We were still alive and breathing, thank God.

Jasmine took the heater out and opened the door to the roof which was on the second floor near our room. All of a sudden there was a lot of fresh air in our lungs and we were okay. My Mom and my sister heard the screams and came running upstairs. Jasmine said, "It's okay, it's okay, they are fine." So Jasmine saved our lives that day. My Mom was grateful that we were alive and nothing had happened to us. She was crying, and she thanked Jasmine.

Mom and aunt Weda sat silently for a while. Then Mom suddenly recalled the story about the snake. It dawned upon her that Jasmine had not been honest about it. It was finally all adding up now. Dad had heard sounds of steps and conversation near Jasmine's room. It must have been someone who had come for her, maybe it was someone from the secret police, the Almukhabarat. Mom thought that when Jasmine overheard that conversation between my parents, she made up the snake story to divert my parents' attention from ever suspecting that she was seeing anybody and conspiring against us. And she indeed was successful, as my parents never doubted her and never made that connection. My parents were so simple and innocent. They did not have suspicions about her.

Mom was silent for a while and was thinking about what my aunt had just said about Jasmine. Then my mother said, "Yes, Weda, you are right. Jasmine made up that thing about a snake when she heard Makki say there were sounds near her room."

"What snake?" Aunt Weda replied. "What are you talking about?"

Mom told Aunt Weda about the snake. And then Mom said, "I think you are right about Jasmine. But since she does not go out by herself it must be that someone comes here to her. You know the only time she waits out alone by the gate is in the mornings. Jasmine goes out at 6 A.M. or so to pick up the bread from the 'bread delivery man.' He brings the bread to the main gate."

A traditional practice in Baghdad was to have fresh bread delivered daily in the morning. The bread deliveryman would come by the various homes that had made a delivery order with him previously, and he would deliver the bread early in the morning. He would get paid weekly for his services. It was nice actually to have this fresh bread daily. We had this order for many years, and when Jasmine came to work for us, she went out in the morning to pick up the bread. Mom thought that maybe Jasmine was going elsewhere too while she was getting the bread.

"I mean, I never check her whereabouts," Mom went on. "I trust her in general. I assume she picks up the bread and comes right back. Some days I am not even awake when she collects the bread so I do not really know. But that's the only time that she can leave the house. That's got to be it."

Aunt Weda was silent.

"And that Zainab," Mom continued, "she must be in it too. I did not feel good about her from the start. She did not look like a maid ... and her frequent trips to Egypt back and forth are not consistent with her being a maid. How can she afford that? And she never told us which family she works for. When I asked her, she avoided the question and changed the subject. I bet that she works for Almukhabarat instead. I do not think she is a maid. I bet Zainab is not her real name either. We do not know who she is."

Mom and aunt Weda were worried about the ideas that they had just discussed.

Suspicions over Jasmine became more intense over the next few days, as she began to insist on going to certain parts of the house pretending to clean up or do some household chores even when these chores were of no urgency. Her normal work duties did not take her all over the house, only to certain parts. So, we were intrigued by her behavior. One of those days we pretended that we were all going out. Indeed we all went out the door on purpose in front of Jasmine so that she could see us. She saw that we were all out and assumed we would be gone for a couple of hours. We did not go very far. Then Mom told my sister Zeena to go in the house quietly, using the guest entrance. A few minutes later, Zeena went in without making a sound.

Actually, because the house was big, that entrance was far away from Jasmine's normal whereabouts in the house. Zeena went quietly into the guestroom and stood there silently behind the door. The room was dark. A few minutes later, Jasmine went into the guest section of the house, the dining part of that section. She started opening cabinets that were normally locked. She went through all kinds of drawers and cabinets. She would not have found anything of interest. The cabinets mostly contained kitchen items and platters and china sets used for guest functions. Zeena stood there for about half an hour and she was afraid. But actually we were not too far from her. In fact my uncle Raid was right there outside the guestroom along the walkway around the house. And he had told Zeena to open the window so that he could hear if something went wrong. We all came back and Zeena told my Mom and my uncle what she had seen. So we all became more aware that we could not trust Jasmine, especially after Mom asked her if she had gone into the guest areas and she denied ever going there.

Out on the patio which overlooked the garden, there was a small storage room which was used for various purposes. Actually, our house had three or four such rooms which were in different parts of the house. But this particular one was used frequently because it was more accessible than the others and it was on the first level of the house. One day Zeena went to look for something in that room, and then, as she was searching there, she decided also to clean up some of the things and throw away some stuff. She came back into the house and told Mom that she was throwing these objects out to make more room.

Jasmine saw that Zeena had been in that room and said, "Zeena, wait for me. Let me help you there.

"No, it's okay," Zeena said. "I won't be long. I am just looking for some old books and if I see junky stuff I shall put it aside to throw it away."

"No!" Jasmine insisted. "Wait for me."

"It's okay, Jasmine," Mom said. "You do not have to do that. Anyway you are in the middle of cleaning up after lunch right now. I will go help Zeena."

Jasmine waited in the house while Mom and Zeena went to the storage room. While they were searching and looking around, Mom saw a package that looked unusual to her.

"Do you know what is in this package?" she asked Zeena.

"No," Zeena answered.

Mom looked at the package closer, and it appeared that there was another inside. It did not look familiar either, but, more importantly, it looked new and not something that would be left in this storage room. Mom opened the packet and saw lots of cash there. There were a few packs of several hundred dinars each. That was a significant amount of money: in total about a few thousand dollars. Mom and Zeena were surprised to see this money and had no idea how it had gotten there. Mom decided to leave the money there. She and Zeena took some stuff from the room to throw away, then came back inside. Jasmine was looking at them.

"What did you throw away?" she inquired. "May I see it?"

"Why do you want to see it?" Mom asked. "It is just some junk."

"Just to see if there is anything I could use or give to Zainab when she comes."

Mom became suspicious of how Jasmine was insisting on going to the storage room to see what was to be thrown out. Mom suspected that the money packet that she had found belonged to Zainab or Jasmine herself.

Then Mom said, "Okay, let's go there and see what you need."

"Oh, madam," Jasmine said, "it's okay. I can go by myself; you don't have to go there again. I will go later."

"No, let's go now, and afterwards I will throw the stuff that you do not need in the trash."

Mom and Jasmine walked to the room. Jasmine went in and pretended to be looking at some old magazines and clothes that Mom had set aside to be taken away. Jasmine saw the money packet was there, but she did not open it. She just looked at it, and Mom was observing her well. Jasmine collected a few items, and then she and Mom took the rest to be disposed of. They both returned inside.

Mom went to her room. She grabbed Aunt Weda and told her about the money.

"I am sure Jasmine will go to the storage room again to retrieve that money," Mom told Aunt Weda.

"I will keep Jasmine busy so she cannot go there," Aunt Weda promised. "Listen, do you have a key for that room?"

"Oh, yes, we have the key. We just never lock that room."

"Give me the key. I will go lock the room now until we figure out how she got this money."

Aunt Weda went and locked the room. The suspicious money was still there. It was safe.

*　*　*

After all those stories of Jasmine, the snake, her visitor Zainab, and her meddling in the house areas where she did not need to go, now there was this money. Mom thought perhaps the neighbors might have seen something or somebody during our daily absence from the house or in general at other times. She went to the Nasers', our neighbors who lived across the street, to ask about this matter. Mom asked Mrs. Naser whether she had seen Jasmine in the mornings with the bread and whether she went anywhere or met anyone in our absence. Mrs. Naser was a home-maker. She usually had her coffee early in the morning before her family was awake. She used to sit on the front porch overlooking the street.

"Yes, Lydia," she told Mom. "I see her daily. But why are you asking?"

"I have become suspicious of her lately after everything that has happened to us. You know after all she is a stranger living in the house."

"Yes, I know what you mean."

"Well," Mom asked, "have you ever seen her go anywhere? talk to anyone? do anything unusual?"

"Oh, God," Mrs. Naser exclaimed. "God forbid.... Yes indeed, I see a man come right after the bread deliveryman leaves. But why? Tell me what's happening. I mean I saw the man several times; I did not think much of it. He just passes her by kind of."

Mrs. Naser stopped for a minute and then said, "Oh, my God. Yes.... Yes indeed. You will not believe this but he and Jasmine do not talk or go anywhere; he just passes by her but he momentarily stops just for a couple of seconds. They kind of exchange something. I have never seen them talk or stay together for long. I have never seen them go anywhere together. Oh, my God, I did not think it was important then. I wish I had told you about this before. Oh, God. I wonder what he gives her or what he takes?"

Mrs. Naser described the man as tall and heavy-built, and he had been wearing a brown jacket recently. Mom could not believe what she was hearing. This Jasmine, this maid, a newcomer to the city, a strange woman in this country, she was also being used by the government against people and to get what they needed from inside people's lives. That was the perfect means to intrude on people's lives without being overt: maids. Jasmine had access to the entire house; there were times, before the events of my Dad's arrest, where she even stayed alone when we all went to school or work. Perhaps the secret police or even her friend Zainab visited her. Mom was shocked. She came home and secretly told my aunt Weda what she had learned from Mrs. Naser.

The next day Zainab came to visit Jasmine to ask her if she wanted to send anything to her family. Mom and Aunt Weda pretended that everything was normal. They let the two women talk as usual. But they kept a close eye on them. Jasmine was talking to Zainab. Then Jasmine pretended that she had to go to the storage room area because she had something there. When she got to the room, the door was locked. She came back. She did not say anything to my mother about the room being locked. But she and Zainab exchanged some looks.

An hour or so later, Zainab left. This time, Mom decided to follow her. Zainab walked a couple of minutes till the end of the road then was picked up by a private car, which was waiting for her. It looked like an Almukhabarat car. It is hard to explain the look such a car had, but Almukhabarat staff often had a certain way of dressing, and they drove the same cars; in fact, certain foreign models were selectively imported for government officials, including them. The closest example to this in the West is when police formulate a profile of a drug dealer, such as what type of clothes he wears and what kind of car he drives. Mom got in a taxi and asked the driver to follow that car. They drove into the city and ended in some neighborhood that had a notorious reputation. Zainab got out of the car and went inside a building. Mom was shocked at how close her suspicions about Zainab had been.

She asked the driver, "Do you know what place this is?"

"Madam," he replied, "I do not know anything. You know very well what area this is. We should not be here. Madam, I will not say anything."

After a silence, he continued. "You know who controls this place … who controls our lives. Look, madam, if you want I will drop you here. But I cannot go any further. I don't want any trouble and you do not belong here either. Let's get out of here."

Mom asked the driver to take her back where she got in. The man sounded honest and that he wanted no harm to come to her. But in those days you could not even trust an innocent conversation with a taxi driver, and that taxi driver probably felt the same way. He probably thought that my Mom was spying on him and trying to set him up and to get him to say something against the government. This severe paranoia and mistrust among people, where you could not have a casual conversation about anything because you never knew who was recording it, was a way in which the Ba'ath regime's tactics seriously changed the norms of society. The driver was referring to one of the Almukhabarat hideouts where they kept some of their aides and employees and even prostitutes. It looked like a residential district but it had all kinds of guards and security around it, from afar even. Mom knew then that her suspicions about Zainab had been right, that she was part of Almukhabarat too.

Mom came home and told Aunt Weda where she had gone. Aunt Weda was mad at Mom. She said, "Lydia, are you crazy? How could you go there? They could have arrested you. Thank God you are safe. You cannot play with fire like this."

Mom did not answer. Aunt Weda continued. "Look, my dear, Makki is in their hands. They could kill him and it means nothing to them."

"I had to go," Mom responded. "See, my doubts are now confirmed."

Later, Aunt Weda told Jasmine that there was no need for her to go to collect the bread in the morning anymore. She had informed the deliveryman to just knock on the door and bring the bread in. Now, there was another shocking event.

The bread deliveryman rang the bell and came to the front door to bring the bread. That morning, Aunt Weda was home and she stayed in the kitchen watching Jasmine. Jasmine went about her normal duties. Later, there was a knock at the inner front door and Aunt Weda opened it. There was a man there. This was strange, because normally in Iraq people were let in through the main gate or were greeted from afar and asked to come in by the residents of the home only. In other words, nobody just entered through the gate unless he was a member of the family, in our case, people like my aunt or my cousins. That was the social norm. So it was strange that this man had taken it upon himself to enter the house. He had not even rung the bell on the outer gate. This indicated that someone in that house expected him. Obviously in this case it was Jasmine, the maid. Aunt Weda was frightened. He was the same man that Mrs. Naser had described: tall, heavy-built and a brown jacket. Perhaps the man had expected Jasmine to open the door. Aunt Weda said, "Yes, can I help you?" The man pretended to stammer and said that he was lost and was looking for someone else's house. He apologized and left. Aunt Weda was afraid and shocked. She waited until Mom came home and told her what had happened. It became clear that Jasmine was the culprit. Mom thought that this man brought the recording materials to Jasmine and she gave them back to him. We kept an eye on Jasmine and the door all day.

Night fell. Aunt Weda told Jasmine that she, Jasmine, was going to sleep elsewhere in a different room that night, not in her room, and that her room was needed for something else. Aunt Weda went with Jasmine to her room to help her get what she needed. Jasmine was surprised at all these changes being made in her life. She began to suspect that she was uncovered. She was confused. She did not say much to Aunt Weda. She did not know how to pass the message to her accomplice, the mysterious man who collected the tapes from her.

By then, Jasmine had become a conniving and manipulative woman. She was now a professional liar, well trained by Almukhabarat and no longer the same innocent woman who had come to work for us months before. Quickly, while Aunt Weda was not looking, Jasmine placed a white handkerchief in the window. It was a mark, a coded signal that she was not there. Then she left the room and Aunt Weda took her to another room where she would sleep that night. Later, Uncle Raid told Mom and Aunt Weda that he would sleep in Jasmine's room that night to see if anyone showed up.

Uncle Raid was smart. He went into Jasmine's room and immediately noticed the white sign in the window. He removed the handkerchief. As he was removing the white cloth, he also noticed one more thing. The screen on her window had evidently been torn by a sharp object—torn on purpose.

Normally in Baghdad homes, all the windows had mesh screens attached firmly to them to prevent the entry of insects and dirt from outside. With normal wear and tear, some screens become loosely attached to the window and may have some holes in them. But this tear was definitely made by a sharp object on purpose. And it was a tear large enough to fit a hand through to exchange small objects. He showed my Mom this screen. Perhaps this was how Jasmine exchanged things with this man. It became clearer that this woman was the villain. There were no more doubts, only more shocking evidence to come.

Uncle Raid stayed the night in Jasmine's room. I was worried about him so much. I thought that he was so courageous. I was scared that someone might hurt him while he was in that room. I kept praying that he would be okay. Meanwhile, Aunt Weda slept close by to Jasmine's new location so that she could keep an eye on her.

Uncle Raid was not afraid. He turned off the lights and opened the curtains slightly. And having removed the white cloth, he gave the impression that Jasmine was still inside the room. Sure enough, after midnight, there were knocks on the window. Uncle Raid looked; it was a man, tall-ish and heavy built, similar to the man Aunt Weda had seen earlier in the day and described. Uncle Raid could not be sure it was the same individual because it was dark. He opened the window and held a flashlight to the man's face and said loudly, "Who are you? What do you want?"

The man was startled. He was expecting Jasmine to open the window. He started running away. The man jumped over the fence to next door and disappeared. Actually the fences between neighboring homes were not as high as the exterior fence on the streets. One could actually climb over them, especially because there were also some steps and rocks from which one could take a jump. Everyone in the house awoke. Uncle Raid quickly got to the door and ran out seeking the man. We ran into the street trying to find the man and to see in which direction he went, but he had vanished. We immediately suspected that he went into Mr. Kader's home, the home next to our house, which Mr. Kader and his family were renting. Mom called the police. We waited anxiously for them but the police never showed up. We called them again several times. They were lying to us straight. They said, "Oh, we are coming, we are on our way...." etc. It was obvious that the police did not show up on purpose. Unlike in the previous event of the break-in at the house many months earlier where the police were diligent and did their best to help, now, about a year or more later, even the local force would do nothing and had dearly become a tool used by the Ba'ath regime in their attacks on people.

Our whole family was shaken; even the police couldn't help us. We felt so defeated. Even the local police who had helped us in the past and who knew us personally had come under the control of the Ba'ath and had been instructed to ignore our call. We were shaken by how involved Jasmine was in these attacks. We felt angry with her. But we could not say anything yet. With all the commotion and running around at night, Jasmine also woke up and was wondering what had happened. She herself was pale and afraid and sensed that she was uncovered after the events of the night. We told her that there had been an intruder just now. She seemed scared too. We were all tired and upset. And we were also afraid that the intruder might come back, so we left many lights on inside and outside the house. We could not sleep the rest of the night. But it was not over, as the next day brought even more shocking events.

* * *

The next day some guests were visiting. My mother was tired. She had not slept the night before. She was pale. The guests were talking to my mother, gently trying to cheer her up a bit, and they were asking about my Dad, and how he was coping and whether there were any new developments. Mom whispered to them what had happened the previous night. They were shocked to hear it. Among the visitors was a couple who had lived in Egypt for many years as former diplomats. They knew the customs and the dialect of that society. They were so amazed and saddened to hear what Jasmine had done. Jasmine came to bring tea for everyone. Without referring to what Jasmine had done to us, the woman confronted her in a general way.

"Jasmine, how could you do this?" the woman asked.

At first, Jasmine did not answer. Maybe she was not sure what the woman was talking about. And we had not confronted her yet about the events of last night, but I think she sensed that we knew of her involvement in them.

"Jasmine," the woman continued, "you know these people, Mr. Makki and Madam Lydia. They are your hosts. They opened their home to you. You lived here with them under one roof … and you shared their daily food … and many moments of their life. How could you betray them? How will you face God?"

Jasmine broke down in an immense show of emotion. She immediately confessed to her involvement in this conspiracy. She just volunteered the whole story without being asked. She cried passionately. "I was threatened," she sobbed. "If I did not do what they wanted they would put me in prison and they would hurt me and I would lose my job. I had to follow these orders from Almukhabarat. They told me what to do, they gave me instructions to place these mini recorders in the house and to replace them daily."

Jasmine took us to the next-door room, the living room, and showed Mom and the guests where she put the recorders. She also said that she placed more recorders in my parents' room. Indeed they were small, she said. No one would have noticed them. She went on to show us where in the bedroom she used to put these small devices.

"They sent Zainab over to give me instructions, and sometimes others came over here," she went on, "I let them in when no one was here. I had to…. I had no choice."

"Madam Lydia … you know I have family in Egypt and they rely on my income to support them…. I am poor, I had to keep my job…. I did not know this would happen, I swear I did not know this would happen. I respect Mr. Makki, and he was kind to me. I am so sorry he got hurt because of me. I wish Mr. Makki would forgive me—I know he is a kind man. Oh, God, please forgive me. I wish this never happened. I wish I had never come to Iraq."

This long, volunteered confession by Jasmine shocked us. It felt like ice-cold water was being poured on us. We could not believe what she was saying. Mom was so enraged with Jasmine. She wanted to kill her and she was yelling and screaming at her. Mom got in the worst fiery mood that I had ever seen.

"You?" she yelled at Jasmine. "You of all people? You ruined my life and family. You cheap slut…."

Jasmine kept crying and weeping and asking for forgiveness. She knelt down at my Mom's feet to kiss them. This was a customary though an old-fashioned humble way of expressing apology and asking forgiveness. It was generally practiced throughout the Middle East but mostly among Arabs. Kneeling down to kiss the feet or the ground where someone was standing was an extreme form of humility and was done when one knew that he had committed a grave crime or an improper act against someone or when one sought profound forgiveness. Mom was not amused by this show of emotion from Jasmine. She was still angry, and she pulled her feet away. This was another tradition, and implied that the apology was not accepted.

Mom was so mad. My brothers had to hold her to calm her down. Haider and Samir took Mom away to her room and forced her to stay there to avoid any more emotional outbursts. But she was so angry.

"I will kill Jasmine," she hissed.

Meanwhile, my aunt was looking after the guests, but they eventually left. And then she came and yelled at Mom to be quiet. Aunt Weda screamed at Mom, "Lydia, stop this now. Stop it. You know they [the regime] will come after your sons too. Do you want to lose your children too? Look … Makki is still in their hands. They would kill him in a second and it would mean nothing to them. And then you would lose him and your children and everything. Stop it and be quiet. Jasmine is their accomplice and there is nothing we can do about it."

Mom was still upset and shaken. Shortly, Uncle Mizhar came over and quickly realized what had happened. He came storming at Mom and said, "Lydia, you will not harm Jasmine. She will be leaving Iraq in a few days and you will give me all documents pertaining to her work and her passport and her payment." He paused for a short while then continued, "Jasmine will go to my house for the remaining days until she leaves Iraq."

Mom and Haider and Aunt Weda were shocked to hear this. They looked at Mizhar with dismay.

"Mizhar, what are you saying?" Mom asked. "What do you mean? Tell me, why are you protecting Jasmine? What have you got to do with this?"

Now her suspicions about him were confirmed.

"Mizhar … talk now," Mom ordered, coldly. "Tell me that what I am thinking now about you is wrong; tell me that I am wrong…."

He did not answer.

"You knew?" she continued. "Mizhar…. You were in on it from the start? And we trusted you like family?"

She was crying in vain.

"Uncle, what's going on?" Haider asked.

Uncle Mizhar did not answer.

"Get out!" Mom screamed at him. "You sick pig. Get out of this house. You are too filthy to be here. You are not worthy to be looked at. You betrayed us…. You pig…. Get out!"

Jasmine went to Mizhar's house. A few days later, she was flown back to Egypt. Her role in this conspiracy had been uncovered; her mission was over.

*   *   *

The involvement of Uncle Mizhar in this matter broke the family. Mom and Aunt Weda were angry with him and with their cousin. My Aunt Kamila cried for days and told my Mom she had not known about this. She was reluctant to come to our house. She was caught in the middle between her husband and her cousin, my mother. It was a dramatic conflict that split the family and brought about strong emotions and quarrels. Many days later, Aunt Kamila resumed her visits. But Mom was cold to her. Our family was a victim of a big conspiracy that developed to involve even family relatives, let alone the local police, the maid, and many others. In their scheme to set up and arrest my father, they used anyone and everyone whom they could lure with money and prestige or anyone whom they could threaten and frighten.

People obeyed Ba'ath orders out of fear or for greed or love of recognition. For example, I think that Jasmine was not a vicious person herself but her conduct was wrong. I do not think that she hated us, because she did some kind things here and there such as save our lives, my sister's and mine. But what she did was unforgivable and could have no possible justification. She followed these orders from the Ba'ath regime because of fear and because of greed and she also did not want to lose her employment. And Uncle Mizhar's conduct was even more hideous and more shocking because he was part of the family. And to be betrayed by your relative is so much more painful. These shocking episodes made it impossible for us to trust people, even relatives and neighbors. We never hired a maid after these events. We did all the housework by ourselves. Also, we became suspicious and analytical about the intentions and the conduct of whomever we dealt with.

In all cases, however, whether it was Jasmine or Uncle Mizhar or Mr. Isam Izat, the student whom my father wrote a letter for, or the other colleagues in my father's office, we knew these people and visited with them, saw them daily sometimes. These were people whom we trusted and thought of as family or friends. All of them betrayed my parents and our family. All of them stabbed my father in the back for some materialistic benefit or a prestigious award or to protect their own skins. It is a horrible facet of human nature to surrender to one's greed or other personal interests without looking at the damage such a surrender inflicts on others. I think all humans have such tendencies, but we strive to keep them under control. Those of us who have principles and moral values, hold them high as our guide. I think that it would be very hard for most people with even the least moral strength to enjoy any benefit or materialistic gain which came from the misery of others. However, the Ba'ath regime used this human tendency to pursue personal gain or safety, in order to inveigle or coerce people into conspiring against our family and many, many others.

* * *

My father was released from prison in the summer of 1975. It was a joyous occasion, a day that we anticipated and dreamt of all summer. In fact we knew in advance of that day, although it was changed and rescheduled a couple of times. It was a long awaited day. It was like a dream, like preparing for a wedding. It was the happiest day in that summer and the best day we had had in a long, painful time. It was a day that made me feel alive again and brought new hope and joy to all of us. We were counting the minutes and hours until that day came and that hour arrived.

It was a delightful day. We prepared the inside of the house for a big celebration but we had to be subtle and keep a low profile outside: You never knew who was watching and listening. We just did not want to provoke any confrontation with the authorities because they might stop the release of my father or simply complicate it. We cleaned the house and we decorated it. We invited only the family and close relatives. Uncle Mizhar was not invited. I think my aunts Weda and Najia and my sister Zeena cooked and prepared everything, as my Mom was gone all day at Abu Graib.

I must say that throughout the ordeal, which lasted many months, I saw beautiful devotion from my mother's family, especially her sisters, towards my mother. It was so touching and inspiring to see sisters supporting each other at a time of crisis. I give so much credit to my aunts and my grandmother for keeping us company during the horrible time that we went through and for helping my mother in various ways, whether it be running the house or lending her money or staying with her during those long awful days and nights. They also looked after us children and tried to help us have a normal daily life by having lunches and dinners together and by taking us out sometimes. It was their love and support that kept us alive during many horrible moments. Although my Mom and her family had their own silly quarrels and fights once in a while and they were divided on some family issues, I think these disagreements were superficial and mediocre and did not mean much to anybody. My mother's family was truly there for her when she needed them. And that is what is important. They helped her in many ways and various ways. They helped her just by being there, by surrounding her with love and support, and by contributing to various house matters. It was so beautiful.

I think the love and devotion of my mother and her family, especially her sisters, to each other as sisters was very admirable and unique and it is perhaps the only happy memory that I have from those awful days. I do remember being surrounded by my aunts and uncles and I remember a few happy moments. On the day that my father was finally coming home, it was only adding to the joy that my aunts were there. It was like they stood by the family during my father's absence. They took care of us. And they were there to deliver the family back to him intact. It was very touching and beautiful.

My other aunt, who was my father's sister, came to stay with us a few days. She was handicapped and it was hard to bring her over to our house and to adjust the place for her needs, but she came and joined us for those few days. And she was so happy that Dad was coming home finally. Although she could not help us because she was handicapped, her presence was very special and meaningful and we were happy to have her share this day with us. She was so excited to be there with us. It was like a long awaited joy. We prepared for the lunch and we had all the fancy plates and decorations out and we were waiting.

My mom, my brothers and uncle Raid went to the Abu Graib. They were anxious however. They just did not want anything to go wrong and delay the release of my Dad. They got there. They first collected Dad's personal belongings from his room. He said good-bye to his prison mates. They were overwhelmed with emotion. Dad told them it would be their turn soon to be released, God willing, and that he would come to visit them. Dad changed into a new pressed suit that Mom had brought for him. He looked nice. Then they had to go to the prison office to sign documents to formalize the release. These proceedings were lengthy. They had to go from one office to another both inside the prison as well as out when they left. They could not come straight home. They had to go to one more office to process some documents. It took them a long time there. Finally, they got in the car and left.

The drive home was long, as Abu Graib was on the outskirts of the city and this day was during the brutal summer heat of Baghdad. In those days in Baghdad, there were no restaurants and rest areas on the freeways such as this road from Abu Graib to the city. It was not really a highway; it was more like a long two-lane divided freeway without many businesses or neighborhoods along the way. So it was somewhat a long drive and rather tiring; normally you had to take with you some water or snacks from home on a drive like that.

At home, we were waiting with anxiety and anticipation. My aunts were putting the last touches to the food preparations and the beautiful lunch they had prepared. There was some hidden tension. We just did not want to be disappointed. My sisters and I were anxious and kept going in and out of the gate to look for the cars. We just wanted my father to come home, and we were so afraid that they would come without him, that maybe something would go wrong and the release would be delayed. We kept going in and out to watch for them.

Then I went up on the balcony which overlooked the main street so I could see when they came. So, I was looking from the balcony waiting for the car and daydreaming about Dad coming home and what I should say to him and where he was going to sit and so on. Then all of a sudden, I saw them and I was jumping with joy. We had been awaiting that day and that moment for weeks and weeks. The cars stopped. My brother Haider was driving one car, my brother Samir another, and Uncle Sadi a third. The cars stopped at the gate and we saw everyone coming in.

Downstairs, as soon as they saw them, my sisters opened the front door and my uncle and my aunts rushed to it. Everyone got out of the cars. Dad walked in. That moment Dad looked so charming. He wore a black suit and a white shirt and a burgundy red tie. I was looking down at them from the balcony. My sister and I had prepared colorful "paper confetti" and I had some with me. When I saw Dad walking through the gate I scattered the paper confetti all over him from up on the balcony. The colorful paper was so pretty and Dad was surprised and looked up at the balcony briefly. Meanwhile my sister was doing the same in the patio between the gate and the door. My uncles and aunts threw candy all over. It was a small festive event outside, really a bit subtle; the exuberance was mostly kept for inside the house. Normally, such celebrations would have been louder in public. But because of all the events and our continued fear and anxiety, we kept the majority of our festive mood within the house.

Inside, Dad was greeted by all of us who were at home waiting. His brother and sister, us children, my other uncles and aunts. It was only family members. Dad embraced each and every one. They all said welcoming words. It was a blessing to have him back. There were so many tears and embraces and prayers. For me, it was like the best gift in the world, holding Dad and kissing him and feeling his warmth and kindness all over again. My brothers walked in afterwards. They were unloading the car and joined us later.

Dad sat down; he was calm but a bit tired. The ride home was in the summer heat, so when they arrived, they were all tired and exhausted from the dust and heat but nevertheless happy. The house was cool and comfortable. He rested a bit and then we had a nice family lunch. But he did not talk much. Neither did my Mom. They were unusually quiet. It was like all the pain and agony of the past year and a half was only beginning to show its effect on them and on the rest of the family. It is like when you are in pain so much that you do not feel pain anymore. And then when you feel better and recover, your face shows the agony and the suffering that you had been through. All the conversations were general. At lunch, my uncles and aunts offered prayers and wishes that our family would recover from all this agony. They told my father how much they loved him and wished that we would all have many happy days ahead. They said beautiful things in his honor and to celebrate his safe return. They wished that he would always be there with us and that we would all be there for each other all the time. It was an emotional reunion.

Also, my mother had prepared some food and money to be given to the poor. This is a tradition in Muslim countries in general. When you are done with some ordeal and you thank God that it is over and pray that it will never happen again, you offer charity to the poor in the form of cash or some meat or other foods. It is a belief in the Muslim faith that providing charity to help the poor brings you blessing and relieves you from bad events.

Dad was enjoying being at home surrounded by loving family and having a home lunch after nearly a year and nine months of being away. I went to sit by Dad every few minutes, as if I was afraid he would disappear. I wanted to have his attention and tell him some stories and catch up on so many things. But there was no opportunity to talk at length because we had relatives and it was a busy afternoon. It was a special day. Everyone went home later that evening to give us all some private moments. Dad talked to each of us about school and other things. My sister and I took him on a tour of the house to show him his way around again, and we took him to our room to visit and to show him some books and stuff. Dad looked at each of us with joy and thanked God that we were alive and they did not hurt us even though they came very close. He was grateful that we were all fine.

My father spent the next few days resting and trying to get back to normal. Having spent so many long months away from home, his return was a major adjustment. We began to have many visitors again to greet him and to congratulate the family. Many visitors came by over the weeks. Some of them were the same people who had visited us before. Others were newer friends. I think some people were sincere. They genuinely wanted to greet and celebrate my father's release. They wanted to see him and know what he had been through. But Dad was cautious; he did not talk to everyone about the details of the ordeal. He was afraid there would be someone spying or recording again so he was reserved and not as outgoing as he used to be. It was fun to have all those visitors. At least this time it was a happy occasion.

The visitors brought many gifts. On such occasions the gifts were not unique or personal in nature. And I do not know why people gave such gifts. But this was part of the culture in Iraq. The gifts would be more of a general nature. They included flowers and big huge trays of cake and baklavas (the traditional sweets in the Middle East). I mean huge trays. The trays were round with a diameter of about two and half feet or three feet. Also, they included things like large containers of sugar or dates. Sometimes people, especially from outside of Baghdad, brought a sheep with them. Yes, a sheep. I know that it sounds very strange.

In the Middle East, it is not that uncommon to bring a sheep as a gift. At least that was the culture when I lived there. I do not know whether it is still practiced. I know that this sounds bizarre if you have lived in the West all your life and you have never seen anything like that. Such a gift would be given on important occasions only and not at regular events such as birthdays or anniversaries. At important events such as weddings, coming back from the pilgrimage or recovering from a major surgery, it was possible that some people would bring you a sheep as a gift.

When you had a very important guest coming to visit you, you might also serve a whole cooked sheep stuffed with rice and luscious nuts. It signified the importance of the visit or the guest. This was less common in Baghdad and practiced more outside in other cities, but we did see that in Baghdad also. First of all, people were used to this. It was not like they did not know what to do with the sheep. They most likely would keep it in the back of their garden for a day or two. Then later, they would hire someone, a butcher who worked in the meat shops, to take the sheep and kill it and prepare the meat in small portions.

The meat would be mostly given to the poor. Only a small portion of it would be used by the family itself and it was important that the family only take a small part and not the whole thing. Again distributing food and money to the poor is deeply ingrained in the culture of the Middle East and is done by individuals and families, not necessarily by organized charity organizations like it is here in the West. For example, in Western culture, you would donate your money to some charity organization and it is they who prepare some meal or offer some service to the poor.

In Iraq, it was mostly individuals and families who did that. They took the meat or the cooked food and distributed it directly to the poor. The poor would be found in some particular areas of the city; sometimes they would stay around the holy shrines because they expected to be given food and charity money there. I remember going to the holy shrine of Alkadimain in Baghdad, to distribute the money and meat to the poor who were lined up around the courtyard of the shrines. My brother Haider took me and my aunt there to give out the meat. There were many such poor families with babies and children. It was so sad to see that. When we gave them the food or the money, they said words of gratitude and some prayers for us. Charity organizations were not that common. The Ba'ath regime restricted the formation of any club or society outside of the party and its affiliated and approved organizations.

This culture of sacrificing a sheep for someone developed from an old Abrahamic tradition and is related to the story of the sacrifice that the prophet Abraham made for his son Ishmael. This story is related in the Holy Quran, the Muslim holy book. Abraham made a sacrifice of a sheep instead of killing his son as he thought he was instructed to do. And God ordered Abraham to kill the sheep instead. So when you endure a life threatening ordeal, like my father did, or recovering from a major illness, visitors and well-wishers often bring a sheep to signify your conquest over your ordeal or illness and to express the hope that you will have a new start in life.

* * *

Our life never went back to normal, however. Dad regained his charming style and lively spirit, but his health had been damaged. He was like a fortress which looked strong even though it may be old and damaged. Dad's health was affected severely by that ordeal and all the torture that he endured. The torture and abuse that he went through would haunt his health even years later. During his torture he was hit on the head numerous times; some of these blows made him pass out. Also, it turned out that he had suffered a stroke at Almukhabarat center. In addition, he had a minor stroke several months after his release. But both of these were transient and mild. He had grown ill and frail but most importantly his soul was injured by the injustice that he had endured.

Moreover, he lost the prestigious position that went with his job. He lost not only his position but also the *right to work* for about a couple of years after this event. This is hard to understand for us living here in the West. But the government at that time had control over all professional jobs. There were very few private businesses in Iraq and mostly those were merchant and trade related. All the professional positions were in the hands of the government. So, basically they denied him his work as further retaliation against him and also perhaps to distance him until his story died away. Otherwise his story would have provoked attention and talking among people and colleagues.

It was a difficult transition at the personal level for my father. Not only was he falsely accused, imprisoned, tortured and harmed, there was now further retaliation against him that he had to deal with. The government's refusal to return him to his prestigious position and any similar employment must have been very hard for him, especially because he was at the pinnacle of his career and had enjoyed so much success before his arrest and the collapse of it all. He had lost all that he had worked for so many years; it was all unappreciated and unrecognized now by the Ba'ath regime. This was upsetting to him and to my mother.

The whole ordeal from the beginning was a painful time for my father. However, like all crises in life, while one is going through them one copes and maintains some strength but when they are over, the lasting impact begins to show on one's face, to have an impact on one's health, and sometimes we remain scarred for a long time. For my father, he thought and felt that it was so unfair to be wrongfully accused, to be set up, trapped by ruthless people and by people whom he trusted as colleagues or friends. It was even worse: Dad's losing his position and the right to work again was a new ordeal that he had to deal with. So it was not even really over for him. And it was hard to go through that and to live with its impact on his life. It was very unfair to be treated that way and it was hard to accept. I can imagine how Dad felt. He perhaps felt betrayed and stabbed in the back. These people used his kindness and sincerity and then they got rid of him. He was frustrated because he could not pursue this matter with anyone. There was no law that could protect him from the wrath of the Ba'ath regime. There was no judicial system that he could lean on. We were all glad that he had come out of the ordeal alive, but we could see the effects of this ordeal on his life, his profession and us as a family.

Because of my Dad's imprisonment and later the denial of his work, my parents incurred many debts because we had to survive without my Dad's income for a few years. The ordeal also took an emotional toll on my Mom herself and she aged so much during those few years. I think that my mother was also feeling angry and sad to see my Dad in that position. It is very hard to see the one you love, the love of your life, hurting and there is not much you can do to help them.

Although I was a child of nine or ten then and may not have understood the impact of those emotions on my parents, I do remember them being chronically concerned and worried in general. Also I think that in spite of the fact that many people came over to visit our family and wish my father well after this ordeal, I do not think that many people really helped him and supported him in the aftermath of his ordeal. I think many of these friendships he and my mother had were superficial and did not translate into real help and support. I think some of their friends were false friends and they only enjoyed the company of my parents during happy times and when they had no problems. And maybe others were simply afraid. Moral cowardice is another disturbing feature of human nature.

My parents tried to bring the happy days back. But it was very hard. In fact, their happy glamorous days never came back. My father was struggling on many fronts: his health and his work as well as dealing with the daily problems of living in Iraq such as the imminent mandatory military recruitment for two years after college that my brothers, Haider and Samir, faced as did all college aged males. Also, then in Iraq it had become impossible to conduct any business without Ba'ath approval and connections. Things had gotten many times worse since before the arrest. Dad was convinced that after what he had been through, life would not go back to normal. He could see matters getting worse for the whole country. If the government could get away with the crimes they plotted and eliminate anyone who knew about them, then many horrible things were coming our way. From that time he began the awesome task of finding a way to get my brothers out of the country.

From the events surrounding my father's arrest onward, things deteriorated in Iraq as the weeks and months went by. It was becoming more difficult to travel even when you had favors and contacts in the government. My older brother Haider was already drafted into the military. He had no way out of it. Military service was mandatory in Iraq for all young men. After college, everyone must go unless he had a compelling medical reason or had some powerful contacts in the government. In fact, in those days in Iraq, the biggest crime for a young man in his early twenties, was to delay or miss his mandatory military service.

Military service was not perceived by most people as a patriotic thing. Most people hated it for several reasons. First, it was a forum of revolutionary propaganda. It was also thought of by most people as a period of service to the unpopular regime. The military, the army and the other branches, were used not so much to defend Iraq against foreign enemies, but rather, to quell civil unrest. For example, during the "War of the North" with the Iraqi Kurds, the Iraqi army lost fifty thousand men fighting its own citizens. Also, military service was a way to implement the regime's agenda. In the cases of various insurgencies, the military was used against the people. And thus many people did not want to be a tool in the hands of the government. In addition, some people simply did not want to serve in the military. They wanted to pursue the goals and dreams of their lives away from militias and wars, and they thought that joining the army should be by choice as it was in many other countries.

My father's goal was to get my bothers out as soon as possible. It was his mission. He suspected that the country was headed for disaster. By using all the contacts they had at that time and paying a lot of money and signing any affidavits for the government, my parents were able to get both my brothers, Haider and Samir, out of Iraq. It was luck, a miracle, providential intervention and a lot of diligent effort from my parents and some lucky contacts from Uncle Sadi that contributed to this great result.

I think that my father remained wounded from that ordeal. He must have been hurting so much over it. But it was hard to see for me as a child. Over the years, he managed to go on and pick up the pieces and have some other achievements. But deep in his soul he must have still been hurting. I know that he wanted this story to be known. There is no way to obtain justice in Iraq. There is nothing worse than an open wound that is ready to flare up. It is so true that the grievances one has must be resolved before they can be put to rest.

The few years after Dad returned home were hard. I almost became a parent to my parents. I worried about them incessantly. I was afraid for Dad's health and his frustrations at the continuing consequences of his ordeal on his professional life. It was not fair what they did to him, but my parents thought that now there would be some peace for a while with the Ba'ath government and hoped that they would leave us alone. But it was not over. He was still suffering the consequences of that ordeal for a couple of years. He and my mother did not really talk about their feelings and agony with me perhaps because I was young. But I wonder so much how they managed to survive this big blow and keep going. They must have been so strong and willing to live.

A few years later, they re-instated my father but gave him work in a different agency. In a matter of months he excelled and became a star again. He made new friends and contacts and was successful again. These new people did not know much about the previous events. But they worked well with him. He was happy for a while.

It is really unclear why the government let him work once more in a government position. I think it was because they expected that he would never stand in their way again, that he was too weak and had a lot less stamina than before; and of course now they were totally in control of all the country's affairs. The Ba'athists knew that he was not going to be a threat to them. Moreover, during that period Iraq was embarking on a rapid modernization of its infrastructure. There was a lot of wealth from oil revenue. And Dad was a forerunner in his field. They needed his expertise and skills. He was the mentor of many of his colleagues and staff, and his knowledge and experience of some thirty years was rare in Iraq. After all, they did want some educated people running the technical and scientific affairs of the country after the deterioration that they had caused earlier in the 1970s.

Nevertheless, the wrath of the Ba'ath regime was not over for us yet. There was more coming our way.

CHAPTER 5

A Deep Dark Well

After all we had endured, we though the Ba'ath terror was over. But there was more of it waiting for us. In 1979 we had yet another ordeal with the Ba'ath government. My brother Amer went to the holy city of Karbala and did not come back. During the period from the time my Dad was detained until the late 1970s, there was tremendous escalation in the viciousness and cruelty of the government and the way they dealt with any potential political opposition. People were being detained and executed by the hundreds. In fact many people vanished during this period. We heard about people who were arrested at college or school or even right in their homes. We heard about many young men who were executed. I have to say that the period of the mid and late seventies was a horrible time to be living in Iraq. So many good people were victims of these atrocities; all of them were well educated, and many were from upper class families. Every week or so we would hear about some mother whose sons were missing or detained. And later we heard about such young men being dumped as corpses at the doorsteps of their homes. They were all "shaved off" and vanished. We heard one story of a leading opposition figure by the name of Abu Esam: they threw him in an acid bath to torture him and he died screaming in the compound. We heard stories about women who were brought to the prison to be gang-raped in front of their detained husbands or fathers just to intimidate the prisoners and make them say something that they did not want to say. There were episodes where the secret police would detain someone and shoot him right there on the spot—no charge, no court order, nothing. Alamin people were allowed to kill anyone without further responsibility. I can only imagine what that trauma would be like for the families. We heard of some families who had this happen to them. The government could arrest you simply because someone " reported you" to Alamin as anti–Ba'ath, or your neighbor betrayed you and said that you bought some magazine or book which was censored by the government. In fact, books of the scholar Muhammad Baqir Alsadr, who was an antigovernment charismatic religious leader, if found in your home, were grounds for arresting an entire family and naming them as anti–Ba'ath reactionaries. It was madness. In fact we had such books at home. My brothers had bought these books in the past, before the censorship of publications became prevalent. These were not political books, as political books did not exist in Iraq. They were more books of religion and philosophy. The publication and sale of all books and magazines in Iraq were controlled by the government. Because Alsadr's books had become illegal and owning them was a crime and could jeopardize your life, we were in a dilemma. We had to get rid of these books. We decided to bury them in the dirt of the garden to hide them. My sister Zeena went out in the garden at night. She dug in the dirt and hid those books away. Later, we heard that the secret police knew about this trick, which many people were using to hide books and other materials. A friend of Zeena's told her that the secret police had come to her house and dug the whole garden up in order to find what was hidden there. They found some books and magazines and they arrested her brother. After hearing this, my father was alarmed. He went out in the garden with Zeena and took out all those books that she had hidden there. We collected the books and burned them in the trash. It was such a shame that we had to burn these books to protect our lives. It was sad to see books burning in flames. The books turned into ashes. It was a somber moment.

Many people became suspects simply if they had any religious or political inclinations. This was not because the government was anti-religious per se, but because the most serious threat to the Ba'ath government at that time was a religious based opposition by the name of Dawa party. Many educated youth who were influenced by religious leaders belonged to this group. The group advocated freedoms and some openness in the political system in Iraq. Many young people were drawn to this group because they were fed up with the corruption and the lack of opportunities for ordinary citizens who were non-Ba'athists. All colleges within the prestigious University of Baghdad had many spots for Ba'athist students even though they may not have obtained adequate marks for the entrance exams. People were tired of the lack of simple freedoms that the rest of the world had. When people traveled abroad, they were exposed to these ideas, which is why the Ba'ath government banned or severely restricted traveling for ordinary citizens outside of the country. There were times when all travel was banned unless it involved a life-threatening medical case. But such a case had to be verified and approved by a *revolutionary medical committee* composed of some doctors who were loyal to the Ba'ath. This way, no one could bring a letter from any doctor as an excuse for travel. This way, no one could travel just for the sake of tourism and a vacation. People wanted simple basic freedoms such as not being harassed and coerced into joining the Ba'ath party, being able to travel, being able to attend a private school instead of a government school, being able to listen to foreign broadcasting (short-wave radio was banned so that no one could listen to news from the outside world). People wanted freedom of the press, freedom of speech, elections, representative government, and appreciation of talent and education as a basis of promotions instead of loyalty to Ba'ath. But no one dared to speak about that. It was like the Ba'ath stepped all over people's lives. They denied them all rights and freedoms to the point that just asking for simple harmless things, such as owning a short-wave radio, became a crime. There were many frustrations among ordinary people who did not have political aspirations, who merely wanted to live. So the government kept a tight eye on all sectors of society who had aspirations to change the system, especially the youth both in high schools and universities.

The viciousness of the government did not stop there. In about mid 1979 and for a few years onward they came up with another scheme. The regime deported Iraqi citizens who were of Persian ancestry claiming that they should go back to Iran. This was a complicated matter. Iraq, being a center of civilizations for thousands of years, was a unique social mosaic and a crossroad for many people of various ethnicities and races. Many people in Iraq today are of non-Arab origins. In fact, the original inhabitants of Iraq were non-Arab. There are many ethnicities and religions in Iraq because people have migrated to Iraq from many other neighboring and distant places since the dawn of civilization. Indeed there are Iraqis who are of Persian, Turkish, Kurdish and Arab origin as there are Iraqis who are Armenian, Assyrian, and Chaldean. There are Muslims, Christians, Jews, Sabians, and even fire-worshipers. So Iraq is a colorful mosaic of religions and ethnicities. Some people have dark complexions, others are fair and blond, and many local languages and dialects are spoken by all these people. Indeed some Iraqis were of Persian origin but they were Iraqi citizens. There were also a few families who were Persian Iranians but were living in Iraq. Anyway, the government started a massive campaign to deport those people of Persian origin or ancestry to Iran. This was around the time when conflict between the two governments seemed inevitable but the Iran-Iraq war had not begun yet.

The government deported those people in the most inhumane way. A whole encyclopedia of tragedy could be written about this sad chapter in the Iraqi history. It was *ethnic cleansing* at its worse. And the world community was silent about it. There are many ways to tell the story of these people: how they were seized from their homes or from their workplaces; how they were terrorized during their transportation to Iran; how they got separated from their family members. These people experienced the horror of walking in the wilderness without food and shelter. If they were lucky they made it to Iran alive. Some of them were able to start their lives over in Iran if they knew someone who would help them. But many of them withered away. For us in Baghdad, the sudden absence of many families terrorized whole communities who were left behind. It was cruel. One day for example, some girl would not show up at school. Everyone thought she was ill, but she remained absent for days. Her friends would call but there would be no answer at home. Then later we would learn that this whole family had been deported. Similar scenes would be repeated for teachers, neighbors and so many others. It was frightening to drive around in Baghdad or walk around some neighborhood and learn that this house had been "sealed" by the government because the family had been deported. Deported was a kind word to use. Those people were not "deported"; they were attacked in the middle of the night and told to get in a bus that was waiting outside. They had to go, no matter who was ill, who was asleep, and who did not want to go. There were no options under Ba'ath brutality. People were loaded on buses literally in their nightgowns. There were babies, pregnant women, older men. In some cases, they took the young men to separate locations from the women and older people. Sometimes they separated children from parents, men from wives. Entire families were dispersed with no money, with only the clothes on their back. People were screaming, begging with the driver and the guards just to let them get some money or medication or their valuable items, or to wait until they found their family member. Buses and trucks filled with people were driven to the border region with Iran. People were simply dumped there in the wilderness and in the cold where there was no food, no shelter, and no mercy. Babies died. Pregnant and lactating women died. Older men and women died. These dead were left behind. Their companions may have buried them. In the mountainous terrain between Iran and Iraq, where those people were dumped at the border, lie the graves of many men and women who perished so horribly in this harsh trip. They died shivering, of hunger and thirst, of frostbite. Sometimes the people who died left children behind. Such children continued the trip with the group that they had come with. They remained without parent or guardian.

Many people adopted these children who were left with no one. The ones who remained alive had to walk to the nearest town and wait there until they were received by the Iranian authorities. It was waves of humans walking, distraught, hungry, cold and just barely alive. Deporting these citizens became very intense and apparent in 1980; this deportation scheme continued until the mid 1980s.

My brother Amer went to Karbala to observe the religious activities of Ashura, which many people in Iraq observed: old, young, educated, uneducated, Sunni and Shia. It was not so much an ideological thing to observe these traditions. It was socio-political. These rituals had become a vortex for antigovernment sentiments. So while people were reciting their religious chants commemorating the death of Imam Hussein, who was murdered many centuries ago by a ruthless ruler of his time, some people also chanted anti–Ba'ath government slogans. The youth in Iraq had grown tired of the lack of freedom and, as in many countries, were more apt to participate in such activities against the government. They had no attachments or responsibilities to families, they were emotional and carefree; they demanded more freedom and political rights; and they still had their whole lives ahead and it was important that they bring about change to this repressive system.

During those events my brother was in the vicinity of the demonstrations which involved some one thousand people or so. He and the demonstrators were chanting: "God is Great. God is Great...." It was peaceful and they were simply chanting slogans demanding more freedom: freedom to travel, to buy books, to talk freely and gather, to form non-governmental organizations and so on. These aspirations seem so normal when we talk about them here in the West. But how dare anyone in Iraq even dream of freedoms. The government forces were watching for such an event; they immediately intervened and crushed this demonstration, detaining or killing dozens of people on the spot. The place was swept quickly by thousands of armed security officers. There was chaos. My brother was detained and transported to Baghdad to the main Alami headquarters.

This demonstration and the arrests were significant in the political history of Iraq. It is known today as the Uprising of 1979. The government intervention was much more severe than that in China in 1989 in Tiananmen Square, events by which the whole world was enraged and rightfully so. Of course people in the West never heard of this event in 1979 in Iraq because all news was controlled by the government. In fact the Iraqi news service did not report such activities. We and others knew about these events via word of mouth and from people who lived in Karbala and others who managed to escape the events. In Iraq in those days, and even today, no foreign news agencies were allowed to attend such events unless they were specifically invited by the government, and they would be escorted all the time by government officers. The government crushed political events like these before they expanded. It is sad that no one knew about it or reported it and no world leaders were enraged by it.

Amer left home Thursday afternoon and was supposed to be back Friday around noon. Well of course he did not come back. Fear and agony hit us again. My mother feared that something was wrong. She said that my brother had told her he would be back as soon as the rituals were over. Also, he did not call home as he promised if there was any delay—he knew how much my parents worried about him. We spent Friday in distress and agony as it became obvious that something had gone wrong. That day was sad and gloomy. It felt awful. I too was worried about Amer and I thought that my mother's fears were well placed. Actually, both my parents were now worried and very concerned. My Dad was usually calm and cautious and not as emotional as my Mom, but even he was worried.

My father felt defeated that his son may be in the hands of the regime. He had been planning for all my brothers to leave. But it was getting harder by the week. Every couple of weeks or so, some new law or regulation was announced that made it impossible to plan any travel or any way for young men to leave the country. Dad felt that he had failed in this task. He now just wanted to know that Amer was safe. Dad knew of their atrocities because he had had firsthand experience of them during his own ordeal. Dad was dismayed that he had failed to get Amer out sooner, with my other brothers. But because Amer was still in university, it was nearly impossible to get permission for him to leave.

My sisters and I tried to help my parents in this terror that was befalling us. We called some friends of Amer to see if they had heard from him or whether they knew anything. Their response was in the negative. They had gone to Karbala too but had come back before the events. They had seen Amer there in Karbala before they left. We were not sure whether they were telling us the truth or were afraid also to speak on the phone. My mother could not sleep that night: She wept and cried and prayed.

The next morning, my father drove to Karbala. He did not go to Karbala that often. As he was driving to find the police headquarters, he saw some shops and homes with broken windows; glass was shattered on the streets. There were damaged cars. It was obvious some battle had occurred. Dad had a thick feeling in his chest. He knew it was going to be bad news. He went to the police headquarters. He got to the office. It was a small building and there were a few armed men in military uniform. He explained his case and pleaded with the officers there.

"My son is missing, he told them. "He came to Karbala and he is missing. I came all the way from Baghdad to look for my son."

"Oh." one officer responded. "Why was your son here, if you live in Baghdad?"

"Yes," Dad replied, "He came to Karbala to watch the Ashura processions."

The officers laughed and said, "Oh, yes, we detained many young men. They are hooligans, and they are not sincere Iraqi citizens. They were arrested and taken back to Baghdad to the main Alamin office."

Dad was shocked and enraged but he maintained his composure.

"My son is not a hooligan. He is an educated young man, he attends the university of Baghdad. He was just here to watch the events like people have done for hundreds of years. Can you show me whether his name is among those whom you arrested? How do I know otherwise whether my son was among them?"

"Look, mister," the officer said, "we do not keep records. We arrested hooligans. We shipped them to Baghdad. They will be processed in Baghdad. We do not know who they are.... They all deserve to die."

Dad tried hard to get information from them. He spoke to their chief who was just as crude and negligent. They told him over and over they couldn't verify who was detained or say who would be released, that it all happened in haste and there was chaos. As Dad walked out to leave and drive back to Baghdad, he saw a small truck being loaded with young men who were being harassed and mocked and kicked. They were being pushed into the cargo area of the truck like cattle. It was a frightening scene and so heartbreaking. There had been no such brutality in Iraq in the memory of my father's generation. They had not seen such viciousness from any previous regime. Dad was distraught and dismayed by what he saw. He and so many other parents had spent years of their lives raising their children, but here they were, grown men and women now, being slaughtered by the Ba'ath regime and treated like they were less even than animals. Dad could not get any information about Amer. They would not tell him anything. That was typical of the regime. They arrested and killed and maimed people before they knew who they were and what they did. In fact there were incidents where people were arrested or executed simply because of mistaken identity. They might have had the same first and last name as another person who the government wanted. Anyway the officers advised my Dad to go back to Baghdad to search there.

Dad came home with no news about my brother. He knew it was no

use to go through the normal channels of checking. No one would tell
him anything even if they knew. Those days in and around 1979 were
awful. Everything that we had endured in the previous ordeal when Dad
was detained was now considered mellow compared to what was unfold-
ing. There was nowhere to turn. There was no one to check with. You
were literally at the mercy of the thugs who ran the two notorious institutions Alamin and Almukhabarat. These were professional killers, their
purpose and goal was to eliminate anything that could become a threat
to the Ba'ath party. They were like savage hungry animals. They had full
authority to kill and instantly shoot anyone they suspected was against
the government, even an entire family together. They mocked the people they were killing, they even enjoyed it. This created fear and trauma
in so many neighborhoods where such things took place and paralyzed
people from even thinking of moving against the government. By the
same token, it inspired and mobilized others to rise up and face this monstrous regime. Both groups suffered. The former perhaps lived longer, but
not with much peace and security. The latter died instantly when they
were caught. The authorities invented a new kind of terror and agony in
Iraq: So many parents of young men and women suffered the loss of their
children in a second when the regime caught them. It was so unfair. Those
parents had spent years and years raising their children only so that the
regime could kill them so easily and so mercilessly in seconds. Lives of
these youth meant nothing to the regime. In a flash of a second, these
young men were shot in front of their parents or on the college campuses
or even at the doorsteps of their homes. It was absolute terror.

We had to rely on anyone who had pull and connections in the government to get any news. It was impossible to get anywhere otherwise.
But this time my Uncle Sadi was unable to help us. Indeed by this time
in the late seventies, the composition of the Ba'ath regime had changed
dramatically. There had been many internal feuds within the regime itself.
This was manifested by the fact that many senior Ba'athists were shoved
out of their positions and replaced by new Ba'athists and especially those
close to Saddam Hussein. Although throughout the 1970s Hussein was
the vice president, he was actually the one running the country. He had
more power than president Ahmad Hassan Albaker. He was very feared
and revered even before he made himself the president. A split had arisen
in the government. This split became clear with the removal of the president from his post and the succession of Saddam Hussein himself in
1979. Although president Albaker gave a speech in which he announced
his resignation, it was widely known among Iraqis that he was shoved from
his post because of the power struggle with Saddam Hussein. Albaker died

abruptly a few weeks after. His death was orchestrated by the new leadership of the Ba'ath. It was rumored in Baghdad that Albaker was poisoned. Throughout these political developments, Albaker's circle of influential men were also reduced or removed from their positions. People who used to be high-ranking officials such as Munther Almutlig and Hardan Tikriti were no more. They were either killed or removed from their posts.

For Uncle Sadi, most of his contacts were among this older circle of influence. So he indeed was cut off from the new contacts of influence which explained why he could not help us. In addition, it just may be that he chose not to. This time, he said that my brother had incriminated himself by associating with these hooligans against the government. So Uncle Sadi was mad at Amer and about why he went to Karbala in the first place. He was accusing the victim, my brother, instead of the ruthless authorities. My mom defended Amer and told Uncle Sadi that it was not a crime to go to see the Ashura processions. People in Iraq had seen those processions for centuries and centuries. It was a tradition and many people, even children, went there to watch; it was an exciting event.

Those days were lonely for us. We were isolated even by our relatives and the closest people such as my uncles and cousins and aunts, except Aunt Mona who stayed with us throughout this period and Aunt Weda who visited us frequently; other relatives were afraid to associate with us. Maybe once in a while or so my Aunt Najia came by. It was hard for us. We did not go out that much either. We could not do anything fun and there was no laughter, no happiness. Those days also taught me a lot about true friendships and true family love and sincerity. I think that you know your true friends and relatives in times of difficulty. We were abandoned by some friends and relatives. I think that many people avoided visiting us because they were afraid for their own safety and security. I do not respect such attitudes. And I do not think that such behavior is to be forgiven. I think that people should be truthful in their friendships and they should endure with their friends in good and bad times.

In addition, I think some of the few people who did visit or call us were sent by the secret police to spy on us. This was a common way for the regime to get information about people. They would recruit some of your friends or even neighbors. They would instruct them to visit and to make certain comments to provoke a discussion about the affairs of the country and the political situation, and that would be the trap. People might just be innocent and too trusting and speak what was on their minds. Then these conversations would be reported to the authorities and even recorded sometimes.

In fact one of my own friends at school did that with me. She asked me about Amer—she said that she had heard that he had been detained. She was trying to get some information about Amer from me. Also, they used family members of people who were detained. For their spying on other people, they were promised that their son or family member would be released. I do not know whether the Ba'ath kept their promises. But we did have such an experience with a woman whose son was also detained. I do not know whether the detention of her son was a fiction for our benefit or he had actually been detained and she then recruited to spy on us. But she came to visit us and she said that her son was also detained like Amer. And she started to cry and to criticize the government in order to provoke one of us to say something bad about the government. It was a dirty tactic. We did have a few suspicious encounters with people whom we knew. But then by that time we had had experience with these tactics and we were more aware than other people.

My parents were desperate to find someone to help them get a hint of what had happened to Amer. They were seeking help from anyone and everyone who might be able to tell them whether Amer was alive. It is a strange feeling to be in such limbo, not knowing whether your son is alive or dead, not knowing whether to mourn or to wait and be patient. My parents were like someone who was lost in the dark and who was following any glimpse of light, any sign of hope. They were restless. They were occupied with this matter day and night.

One of Mom's friends was really disheartened about how sad my mother was and she had a lot of empathy for her. Her name was Hana. She whispered to Mom that she knew of a woman with some special gift. She told my mom, "Lydia, I have to tell you, there is a woman in Baghdad, she is blind but she is gifted with this knowledge. You've got to go there. She will tell you about Amer."

Mom looked at Hana with surprise.

"I swear, my husband's brother was also missing," Hana continued. "This woman told us about him. I will go with you. Lydia, you've got to go, you've got to find out about your son."

"Hana?" Mom replied. "What are you talking about? How can that be? Maybe that woman is put there by the government? How can you trust her?"

"No, Lydia, no…. I have heard about this woman from many people. And when my brother-in-law was also arrested, just like Amer, a few months ago, that's where we went. And she told us that he was alive and that he would be released."

"I really don't know what to say. I do not want to go to a fortuneteller. Only God knows the unknown and the future."

"I know, Lydia, but this woman is humble. She does not even ask for money. People give her money usually as a donation to her. She does not do this in order to abuse people's pain and agony. She had told someone that when she was young, both her parents died. She was orphaned. She lived initially with her uncle. He was not kind to her. And she used to pray a lot as she endured ridicule and neglect from her uncle. Then she had a visionary experience. An imam, a religious saint, appeared to her and told her that she would have a gift from God, which would help her sustain her in life. And then a few years later she started doing these services."

"Okay, I will go," Mom said. "Oh, I do not really know. Oh, God; I am dying to have any news about Amer. It is so unfair what they have done to us. We raise these children, we are happy when they are all grown up. And then the Ba'ath just takes them away. Oh, God, please make him be alive."

Mom went with her friend Hana to the house of this woman; she was known by the name Rifa, the blind lady. When Mom and Hana got to the house many other ladies were there. It was such a sad scene. All these desperate women had come to seek some divine information about their children. It was disheartening. When people are desperate they will do anything. Even though my mother was not superstitious—she was educated and had traveled the world—she still went to this woman out of desperation. Mom was torn about Amer. It was even worse than when my Dad was detained. I think the loss of a child is a horrible thing and all these women had come to visit this lady to see if there was hope of finding their children. Mom sat and waited. The blind woman was not really that old, she perhaps was in her late twenties or early thirties. And she was just sitting and talking to another woman. The visitors would go and sit by her and say the first name of their son or loved one. When Mom's turn came she went and sat by Rifa.

"I am mother of Amer," Mom said.

"Tell me more about your Amer," Rifa responded. "There is another mother of Amer here. [Indeed Amer was a common name. There was another woman in the crowd whose son's name was also Amer.]

"Amer, my son, he is twenty-two years old. He is in his fourth year at university and he is missing."

"Okay .... Yes, I know about him."

Mom was silent. Her heart was racing.

"He is alive...," Rifa continued. "But he is in a deep ... dark ... well."

"There is an informant that caused his trouble," she went on. "A man, a man whom you know, a man who comes and goes to your house. He is the one who set up Amer. That's all I have."

Mom thanked her and said some prayers for her. She also gave her some money. Another lady came to sit by Rifa and had queries about her husband. Mom and Hana left. Mom was intrigued by this experience and by what she had seen: all these women, worried, crying, desperate for any news about their loved ones, hanging on anything that gave them hope, anything that relieved them of their despair. Mom came home and told Dad and us the news. She kept wondering about this informant and who he may be. Dad was not into these things and did not take what the woman said very seriously. My sisters and I, however, were intrigued by this woman and her capabilities. We had never heard of such a thing before. We kept praying that Amer was still alive.

One night, we were home as usual. There was a knock at the door. We went to see who it was. A young man stood there. We did not recognize him. He said he had news from Amer. My parents quickly went out to greet him. After a few minutes they let him in. He appeared to be in his mid twenties. He seemed simple and humble. My parents were reluctant to talk to him at first, since this visit could be some kind of setup. My parents listened as he introduced himself; they did not say much.

"Sir, you don't know me," the young man said to my Dad. "My name is Jasem. I was in detention too, in the same place as Amer. I came to tell you that your son Amer is alive."

"Where, where were you at?" Dad demanded.

"I was in Alamin. Right here in Baghdad. And Amer is there too. I did not see him. I do not know what he looks like. We were in separate rooms. I only talked to him through the door. He heard that I was going to be released. He gave me your address; I wrote it on the sole of my foot."

"What did Amer tell you?" Dad asked. "Please tell me."

"Well, Amer overheard that I was being released. My prison cell was next to his. And he told me to please go deliver this message to his family—he told me to come to this house to tell you that he was alive."

My mom said, "Please, tell me what he sounded like. How do I know it's him?"

"I just talked to him once," Jasem said. "I did not see him. He gave me this address. It's him."

Mom hugged the young man. He was the first to give her news that her son was alive. My Dad asked the man to give any other details about what Amer said or how he sounded. The man said, "I swear by God that is what he told me. I am honest. He just wanted me to deliver the message. He is alive. Your son is alive." After this conversation, the man left. He said that it was better that we did not stay in touch because he himself had just been released from detention. He was being observed by the secret police for sure and it was better to stay away from trouble. We did not see him again

My parents were slightly relieved to know that Amer was alive. Now they were determined to use any government connections to release him. A friend of my mother's at school knew some top people in the government and she tried to help us find out what had happened. She indeed got news that Amer was in Alamin and had been there for nearly two months. We were not allowed to visit him. This time around there were no such things as visitations. In fact, my parents went once to see if they could try to talk their way into seeing Amer. Mom had been to Alfidailia detention center many times, ironically with Amer, to visit my Dad several years earlier. Now she and Dad went to Alamin detention center trying to find Amer. It was heartbreaking. All these mothers and fathers, begging the guards for any news, any hope, even paying money to the guards just to get them some information. My parents left with no news. We waited days and weeks in that condition. It was a long hard wait. We could not trust anybody in those days. Sometimes, Amer's friends would come to ask about him. But we did not know whether to trust them. We could not speak freely with them. Maybe they too were being used as spies and informants. So we could not say much to them.

* * *

When Amer was released, we did not know beforehand. He just came one day and knocked at the door. It was one afternoon unlike all others. We had just finished having lunch and were cleaning up. We were sad in those days but we tried hard to continue our daily life. As we dispersed into the house each going to his room to change and rest, the doorbell rang. Mom was still in the kitchen tidying up the place. She went to see who it was. She saw a taxi at the door and then she saw Amer walking through the gate.

Mom screamed, "Amer.... Amer is here."

My Dad heard her because he was the last one to leave the kitchen. He came back running to see what had happened. He thought he had heard Amer's name. When Dad walked in, he saw my Mom embracing and kissing Amer and kissing the ground. She was in tears. Both Mom and Dad were crying with joy that their son was alive. Amer was in bad shape. He was all bruised and had lost so much weight. His face was pale. His feet were swollen. When Mom and Dad saw him, they could not believe this was their son. He looked different. He was barefoot, and all beaten up. Both Mom and Dad were crying at what had happened to their son. Mom looked at his wounds. She was kissing his bruised hands and holding his head to her chest, her tears flowing over him.

Dad put his arms around him and said, "Amer, son. Oh, my God.... Thank God. Thank God. You are alive.... Oh, God. What have they done to us?"

Even Dad was extremely emotional. "Amer, listen to me," he continued. "You are leaving this crazy country. I promise. You must leave ... I want you to leave. Oh, God. You are not staying here anymore. These thugs ... what have they done to us?"

The taxi driver who brought Amer home was waiting outside to be paid: Amer did not have any money on him. We were so overcome by emotions, we forgot about the taxi driver. "Mom," Amer said, "I need to pay the driver." Dad went out and paid the driver double his charge for the ride.

We could not believe that Amer was home with us. In fact, Amer later told us that being released that day was a total surprise to him too. Amer woke up that morning and was told that he was being released that day. He thought they were playing a game on him. They did that often to agonize people. They told them that they were being released and then nothing happened. But actually Amer was released.

We sat around Amer to look after him.

Later, over the following days, he told us many awful stories about how he was arrested and what he saw at the detention place. During the events at Karbala, there were hundreds of police. But they were disguised in regular clothes and some were even milling among the demonstrators and the bystanders. The secret police picked anyone who was in the vicinity of the demonstrations. They did not even verify their names or what they had done. They just grabbed them and threw them on the ground face down. They could not move. Anyone who moved was shot. Amer also told us more gruesome details of his ordeal. The dungeons of the Alamin were another world. They comprised the ugliest face of the Ba'ath regime. These dungeons were beyond the imagination of anyone. The terror that went on there was beyond our capacity to believe. It was like the underworld of the Ba'ath regime. It was like the core of the regime's hatred of the people of Iraq. It was so unbelievable that even my Dad, who himself had been inside these dungeons years earlier, could not believe what he was hearing.

Amer said that they were first loaded in a small bus. There were forty or so men in his group. Initially they were taken a short distance away to some security office for half a day or so in Karbala. There, they were kept in a small room. All forty of them. The room was so small they could only stand up. They could not sit or lie down on the ground. They were standing for many hours. Amer said the room was awful, it was hot and stuffy, and there was no air. Some people were coughing and the place was unhygienic. The officers terrorized him and the others one by one. Amer was taken for interrogation. Without being asked anything, he was pushed against a wall. One of the officers held a gun to his head and said, "I shall kill you now. I want you to count from one to ten aloud."

Amer started counting. Then as he reached ten, his heart was racing—he was expecting to die at that moment. Then the officer, who was drinking beer, said, "No, I changed my mind." He asked Amer, "Why are you plotting against the government?"

"I did nothing like that," Amer protested. "I was just standing by watching the procession."

Amer was hit all over, on the right and left of his face, on his back, until he fainted. When he woke up, he and the other men were loaded in the bus again and taken to Baghdad. Amer said that on the drive to Baghdad, there were members of the secret police (Alamin) in the truck. They were armed. They were looking at all those young men and pitying them and sometimes cursing them with swear words. Those moments were frightening. Amer said he had a wish during the ride. He wished the bus would get in an accident and he would die. Death would be easier than what was coming his way. He did not want to be detained and tortured.

They arrived in Baghdad a couple of hours later. As they reached the outskirts of the city, and right before they entered it, they were all blindfolded. This was so no one would know exactly which building they were going to. Alamin operated from more than one location. Some of Amer's bus mates told him that they could see through the fold and they knew where they were going. It was indeed the notorious headquarters of the Alamin, the division known as the *fifth section*, a special place where they kept all the citizens who were suspected or accused of actively being against the government and the party. They removed the blindfolds. Amer and hundreds of young men were all marched into a big hall, into which led a few hallways that were lined with small rooms and cells. Some were rooms with doors, some were rooms without doors, and others prison cells. Some of those rooms were chambers of torture in which there were many frightening instruments. There were live electric cables; there were bottles with broken sharp necks, batons, chains, irons and barbed wire. Other rooms were holding stations where people were kept between torture sessions. In other rooms still, guards and torture operators were just waiting for their jobs to start or maybe resting. They were drinking whiskey and smoking. These were ugly looking thugs. They had the cruelest look in their eyes, as if they were the devil himself. One does not know how a human being can inflict so much pain on others and enjoy it. Those men killed, tortured, raped and committed so many other disgusting acts on the prisoners.

Along the hallways, there were stairways and other smaller corridors that were dark and damp. There were pieces of clothing soaked with blood and vomit. Some rooms especially smelled foul. Amer and others were told to wait there and stand still. They also saw some other equipment which looked more advanced and modern. Some pieces of equipment were stacked on top of one another. Amer was frightened of what they would do to him. He was feeling sick from all the scenes around him. It was nauseating. Later, the big group was broken into smaller groups. Amer was led into another hallway. He and a bunch of men were told to follow a man who was leading them to where they would stay. As they walked along, he saw rooms and chambers crammed with men and women. The rooms were overcrowded. As they walked further, there were more corridors from which he heard sounds of screaming and pleading and laughter and more screams. It was nerve-racking and it was nauseating. As Amer walked, he looked at some of the people in those crammed rooms. He saw many of them with burn marks, many had bleeding wounds. Some were just lying on the floor half-alive. Their feet were blue and purple. It was an awful scene.

As they finally reached their destination which was a medium sized room, they saw some men who looked like devils. They were nearly naked and showed their muscular bodies. They carried batons and hoses and cables and as soon as the detainees entered, they were blindfolded and then were ordered to run. Then Amer and the others were beaten and kicked by these men and spat on by them. The prisoners were pushed against the wall. They were beaten on their heads, on their genitals, on their feet. These young detainees rapidly descended into a near coma. Amer said it was a state of being in which they were alive but numb, unable to stand or to talk. The shock and the pain were so traumatic, some of the young men passed out. Later, the thugs left the room. The detainees were moaning and in agonizing pain. Many of them were sick and just lying there. While Amer lay in his cell with many other men, his cell-mates told him that they had heard that people were placed in coffins for a couple of days where they could only breathe, they could not move; the coffins were dark and they would feel like suffocating. Amer also saw two rooms with a big basin in the middle. The basin was filled with some liquid. Amer had heard that this was the nitric acid and they tortured people there by dipping their legs or arms in the burning compound. And sometimes they even threw people wholly in—people whom they could not release because they had been maimed, for instance. Another form of torture Amer saw involved the jailers throwing the detainees on the floor and using their heads as footrests. They even urinated on people's faces, he stated. It was awful.

It was traumatic for Amer who had lived all his life in the seclusion and relative luxury of our home. It was a shock that was beyond his capacity to imagine. Amer was taken for interrogation many times. His days were divided between torture sessions, interrogation sessions, and periods when they left him alone. During torture sessions, he was hung by his legs from a fan in the ceiling. The fan would spin at high speed; then they would drop him and force him to stand up straight. He would be so dizzy that he could not even sit. They used electric shocks on his back and on his face. They burned his back with cigarettes. Amer screamed and yelled in his powerful voice. During one of those interrogations, a thug by the name of Faisal Hlal was terrorizing Amer.

"Amer, come here," he said.

Amer went and stood before Hlal.

"You are tall," Hlal pronounced. "I am going to make you shorter."

Amer did not say anything. He was scared by the evil he saw in this man's eyes. "Listen up, Amer," Faisal continued. "I will make you four pieces with my own hands. Then you will be smaller in size."

Amer was afraid and he was getting sick from this conversation. Faisal started beating Amer up all over, left and right. "Why do you grow you hair long?" the jailer demanded.

Amer indeed had long hair; it was the fashion among young men.

"I just like to have long hair," Amer replied. "It is fashion."

"Shut up ... shut up...," Hlal screamed. "You want to make yourself a leader.... Ha.... You want to be the Che Guevara of the Shia? Ha? Shut up...."

"Sir ... no...," Amer tried to explain. "Long hair is in fashion."

Amer was also later interviewed by the head of the Alamin directorate, a thug by the name of Fadil Albarak. Amer was afraid. This man was the chief of this dungeon of terror and evil. Amer had heard of him even before his detention. All of Baghdad knew of Albarak as a thug, a criminal and a killer. But Amer had never seen him before and he did not recognize him by his looks. Albarak had a lengthy talk with Amer. When Amer went to see Albarak, Amer was all bruised and beaten up and he was very weak.

"You know," Albarak said, "I feel sorry for you. You live in a nice house in upscale Baghdad ... you have a nice life at home ... how does it feel to be here?"

"I do not know why I am here," Amer responded. "I do not want to be here."

"Why were you with these hooligans?"

"I was only standing by watching. It was the police who started the violence."

"You are an intelligent man," Albarak said. "You are in university. You should not have been near these hooligans and low types. They are not Iraqis.... They are not sincere...."

"I wish to go home, sir," Amer said.

"I am going to give you another chance," Albarak replied. "But only one more chance. If I ever hear anything I don't like about you.... If I ever see you again in any such activities, I myself will see to it that you will be finished. I will behead you with my own hands. Consider yourself lucky that I am giving you another chance to live."

With this, the meeting ended. Amer thought that he was being released after this show of "mercy" from this thug. But they kept him for a few more days.

During those days, as he walked back and forth between the torture rooms and his waiting room, he heard screams and cries all over. He saw many nearly dead people lying at the sides of the corridors in the prison. He saw other people being tortured. There was also psychological torture. They would leave him in the dark for hours and hours, and then all of a sudden they would alternate the pitch black with very bright light, on and off. There would be sounds of screaming and then laughter and then frightening sounds of dogs and coyotes barking and attacking someone. A man would be screaming—he was being ripped to pieces by the hungry beasts. It was meant to frighten him. Amer did not know whether it was recorded or real. There would be the screaming and pleading of a woman being gang-raped, then the laughter of a bunch of men. Throughout his arrest, he was sleeping on the floor. There was no decent hygiene, no air, no sun. They gave him a few pieces of bread once a day. It was dirty and old bread. Sometimes it had things growing on it. They had no clean water. They all got sick. It was awful.

After spending nearly six weeks in this horror, Amer was told that he was being released that morning. He could not believe it at first. He thought that it was another trick just to raise his hopes. He was in agony. Then he knew it was real. They called him. They made him sign a document that said that if they ever caught him in any anti-government activity, he would be executed. Amer signed the document. He just wanted to be out. Then they told him to get out. Amer left. He was so afraid as he took a few steps out of the building. He was afraid that they would haul him back in. He was disoriented. He walked further from the building. He could not believe that they had let him go. It was a miracle.

Amer smelled fresh air for the first time in weeks. He saw the sun for the first time in weeks. He saw normal people outside. He walked a few blocks. He was distraught. He was afraid to look back, maybe they were coming after him. As he walked, he passed by a school and saw all the little innocent children who were on recess. He stopped at the school and looked at the children in the courtyard. Those children knew nothing of the horror building so close by. Amer could not believe that he was alive, that he was looking at normal things and breathing clean air again. He got a taxi and told the driver to take him home. And that is how he was released.

After hearing about what he went through, I though that Amer was so brave and strong. He was a hero. He was my hero. He endured so much pain and it must have been so fearful to him. I think he had a strong will. He told me that he hated the pain and the torture and that he though that death would be easier because then he would not have to suffer anymore.

Over the next few days he rested at home. We could not celebrate in the open. We just had a little celebration for him at home, just for us. My sister and I bought Amer a plate with roses embedded in it and we wished him well in his new start in life, as going through the Ba'ath terror and coming out alive was like having another chance at life. We wished him a new and lasting happiness. Our celebration was quiet and rather small. In those days you had to keep a low profile. You never knew when they would be back to haunt you. But the affair was low key more because it was hard to celebrate. Many of Amer's friends did not make it. Every now and then we would hear about some young man or woman being arrested and detained for many months, and all of a sudden we would hear that he or she had been executed. It was a horrible time to live in Iraq.

That year, Amer was in his last year in university. He had missed more than three months of school, and when he got out of the detention he needed medical treatment for his injuries. So he had missed exams and a lot of work. Because he was a good student and some professors had empathy for what happened to him, and they knew my Dad and about his former ordeal, they tried to help Amer make up his missed work. He was given another chance to take his exams at the end of the summer; he did pass and graduated that same year. This was common in the Iraqi education system. If you missed your work for any reason but had done well throughout the year, you were given another chance to take your exams. This way you would not lose the whole academic year.

My parents were overwhelmed by Amer's agony. They knew it was no longer safe for Amer and even us girls to stay in Iraq. They were dying to find a way out for Amer. They knew that sooner or later Alamin would be coming after him. Alamin did not need a reason or a violation to persecute him. They could easily fabricate something against him. However, my father thought that since Amer had just been released from detention perhaps it meant that he was in the clear for a few weeks. So, this was the only window of opportunity for him to leave. Since they released him it meant they really did not want to kill him at that time, otherwise they would have done so then. Every hour was precious now before any other developments. Mom and Dad thought that Amer had to leave right away. It was complicated, however; not only were there no exit visas given at that time to young men his age who were eligible for military service, but also he had to start his military service soon.

Joining the army after college graduation had been mandatory since the fifties in Iraq. Really Amer had no way to escape the army. So Amer went to the army recruitment office and signed up once he had graduated and got his credentials stating that he had signed up. These credentials, known as *Daftar Al Khidma*, were necessary in Iraq. This document was like your doorway to heaven, or to hell if you did not have it. It really made the difference between life and death. It was like a testimony of your faith to the regime and your obedience to the Ba'ath. If you were a male and they caught you anywhere, say at college, in the supermarket, at your friend's home or even in your own home you had better show your military ID stating your clearance with the military and indicating that you had either signed up or that you were on active duty in the army. And God help you if you lost that document. You would then have to go to the issuing office and they would have you checked out thoroughly: your background, your religious affiliations, your membership in the Ba'ath and so on.

Amer was able to get an exit visa just for a few days. It allowed him to go only to Jordan. He convinced the clerk who issued these permits that he was going to get some spare parts for his car. It was total luck. He got the permit and left for a few days and did not come back. He left via road, not the airport, as my father advised him to do. That meant that he had less chance of being caught; the borders were not monitored as strictly as the airport, mainly because not many people traveled via road. Mom and Dad took Amer to the bus station. They told him that when he made it out of Iraq, God willing, not to call home at all. They thought that the telephone at home was most likely being bugged. They said that when he was safe and sound, to call his brothers who were in Europe at that time and tell them that he was safe, but never to call home. We agreed on a coded message that he would give my other brother, then my other brother would call us and relay that message without saying his name. Coded messages were the norm for Iraqis speaking to anyone outside the country.

Then, Amer went to buy his bus ticket. Mom and Dad watched him as he got on the bus. They could not say good-bye in any emotional overt way. They all had to keep a low profile so as not to bring the plan undone. Mom was reciting prayers for him all the way. They were anxious and had a broken heart as they sent their son off to an unknown fate. They had to, it was the only way to get him out and to avoid having him arrested again by the secret police. It was a necessary risk. They had to try anything and everything. It was hard for my parents that day. When they got home, they were quiet for most of the day. They were concerned and worried. They were counting the hours to when he was expected to reach the border. Mom was praying incessantly and anticipating that he would arrive in the evening of that day. We were all afraid that Amer may be caught or his plan fail. And none of us could talk about this matter in the house because we expected the house was still being bugged even though Jasmine had long left us.

For Amer, it was a long harsh trip, some 1000 kilometers (620 miles) across the desert. He arrived at the border checkpoint, another hurdle one must pass through before one could get out of Iraq. It was a critical moment in Amer's life; he had to pass that border checkpoint. Amer prayed silently—he placed all his trust in the will of God, took a deep breath and walked to the window where the border-control officer was sitting in his booth. Amer told the officer that he was going away for a few days to Jordan and that he was already signed up for his army service which would begin the following month. His military ID was indeed current and he presented it to the officer. He was safe.

Although he was able to leave Iraq, we at home did not know it because my parents had told him not to call the house, because the line was most likely bugged. We spent the following days in agony: we did not know whether he had made it or not. It was a miracle, Amer later told us, an oversight by the attending officer that enabled him to leave. If the guard had taken any small investigative step, he could have held Amer up. But Amer made it safely out to Jordan. Back at home, however, terror from the secret police was coming our way again.

* * *

We had a couple of anxious days since there was no way to know whether Amer had made it or not. We just waited. One evening we were sitting and talking to Aunt Mona and my cousin Sara, her daughter, who were both visiting us. All of a sudden, there was a violent knock at the door. Sara opened it. About thirty or so armed men from the secret police, Alamin, pushed her aside and stormed in. They were all over the house in seconds, immediately spreading into all the rooms. They were looking for Amer. They were shouting: "Where is Amer? Come out now, Amer … or you will be shot once we see you."

Mom thought that they had caught him, because she had not heard from him then.

She said, "Oh, my God. Where is he? Do you have him? Where is my son?"

The lead officer, Zuhair, told my Mom, "Look, lady, if he walks in here I would shoot him here in front of your eyes."

"Oh, God forbid, God forbid," Mom exclaimed.

We had to quickly gather in front of them; anyone who was not would be shot.

I was shaking with fear. I was terrorized. They not only searched for Amer, they were searching for books and leaflets, and even a magazine or a picture would have incriminated us at that time. They went into each and every room. They opened the closets. They threw our clothes on the floor. They went into the carport. They went all over the gardens and behind the big trees. They went onto the last floor of the house, the roof. There were a couple of storage rooms there. They even searched the water tanks which also were on the roof level of the house.

Homes in Iraq typically had "water reserve tanks" located on the roof. The tanks constantly drew water from the city supplies. I do not know why the water system was designed as such. Anyway, our house, like all other homes, had these tanks which were located on a high bench on the roof. The secret police officers even looked inside them. They opened the tanks and shone their flashlights inside. They stuck a big wooden rod into the water tank to be sure no one was hiding there. The only thing they found was water. They could not find Amer.

Back inside, they recorded everyone's name and address and occupation. And then they asked each of us what our political affiliation was. It was such a stupid question. Dad told them we did not belong to any political organization; we were just ordinary citizens. We had to answer all their questions such as, What books do you read? Who are your friends?

Then came more trauma. They wanted to take my father with them for further questioning about Amer. Mom pleaded with them not to take him, she said that he was ill. They insisted that they would take him. We were in a panic. This looked like they were going to take Dad and arrest him and that he would never come back. We were crying and pleading with them to please leave Dad alone. It was humiliating and it was unfair. My father told us to be quiet and he went with them. He did not want any of us girls, and my cousin Sara too, and my Mom and aunt to be harmed. They said they would bring him back in an hour. We had to concede to their will. We had no choice.

Moreover, while a couple of them took my father and left, some of them stayed with us at home. We had to sit all in one room in front of them. We could not go anywhere. We had to ask them even to go to the rest room. When the phone rang, we could not even answer. They answered instead. It was a frightening experience. There were all these armed men in our living room and in the rest of the house, and with Dad gone with them it was just my mother, my aunt, our cousin and we girls. It was an awful hour and a half or so during which my Dad was gone: We were crying silently and praying and just wanted them to bring him back. We were so afraid that they would take him to prison like they did before. We had to remain calm and cooperate with them. Any commotion or scene would have brought retaliation and further harm to us.

Finally, Dad came back. He was fine and unharmed. We were happy that he was back, and most of the armed men then left us. But they said they were going to stay outside the house so that if Amer came they would get him right there. We thanked God that Dad was unharmed. That was a traumatizing experience unlike any. It was my first experience face to face with the thugs of the secret police, but it was not my last. We were all shaken that night. We were safe only by the grace of God. They could have easily shot or arrested some of us.

The secret police (Alamin) came thereafter many times. All of a sudden, in the middle of night there would be violent knocks on the door and the bell would ring a dozen times. We would run like mad people, get dressed, and jump downstairs. The Alamin were pretending to be searching for my brother Amer. They would storm in and scream, "Where is Amer? Okay, come out." They thought or they pretended to think that Amer was at home hiding somewhere. They said that once they caught him he would be executed.

On subsequent terrorizing visits they kept searching for Amer and now they were even asking about my brothers Haider and Samir. They would say, "Where is Haider? Where is Samir? Why are they out of the country? They should be here serving the party and the revolution." They said things like, "Well, two of your sons are away and the other is working against the government and they would be killed right here if we saw them." Mom and Dad would attempt to explain to them, gently saying, "Look, come on, our son has nothing against the government. You've got to be mistaken. Perhaps it is someone else you are looking for." Then the police would search the whole house at night. They were so crude. They made my Dad, an old man, walk all over the house with them, the roof, the garden, and the garages, in the middle of the night. They would go into every room. They would say, "Whose room is this? Who's that in the photos? Who is reading this or that book? Who bought this magazine? Is this your picture…," and so on. Some fifteen to twenty men would come and be all over the house.

They had no respect for privacy, intruding into people's homes at night. They were armed and we were very frightened of them. We avoided eye contact with them. But it was so hard to be calm and behave normally. At the slightest provocation, they could have taken any of us girls or even my parents and then we would have vanished too. My Dad would have given the world during those long moments just to protect us girls and to take us away from this terror. It was rather a common practice of the government to arrest or detain as hostages members of the family, even little kids, when they wanted to terrorize someone or when they could not find the one they were looking for. Now that my brother had been detained once, they were not going to leave him alone; they would be back. They could not hurt my brothers because they were away. But that was no relief because we girls were at their mercy. It was just a miracle of God that they did not hurt us.

This scenario of the terrorizing visits was repeated many times. We spent a few months under this type of terror. Each time they came, it was like living moments from hell itself. They would come, terrorize us and leave. Sometimes they would give us dirty looks and sometimes they would try to befriend us girls so we might tell them something that our parents were not saying. For example, they would ask a series of innocent questions such as: "Where is your room? Which one is your desk?" Then they would demand, "Where is Amer? When did you see him last?" They were looking for an inconsistency. During one of their latter visits of terror, they informed my Dad that the government has issued an execution order for Amer. And they would search for him incessantly. This also made our whole family suspects and placed us under their mercy. Dad tried hard to speak to them but they were so mean and threatening.

These were nerve-racking times for my parents. My Dad was worried every moment of those months because of these repeated visits. He was now mainly worried about us girls. He and my Mom would discuss that all the time outside in the garden. They could not talk about it in the house. Dad was agonized and afraid for our safety. He could not get one restful night of sleep. He shared those thoughts with my older sister Zeena. He told her that he was planning for us to leave. He told her not to tell anybody about the plans. He insisted that after we left, she must take the lead and look after us, my other sister and I, since we were much younger. He explained to Zeena that these thugs were very likely to come after us girls if we stayed. They could arrest us just to hurt the family more. It was only a matter of time.

By then, 1979 and 1980, the government was already arresting women and girls, raping them, harming them, and killing them. It was unusual in the mid or early seventies that they would do that to women or family members. But things had gotten worse over the years. Many women were detained and imprisoned and raped and dumped on the streets. In fact, my Dad knew of one such in a family who were our distant relatives. Their daughter was arrested because of her father's political ideas. She was imprisoned and tortured. Her father was outside of Iraq at that time. She was in Iraq then. She was detained and God knows what they did to her. She was released only because her father knew a foreign world leader who had some personal influence with Saddam Hussein. She was dumped at the doorstep of her house barely dressed.

My parents, however, did not involve us in these discussions. They were planning a way for us to leave but they did not discuss it in the house or with us so that we could not make a slip of tongue and tell anybody.

At that point the regime was also forcing girls to join various Ba'ath organizations to serve some function that the party needed. Every day they came up with a new scam to scare us with. This was at the peak of an era of enforcing socialism and fascism in Iraq. The government was recruiting all society to serve various Ba'ath party functions. One day we were at school as usual. All of a sudden they loaded us on buses. We had to go. We could not call our parents. In fact for such events, they never sought the consent of the parents, as they would normally, for example, when they took us on a field trip or on a day trip that was far away. They would normally list the names of who was going and which bus they were on and so on. That day, we did not know where we were going. They drove and drove. And all of a sudden we were at the main road which led to the airport. There were hundreds of students, teenagers from secondary school and high school. We and other girls from other schools had to stand there lining both sides of the road to greet President Saddam Hussein and President Fidel Castro, who was visiting Iraq then, as they were passing from the airport. We waited and waited in the sun and then we were told to sing and cheer as the motorcade passed by us for a second and went off. We only caught a glimpse of them.

Afterwards, no one came to collect us. There was chaos. Some of the girls got lucky and found places on the same buses that had delivered them. But some buses did not stay for the duration of the event. So there were not enough buses to take everyone back and some of us were left behind. The school officials did not bother to verify who got on the buses and who was missing. About fifty or so girls from our school were left on the freeway and it was starting to get late already. I was among those fifty who were left behind. We were scared. Some of our teachers drove by in their own cars—they also had to come to this event. They picked some of us up. But they could not pick up all fifty of us.

The group scattered and separated. I was left behind with four or five other girls. We had to walk back. Except we did not know the way back to school. We just walked along the main road leading away from the airport hoping that we would reach the city and get a taxi from there to the school. Actually at that time in the late seventies, the airport was on the outskirts of the city and was not in a normal residential area. The road leading to and from the airport was a long highway but there were no services of any kind along it. Not even a telephone. We did not know how to get home and we all lived in different parts of the city anyway. It was getting dark and we were lost. Finally a pickup truck stopped. The driver asked us if we wanted a ride. He picked us up, but it was not pleasant.

Normally in Iraq, girls did not ride in these types of cars. Indeed there were only grown men in the car, some factory workers who were coming home late. All six of us girls crammed into a seat that fit three. I sat on my friend's lap. We had to all fit in that one seat. Otherwise we would have had to sit on some guy's lap as the rest of the car was full and they barely freed that one seat for us. The men looked at us strangely, wondering what on earth we were doing at night on the main airport road. The driver dropped us near our school. We walked about one kilometer and got in the school.

There was chaos at the school. Many girls were waiting to go home on their normal school buses. But the bus drivers had left, and all the girls who normally relied on the school buses to take them home were left behind. And everyone was trying to call their parents. Some parents offered other girls rides when they picked up their daughters. Some girls were still missing. The school director was not there; she had gone home in her car. The only staff there were one of her assistants, a couple of teachers and the school guard. They were kind. They were trying to sort out who could go with whom. It was a mess. We found many parents enraged with the school because their daughters had not come home. It was nearly seven or eight in the evening. My sister had made it back with one of the teachers. My sister was crying about me. She thought I was lost or kidnapped. I collected my school bag and we went home. My aunt had come to pick us up.

My parents and many other parents were angry with the school about leaving their daughters alone like that, especially as we were all teenagers and there was no adult with us. I was thirteen then. It is extremely unacceptable in a conservative society like Baghdad's for girls to be roaming about in the outskirts of the city so far away from home and without the knowledge of their parents and with no adult around. We could go out and walk around in our neighborhoods where we knew the surroundings and the nearby families. But we never went far unless we had made prior arrangements with our parents. My parents and other parents came the next day and complained to the school. They were enraged. They met with the director and other school staff. Some parents were so mad. They were yelling at the director.

One parent was particularly mad at her. He said, "Are you crazy? How could you leave those girls by themselves?" Ms. Aneesa tried to speak but the man continued. "Don't you understand that when you take our girls out of the school, you must bring them back? You don't just leave teenage girls alone on the freeway...."

Mom said, "And you had the audacity to leave and go home while our daughters were walking on the freeway? You left and went home while this school was in chaos last night? Have you no shame?"

"We were doing a service to the party and the revolution," the director, Ms. Aneesa, responded. "We had to go. We are all servants of the party.... And it is nothing to give up your daughters for the sake of the revolution and the party...."

"Give up your children to the revolution if you want," Dad snapped back. "Do not give up our daughters."

The parents left. And we were now afraid of her retaliation.

With all these incidents, Dad was worried about us everyday. He would take us to school and bring us back; sometimes my aunt would bring us back home. They were afraid of all the awful things that were happening to girls whose families were in a situation like ours. After a few of the nights of terror and the airport incident my parents decided that we must leave right away, that harm to us was only a matter of time, was possibly even imminent. So they would have to find a way for us to leave Iraq. Perhaps it was to their decision and insight that my sisters and I owe our lives today. I think it was the most loving thing they did for us, in spite of how difficult it was to achieve and, later, to endure. It was quite a big accomplishment, getting us all abroad away from the Ba'ath. In spite of all the difficulties and restrictions, they strived so hard to make that happen. They worked hard each step as they steadily and silently arranged for each of us to leave Iraq peacefully. It was their mission to deliver us abroad safely and they knew that from there somehow we could manage. At least we would be away from the Ba'ath terror. But until we left, life was still getting worse.

By then, we were being directly terrorized and harassed even at school. My sister and I attended the prestigious Baghdad High School in Almanour district. This was a dream school for all girls. The school recruited top students (only girls) from all over Baghdad. Girls came to this school from far districts. The school required top performance to be admitted. Both my sister and I made it into this school. Many girls were from upper class families but also had to have excellent marks to get in; of course, some girls got in just because their families were among the Ba'ath leaders. I spent my junior high years there and was going into high school but never made it because that was the year that we left.

Even though my sister and I were excellent students and were liked by most of the teachers and students, the Ba'ath officials in the school, including the school director, constantly harassed us and called us names. The school director terrorized us during our final exams too. Her assistant came and interrupted us in the exam and said we had to go to her office. When I got there, I saw my sister was there before me and she was signing some documents. Then it was my turn.

"Yes, Ms. Aneesa," I said. "You asked for me to come here."

"Yes," she replied. "I want to discuss your political affiliations. What party are you a member of?"

"Pardon, Miss?" I stammered. "What do you mean?"

"What is your affiliation? Are you a member of the Communist party? The Ba'ath party? The Dawa party?"

"No, Miss. None.... I am not a member of any political party."

Then she continued and said that our family was against the government. She had a full "*Security Report*" on our family. She knew the details about Amer being arrested, Samir and Haider being out of the country, my Dad's ordeal. She insulted my brothers and said they were reactionaries and they did not serve the party and so on.

"Well, you must join the Union," she went on. (The Student Union was the Ba'ath party's organization for youth and teenagers.) "This is necessary to demonstrate your loyalty to the revolution.... Because you are suspicious people...."

After listening to all that she said, I was fired up. I must have gotten those fiery genes from my mother. So, I argued fervently with the school director and defended my family's name and my brothers. I spoke so innocently but with passion about a basic freedom that was unheard of in Iraq in those days.

"I do not want to join the party or the union. I am only fourteen years old. I do not have to do something that I do not want. Why are you forcing me? People should join the party when they want to, not by force."

Ms. Aneesa was angry with me. She said, "You cheeky kid. Shut up. I am telling you, you must join the party. And if you do not, then you must sign a statement explaining why not."

She made me sign the document, like she did my sister, saying that we did not want to join the party. We were kids of fourteen and fifteen years of age. We were upset because she insulted our family and our good name by calling us suspicious people like we were criminals, and she also disrupted our exams. We went home crying and shaken. My parents were so enraged at what she did. They tried to calm us down.

My mother held my sister and me and said, "Don't cry, darlings. That witch can go to hell. Just try to finish the one exam that you have remaining. Then we shall deal with her."

Dad told us that he and Mom were going to the school to have a talk with Ms. Aneesa. He also said that they would wait a couple of days until we finished our last exam.

They went to the school and directly confronted her. She did not know they were coming. She was surprised to see them because parents did not normally show up at school unless there was some event.

"You disrupted my daughters during their exams," Dad told her. "And you made them sign documents. How dare you make two under-age children sign documents? I want to see what you made these children sign. They are under eighteen. I am their father. I want to see those documents."

Ms. Aneesa immediately realized what the visit was about.

My mom told her, "Aneesa Janns [that was her full name] who are you to insult our family? Who the hell are you? And where did you pop up from?"

Mom reminded Ms. Aneesa of her family's past and how her brother had been sought by the government, the same Ba'ath government, when they first took power, because of his loyalty to Iran in the early 1970s, a time when the Ba'ath regime had a conflict with the shah of Iran.

By then the teachers and the administrative assistants in the office had all overheard this argument. It was quite a scene.

"You scared the girls during their exams," Dad said vehemently. "Have you lost your mind? Are you running a school? Are you an educator or just a party recruitment agent? What are you exactly?"

Ms. Aneesa tried to speak.

Mom was ahead of her and said, "This is not the first instance of your incompetence. You left my daughter at the airport and she had to walk half the way home. She had to ride with strangers to get to the school.

Ms. Aneesa was humiliated because all the teachers and her own assistants could overhear and see this argument. Many of the teachers knew my parents personally from college. They respected my Dad and loved him as he used to be their professor. Some of my teachers were his students. They were excited to see their professor after so many years. Some teachers came out to greet my parents and said that they were sorry to hear what had happened to us.

"Mr. Makki, what a pleasure, what a pleasure to see you," one of them told my Dad. "What's going on?"

Dad told the teacher briefly what had happened.

The teacher was sad over the way my sister and I had been treated. She said, "Oh, my God, Aneesa did that to them? She is cruel...."

Another teacher said, "Oh, my God.... Dalia and Marya, they are wonderful girls. What did she do to them?"

When Ms. Aneesa had harassed us, it was in private. It was in her office. Not many people had seen what had happened. But when my parents came over, it became a public matter. Ms. Aneesa was angry and we were so afraid of her retaliation against us. But we had just finished our exams and passed. That was the end of the school year.

*   *   *

The summer holiday followed all these fears and anxieties at school that we had just been through. But we were still afraid; we did not really go out that much. It was a sad time to be in Iraq. We kept hearing news about people being detained and executed. We were not happy. It was frightening every time the doorbell rang—we thought they were coming to arrest us and take us away. Mom and Dad told us at that time that they had made plans for us to leave Iraq in a couple of weeks. They ordered us to be quiet about it and not to tell anyone. They explained that if we stayed in Iraq, this harassment and terror was likely to continue and become worse. They insisted that not only could we not tell anybody about this but that we could not even give the impression that we were leaving for good. So we could only take with us a few things appropriate for a short trip. They further said that we must understand, and be grown up and learn to be independent.

I kept asking my Dad, "What about you? Will you be coming with us?"

He replied, "Darling, we will leave with you at first, but then your mother and I have to come back. After that, I will do my best to make sure that we can join you. But you must know that it is harder for me because I have to keep my job and I have to secure the house and so many other logistics. They will not let me go easily. First, you go and be safe and later your mother and I will come, God willing."

We started preparing for this trip in a quiet, subtle way. We were all so nervous, especially my parents because any mistake or any bad luck would ruin this delicate plan.

*   *   *

One day during the summer holiday, we were sitting peacefully at home. Mom, Dad, my sisters and I and my aunt Mona. We stayed home a lot. We did not do anything exciting and we were trying to keep a low profile and to avoid any confrontation with the authorities. So we were inside at home just talking and chatting. All of a sudden we heard a big bang sound right at our gate. Just like that: "Boooom!"

We ran to the door to see what had happened. The sound we heard was at our guest entrance. A big American-made car had smashed into the gate. The gate was damaged and slightly pulled off the wall on one side, and the lights on that side of the gate had broken and the glass shattered. The sign on the wall which carried my Dad's name had fallen off.

Typically, homes in Iraq carried a sign with the name of the father or husband in that house. Our house had an elegant golden sign, which stated that this was the residence of my father. It was common in Baghdad to have these signs at the gate. I think people used these signs because the address system in Baghdad was not precise. The signs were to ensure, more than anything perhaps, that visitors and others who had business at a home, would not miss it and have to ask around.

The accident was a mess. My Mom went quickly towards the car to see if anyone was hurt. A young man was in the driver's seat and he had a friend with him, another young man. They both looked like teenagers of sixteen or seventeen or so. Mom looked at them. They seemed unhurt. The front of their car was damaged as it had hit the gate and the wall. Mom and Aunt Mona asked the boys if they were all right and went to see if they were injured. The boys were fine. They were shaken a bit. We brought them some water and sat them to rest on the steps outside. They rested a bit and then wanted to leave.

"What happened?" Dad asked the driver. "How did you run into a big house?"

"Oh, I am sorry, I am sorry," one boy replied.

"Do you have a driver's license?" Dad asked.

"No," the boy answered.

"How old are you?" Dad demanded.

"I am 17, uhhhh … can I call my Dad? My Dad is [so and so], I am the son of [so and so]." He mentioned the name of some Ba'athist in the government.

"Where is your house? Where do you live?"

"My house is in Alkarada."

That neighborhood was actually far from our house.

"So you do not have a driver's license?" Dad continued. "And obviously you do not know how to drive. What are you doing here; this is very far from your home?"

"Well … I. I … I am learning to drive. Look, sir, my Dad will fix this damage. I am the son of [so and so]."

Mom was enraged by now and yelled at the kid, "I don't care whose son you are! I do not care who your mother is and who your father is. You are under age. [The driving age was eighteen in those days]. You do not have a license and of course you don't know how to drive. You could have killed someone at this doorstep."

The boy called his Dad from our house. His Dad later spoke to my Dad and said he would arrange for everything to be fixed.

"You know I will file a complaint," Dad threw back. "As you are aware, your son should not be driving, he has no license."

"I am so sorry," the man said, "but I will pay for everything. If you file a claim you will get the same money, except my son will never get a license. Please wait, I will fix it all."

The boy and his friend left after his Dad sent a car to pick them up. My parents and my aunt were so mad. Now we had to deal with the teenage sons of Ba'athists. They too were above the law. They roamed about the city chasing girls and just showing off their cars.

The next day a building crew indeed came and patched up the wall. They did not do a thorough job. They did not fix the gate or the lights. They were supposed to undo the damaged part of the wall and rebuild it properly. Instead, they just patched things up. So it left the wall looking inclined, and it looked weird. The material did not match the rest of the wall as the wall was decorated with some special rocks, and it looked half and half after they patched it up. Dad called the boy's father, Mr. Riadh, and asked him if they would fix everything properly and return it to the way it had been.

"I already sent a crew today," Mr. Riadh said. "You know, it's not such a big deal. I mean it only needed to be patched. It was not big damage."

"Look, Mr. Riadh," Dad replied. "You know that your son violated the law. I could file a complaint. But you said you were going to take care of it so I believed you. I want the whole thing fixed, otherwise I am filing a claim."

"Are you threatening me, Mr. Makki?"

"I am just reminding you of the fact that your son has no license; he could have killed someone at the door. Fix the damage and keep your word like a man."

Although ironic, it was indeed possible for my Dad to file a damage claim. I think such laws had existed in Iraq long since; perhaps the Ba'ath regime had modified them, but that is all. For most people, however, such disputes were resolved in person and they just agreed on some compensation. If cases were not resolved, they went to the claims department.

The gate and the wall were never fixed. We were all upset by this recklessness from these people. Mom kept pressing on my Dad to pursue the matter and to get this rotten kid punished. Dad had decided to give it up because he did not want a confrontation with the authorities. These were fragile times. Dad was working on getting our passports and exit visas done. It would be detrimental to say the least to our travel plans to have another confrontation with the Ba'ath. Dad told Mom to forget it and that he would hire a crew to fix the damaged wall and gate. But Mom would not give up. She made this a matter of principle. She got angry with Dad for leaving the matter, and she kept pressing him to file the claim and punish these people for their recklessness.

"Makki, why are you giving this up?" she demanded. "It is their damage and they have to pay for it. Look the law is on your side. Go and file it. Let this kid be punished."

"No, Lydia, I will not do that," Dad responded. "I do not want confrontations now with them. Not again."

"Please, you have to do it. I am so angry…. What do they think? They just do whatever they want…. Who do they think they are?"

"No, Lydia. Any confrontation now is bad for us. They will not give us and the girls exit visas. You know that I am working on these applications, we are nearly ready to leave, and we only have a few more days. If we have a conflict now, they could ruin our travel plans."

Mom would not back off. She said, "No, Makki. You have to do it.

Do it for me, even if you do not agree. What do they think? They just step all over people and get away with it?"

By now my father was really angry. It was one of the few times in my life that I had seen him so mad.

"No, no," he said. "The hell with the wall ... and the gate ... and whole house. Let it all burn in hell. I do not care. But I have three daughters. I want to get them out of this crazy country. Any confrontation now would not only mean the denial of their passport application, they would come after us again. I do not want these thugs near my daughters. Lydia, you must listen to me. You must listen. I don't care about anything now. I do not care about the house. I do not want to make a point with them now. I cannot fix everything in this country. God knows I tried to bring morals into this government and I sought justice for myself. I thought that the law would protect the truth and would protect me—not in this jungle, Lydia. I just want my three girls to be safe and out of here. If one of them is harmed, then I will have failed in my life. Then nothing I ever accomplished in my life matters. I will never forgive myself and neither will you."

There was silence. Mom did not say anything. We heard and saw this big argument between my parents, the like of which we had never seen before. Mom conceded to Dad. She realized that he was right. She was being idealistic and trying to prove a principle. We had a few tense days after that argument.

Dad's concern about the travel arrangements was valid. In Iraq, throughout the seventies and eighties you could not just hop on an airplane and travel for personal reasons such as a vacation. You needed to get an "exit visa" which was permission from the government for you to leave. Such permission was usually given for a vacation, medical reasons, or business reasons during a period when travel was not banned. Usually getting this exit visa required lots of effort and connections. Because our family had had various ordeals with the government, it was more difficult for us to obtain such permits. In general however, if you were young, under eighteen, it was not a big deal to get a vacation exit visa. But for adults, who were employed by the government or were business people who wanted to leave for work related purposes, it was rather complicated. You had to go through a long ordeal. First you must have a "security clearance" which was testimony from the intelligence office that they had checked you out and it was permissible for you to apply for an exit visa. Then, you must show all kinds of evidence that you were coming back. In fact it reached the point that you had to do bizarre things to demonstrate that. For example, you had to pay a big sum of money as a bond until you came back. Or another member of your family had to sign a "promise" that if you did not come back, he or she would be liable and responsible. That person would have to pay a big sum of money, or indeed that person might be imprisoned until you came back. Also, in some cases, you had to sign your property over to the government and release them from any future demand that you may have on the property. Dad worked diligently on our applications and passports for days and weeks and his efforts paid off. We got our exit visas.

* * *

We left Iraq in the summer of 1979. We left in haste. We could not say to anyone that we were leaving for good. We could not say good-bye to our friends or our teachers. It was a sad departure. We pretended that we were going abroad on vacation as we normally did most summers when travel abroad was allowed. Because we were teenagers, it was not really a big deal and we did not raise many suspicions.

I must say that throughout my travel during those years to and from Iraq, we, like all Iraqi citizens, were treated like criminals at Baghdad airport. In all the countries that I visited later in my life, such as many European countries and North America, homecoming citizens were respected and treated well. In Iraq it was just the opposite. Foreign nationals were allowed in through one easy step and were treated with respect. But as an Iraqi citizen passing through Iraqi immigration, you were interrogated like a criminal by the special secret police, Alamin.

They had a ton of information about each person. (Alamin had a desk at the airport which you went through both on your way in and out.) They would flip back and forth in many files and lists to look you up. They would ask you many questions as you were leaving Iraq and also as you were coming back, questions like: Where were you going and why? Where did you just come from? And whom did you see? And how are they related to you, what are their names? What are their political ideas? What books do you read? Are you a member of the Ba'ath party? Why not...? and so on. And God help you should you be put aside for further questioning.

In fact, passing through Iraqi immigration as an Iraq citizen was a terror ordeal of its own. These are the longest moments of your life. This experience typically ruins all your happy memories from your trip. Or it makes your anticipated trip so worrisome and full of stress. Sometimes we were lucky and were greeted by Uncle Sadi who would let us through via his connections and contacts and all the people he knew at the airport because of his high-ranking position. So when we left Iraq that last time,

just the ordeal of passing through the Iraqi immigration during our departure was quite frightening. We were afraid that they would stop us and
harass us. But we made it through.

Having left home in haste and under such abnormal circumstances,
I left many dear things in my room. One thing that I especially miss is
my autograph book, which was signed by my teachers since primary
school. This was a common thing that girls did in those days. We would
have our teachers and elders such as relatives and aunts sign this book
and we would keep it forever. We cherished these words of love and wisdom from our teachers and elders and we would read this book over and
over. Teachers and elders would write sweet things to you and give you
many good wishes. Over the years we would go back and read what was
in it. It was like a book of compliments from your favorite people and
teachers. I have not seen anything like it here in the States. Perhaps the
yearbook in schools is the closest thing to it. But really the autograph book
is much more special and more personal. It is handwritten and the only
copy that exists is the one that you have. Mine was very special to me.

I also left my collection of stamps, which I was proud of and which
I had organized in a meticulous fashion in various stamp books, and so
many books and things from childhood. I did not have that many things
really. But I do miss these few precious memoirs. I can only imagine how
my mother missed her things of a lifetime: albums, memoirs from our
childhood and of her own family, family pictures, her gifts for us ... and
so on.

So, that's how we got to Europe.

*   *   *

Having delivered all of us abroad, my parents had to go back to Iraq
because they had signed all kinds of statements that they were only going
for a vacation, and because they would be held legally responsible and be
in more trouble if they violated those agreements. They left my sisters
and me with my brother, who was living in Europe at that time. They
were happy that they could deliver us safely to my brothers. When they
were leaving, it was tough to say good-bye to them. We cried and we had
an aching heart. Although we all knew in advance that they were going
to leave and go back, we sort of pretended that this day would never come
or that it was so far away. But that was wishful thinking. That day came
and went so quickly. That was the day that my parents and I were separated. I really did not think about it so much then. I thought that I was
tough and that I could endure this cruel separation. And perhaps I did
on the outside. But today some twenty or so years later, I think that it

was very hard to say the least. From that day my sister and I had to get used to living without our parents. We had to rely on ourselves a lot. It was a harsh jump to being grown up and independent for me. Just like that, so quickly.

My parents went back and they spent a few years alone in Iraq while all of us, their children, were abroad. My mother told me later that these were very hard times for her and Dad. She and my father too felt alone after having had the house full of their six children for many years. All of a sudden, it was empty. And to make it worse, they could not really discuss our departure with anyone; they had to keep a low profile about it.

It was a painful emotional ordeal for my parents too. On the one hand they were relieved that we had left Iraq and were safe. But it was hard for them emotionally. Mom told me later when I saw her that it was a cruel decision for her, sending us away. While she had gotten a bit used to my brothers being gone long before us, it was our absence that made life so lonely for her. She worried about all of us girls very much.

My older sister Zeena had just had her first baby. And my mother worried about her daughter being a new Mom and the baby and that she could not be there for them. She kept worrying more especially about my sister Dalia and me because we were so young. We were still growing up; we were only fourteen and fifteen. We still had a long way to go. She wanted to be there for us like any Mom would. But she and we were denied that chance. It was very hard for her to deal with our absence. She kept longing for us. She wept and cried over this abrupt departure. Such a short time to be there with us as a mother and to look after us. She told me that she used to walk into our rooms and kiss the beds and the walls and imagine that we were still there. I had always known my mother to be emotional but I really thought that she could manage this departure. She said it was the hardest thing for her to leave us when we were so young and innocent and inexperienced. It was a cruel separation.

It was very hard for my sister and me too. It was a scary prospect to be living away from my mother and father. It certainly was a tough jump into the adult world. Even though my sister and I stayed with my brother and were safe and sound, we had to learn many new things and be independent and be responsible. For me, I had to think about then major decisions such as which school to attend, how to manage money, how to do laundry, and how to manage without having my parents around. But I think we adapted well. I think we looked forward to our new life and what it might be holding for us.

Living abroad was not free of difficulties, but as long as it was not

Ba'ath terror, it was okay to deal with. But the Ba'ath menace haunted people even when they left Iraq. Now, we had to deal with things like having to renew our passports. And of course if you were not a sincere Ba'athist, even that simple procedure was used against you as a weapon. Because if you did not have a valid passport, you could not stay in any country that you may be in. Also, it was then forbidden for Iraqis to transfer money to anyone abroad. So now, my parents had to deal with how they were going to support all of us abroad when there was no legal means for them to send money for us. For that, they relied on some friends who transferred money via their travels and money which they had abroad. But this was not a reliable method and its availability was variable.

*   *   *

Those years were not free of terror and harassment for my parents. It was now during the Iran-Iraq war and everyone had to send their children to the war. For my parents, none of their children were in Iraq, so they were penalized and persecuted for that. Literally, recruitment officers would knock on the doors to recruit people to the war. They would ask my parents how many people in their house were in the army. And my parents would say none. And they would make them pay money as a donation instead. Moreover, the secret police never stopped harassing my parents. A member watched our house all the time to check who came and went. Many people abandoned my parents. Even our relatives and friends did. People were afraid to come and associate themselves with Mom and Dad because of the accusations against my parents. People were afraid that they would be penalized for these visits. When my aunt Kamila came over with her son one day to visit Mom, the secret police stopped her and asked who she was and why she was visiting this household. My aunt Kamila told him: "I am coming to visit my cousin; is that illegal too?" The guard let her in after more questioning.

My parents were accused of being disloyal to the Ba'ath party because they had arranged for all their children to leave Iraq. They did not give any of their children to the war and to the party and so on. Both my parents were old by that time. The regime had no respect for anyone: an older man or older woman, the innocent. They harassed my mother at her job and ultimately removed her from it; their official reason was that she promoted dissent in her classrooms and had not given any of her children to serve the Ba'ath party and the war.

Mom was home one day and the security men came over and took her with them. She was afraid. They did not let her call Dad or anyone. They told her she would come back home soon.

"Where are we going?" she demanded.

"To headquarters," an agent told her. "We need to ask you some questions."

"Why can't you ask me your questions here?"

Mom was afraid. She wanted to call Dad or one of her sisters. But they would not let her. They told her it would not take a long time.

They asked her the same questions that they normally asked when they came over to the house, such as, Where are your children? How many of your children died in the war? He began insulting her and my father and would not stop. Mom, being her feisty and fiery self, could not keep quiet and that was a big mistake this time. She kept talking back to the men who were interrogating her, especially when they insulted my Dad and our family. She told the men: "Who are you? Are any of you even worthy of saying my husband's name? All of you were poor and helpless with no hopes and no education and the Ba'ath gave you money and guns and now all of a sudden you are somebody and you know how to say a word? Who are you?"

Then all of a sudden Mom was hit on her face so hard that she fell down and fainted. When she woke up, she found herself on the outer steps of the building. She did not know what had happened. She could barely walk and she could not speak well. She felt her face was heavy and dull and swollen. She got into a taxi and went home. She had been gone for three or four hours in total. She was afraid when she remembered what had happened to her. When Dad came home, she told him about her trip to Alamin headquarters. Dad was shocked. "What?" he gasped. "They came here and took you? You should have called me. Oh, my God! Are you okay?"

"They would not let me," Mom responded. "I tried to call you or Najia or Weda."

She continued and told Dad what she remembered of the ordeal. She said she was not feeling well and went to sleep.

Dad was worried and frustrated that he could not protect my mother from these savage people. That they came home and took her, was a vile move. The government had become vicious and more aggressive than before. But this was the first time they had taken Mom. They had come after him a few times. But by now he knew how to appease them and stay calm. But Mom had probably gotten wordy with them and answered them back. So they had slapped her many times and hit her. Dad was concerned because Mom told him she was sick. He waited for her to wake up to see how she was. He called my aunts and told them to come. Aunt Najia came over to see what had happened to Mom. Mom was asleep.

Mom got up a few hours later. It was already the evening by then. She could not talk well. She felt her face was solid like a rock. She was off-balance. She went to see Dad. He screamed: "Lydia? What happened to your face? Say something. Speak."

Mom was awake and conscious and said a few words but her speech was not normal. Dad went to our neighbor, Dr. Anwar, who was a doctor and asked him to come look at Mom. Dr. Anwar came over; he was very concerned about her. He examined her and then told Dad that Mom had a lesion in the facial nerve.

He asked Mom and Dad what had happened. "What happened? Please tell me. An accident?"

Dad told the doctor about the episode with the Alamin. Mom was able to say some sentences but they did not sound normal. So she wrote down for the doctor that all she remembered was being hit severely on her face and head and passing out after that.

Dr. Anwar was so mad at what they had done to Mom. He said: "Oh, God, those criminals. Madam Lydia, you cannot argue with these people. Look how they hurt you. They could have killed you and it means nothing to them. They are savages … animals. They have no mercy … no respect for anyone. Look, please stay home and do not go anywhere. You are lucky; this is not permanent damage. This will heal in time. But come tomorrow to my clinic. I shall send you to have physical therapy and massage. It may take a few weeks to heal."

*　*　*

A few weeks went by. My mother recovered slowly from the incident. She had to continue her treatment. Life had become different and very hard. It was a struggle to just keep the wrath of the government off their backs. One day, my mother was at home and there was a knock at the door. A young man stood there, in his late teens perhaps. My Mom did not recognize him immediately though he looked familiar. He was dressed up in a military fatigue suit. His uniform indicated that he was a member of the *popular army*; this was a special Ba'ath militia of youth from poverty stricken families. Mom kept looking at the boy's face trying to remember where she had seen him. In a rough crude tone he said: "Where is Makki, is he home?"

My Mom was shocked at this rude behavior. This kid did not even greet her, did not introduce himself, and on top of that referred to my Dad by his first name. It was extremely uncommon in Iraq to refer to people older than you by their first names without saying Mr. or Uncle or Mrs. It was considered rude and indicated disrespect. Even if someone were a stranger in the street, you must say Mr. or Uncle. So it was very crude of this kid to be asking about my Dad by his first name.

"Pardon?" Mom exclaimed. "Who are you? What's your name?"

"Oh, I am Hassan, Obaid's son. The gardener's son. I am now the personal escort of Master Taha Yasine."

Hassan was referring to the deputy prime minister, Taha Yasine, a senior government official.

Mom immediately remembered him then. He had grown so quickly. He sometimes used to accompany his Dad to our house. Mr. Obaid had taken care of all those trees and flowers that we had in the garden. He worked for many hours and we saw him every week. My parents were always kind to him and his son. But my Mom was enraged by this kid's crude tone and style now.

"Shame!" she told him. "Is this what you have learned from your training? To be crude and to insult your elders, not to mention this household which looked after you and your father so many years. And you don't even know how to say Mr. or Uncle.... Get out of here. Get out."

Hassan was so ashamed he started crying and left. He could not even say a word. Mom was enraged at what had become of society. Even the youth had become corrupt. They had lost their manners and principles. Our gardener, Mr. Obaid, was a poor man. He lived on the outskirts of the city. His children did not have schooling and formal education. He used to bring his son, Hassan, with him sometimes. My Mom would always serve them some lunch and drinks. During the Eid, the religious holidays, my parents always sent money and gifts to Mr. Obaid's family even though we had never seen them and we did not know them. We only saw this one son. During that incident when he came to ask about my Dad, he was just in his mid teens but had already been recruited by the Ba'ath militia. They had taught him to be crude and disrespectful of society and its norms and principles. These kids roamed about the city to collect donations for the war or performed various other tasks as instructed by the regime. There were so many youth like that. Even girls were recruited into such organizations. Poor or lower class youth, given weapons, trained how to use them, trained to abuse and terrorize people, trained to disrespect all familial and social and religious symbols of authority—it was appalling. It was appalling to see those kids in uniform and with guns, able to terrorize entire families and neighborhoods.

CHAPTER 6

A Letter of Love

My parents left for England about 1985. It was so great that they were allowed to leave. They had a "medical reason" to leave and they were granted a "medical exit visa." My father had made arrangements to see his doctor in London, whom he knew from before. The doctor had to send a letter of appointment to my father to come to see him. So, Dad was granted a medical exit visa and my mother was able to join him on that visa as an assistant companion who would help my Dad in his travels.

It was relief, the government giving you permission to leave the country. It was as if they granted you a favor by allowing you to leave. My parents were able to leave Iraq only with the little money that travelers were allowed to carry. This was another way that the government restricted you and made sure you could not go very far for too long. They limited the amount of money you could take with you to a minimum that could not sustain you beyond a few weeks. If you exceeded that you risked being arrested and executed for money smuggling. The Ba'ath regime thought of everything. They thought that if you did not have money, you were bound to come back.

Having gotten their exit visa, my parents had to leave in such a way as to give the impression that they were coming back. Otherwise they would have never been able to leave. Because of that, they had to leave the house as it was. They had to leave everything that they loved and cherished so much, the photos, the art, the books, the world collection of art and objects, and the gifts which Mom had prepared for us for our weddings and our future children when they were born. Mom was so sentimental. She had gathered things and gifts and dresses and exquisite things for each of us, her children, for our weddings, for our future homes, for our future children. In fact, she had a whole section in her room where she stored all these little treasures from all over the world: dresses from Japan, fabrics from India, baby clothes from England, and so on. I remember looking at those things with her a few times. She would show me some beautiful item and say, 'This is for your wedding, I got it from Japan," and "This is for your first child," and so on. She had the same things for my sisters and my brothers. But when she and Dad left, she had to leave behind these things and pretend that she was coming back. It was sad for her. She kept saying, "I want to give all of you these gifts for your weddings; I collected them over the years. It was my joy to prepare these collections for each of you to surprise you with them later. I wish you will get them somehow; I do not want them to go in vain," and so on. It was a shame to lose all those sentimental things and it must have been hard for Mom to let go of all that. But the threat to them was so real and so close that all these things did not matter. Being sentimental in Iraq was now a luxury one could not afford.

I think it is hard for older people to immigrate to another country. Even in the case of my parents who had traveled extensively abroad, and specifically my father who had lived abroad for many years, it was still hard to adapt. Although my parents were grateful to be out of Iraq and away from the terror of the Ba'ath regime, it was difficult for them to adjust to their new life. I think this is because older people yearn a lot for their memories and homes and friends and neighbors and they feel that they are being uprooted. They were indeed like a big tree, which had lost its roots. I think that my parents had such feelings and sentiments. I sense such sentiments from the older immigrant people I have met over the years.

In contrast, for younger people and children, it is usually much easier to adapt to the immigrant life. This is because young people get busy right away with their education and fitting their goals into this new life. And most people who immigrate when they are young find a new life in their new homeland. Young people finish their education, get married, have children and form new roots. They thrive on these new challenges; typically this pressure drives them to excel and to be happy.

I think that, in their heart, my parents thought they were going back to Iraq fairly soon; or, at least, that was their wishful thinking. They were in a dilemma. On the one hand they missed their home and their friends and their own families. But on the other hand they wanted to see us and to be with us and they were relieved that all the family was finally abroad. I think that they probably thought that they would stay a few months and somehow things would change and they would go back and all of us would too. This was a fantasy. They stayed in England and never went back.

Perhaps this was because all of us insisted that they stay and not go back, but maybe it was providential intervention that kept them in Europe. God knows what else they might have endured had they gone back. They would have suffered even more. Especially because now all of their children were abroad, and none of us had participated in the Gulf War (the first Gulf War, the Iran-Iraq War, 1980–1988) then. This by itself was a sign that the family was not loyal to the party and the revolution.

Mom told me later when I saw her that during the time of the war you showed your "loyalty" to the Ba'ath regime by how many of your children had died in combat. Saddam Hussein used to visit families whose sons had died in the Gulf War. Mom saw such visits carried live on television sometimes. Saddam Hussein would be with his guards and entourage and they would visit a home suddenly. He would ask them how many other children they had. They would present him their other son or daughter and chant: "We shall all die for you master"; "Our children shall die for you master." These people would then be promoted or given cash or a car or something as a gift instead of their lost child! No normal person would say such a thing in their right mind. But, the social norms in Iraq had been altered dramatically because of Ba'ath policies.

Moreover, if people did not have children or if all their children had died in the war, they still were not off the hook. They had to volunteer money and material support to the war. Women had to give up their golden jewelry as a symbol to sustain the war. The authorities would come to the schools and offices to collect the jewelry. It was so bizarre to see all these women taking off their wedding rings and their other jewelry and donating it, by force, to the war. Young girls were recruited, not for combat but to various other war-related activities. It was a bizarre era of nationalist frenzy, as if people were hypnotized to obey the government and just accept that two or three or all of their children should die for the sake of this war, which was meaningless to most people. I know people had no choice but to obey. The whole of Iraq turned into a machine of human onslaught. If your children did not die in Almukhabarat, then they had to die in the war. From 1979 until the mid eighties so many young men and women were detained, tortured and killed because of their lack of loyalty to the Ba'ath. And many others died in the war. Thousands of young people perished this way.

During the (Iran-Iraq) war, all college-aged men were forced into recruitment and even men of younger age. Literally, teenage boys were pulled from their high schools and forced to join reserve units of the army. My cousin was recruited like that; he was in high school and it was recruitment by force. People did all kinds of desperate acts just to avoid going to the war. In fact, a man we knew who was about thirty years old then was also recruited, even though he was older than most. He was so desperate not to go to the war. He injured himself in the arm, to disable himself, so that he would get a medical exemption from joining the army. It was awful. It was crazy but people did that to avoid being recruited. Young men also purposely failed in high school so that they would be held back a year and would not have to join the army. If someone did not join, he and his family would be punished. If someone joined and then deserted, his family would be punished. If he were caught later he would be executed in a public arena. The family would have to denounce and disown their son for deserting. Otherwise they themselves would be punished—publicly humiliated or, as in many instances, executed. Such things were even carried on television sometimes. Fathers and mothers had to denounce their children, women had to denounce their husbands. It was so cruel. Sometimes they would even force the family members to participate in or witness the public execution. In some instances, the executed body would lie out in the square as a symbol until it rotted. The family was not allowed to prepare it for burial. I did not think the world had known such cruelty and brutality before the Ba'ath employed it. It was a mockery of people's lives. A whole generation of young men and women were wasted in the prime of their youth through no fault of their own. Because of these widespread deaths, nearly all the women in Iraq were dressed in black as a sign of mourning. (It is traditional in Iraq and throughout the Middle East for women to wear black clothes when someone in their family has died. Donning black continues for about one year, then they go back to their normal clothes.) This black dress phenomenon became a disturbing issue in society, as nearly every family had suffered a loss. So the government banned people from wearing black to mourn the death of their men. And as if that were not enough, later people were not allowed to hold a funeral gathering to mourn the dead. This was a painful and a shameful era in the history of Iraq, with such a lack of basic rights and such a mockery of people's pain. A famous Iraqi singer from the 1980s depicts this pain in a song, which goes something like this: A guest is coming over, And we are celebrating, But don't go into that forbidden road, And don't cry aloud Because the sound of mourning is forbidden.

* * *

While my parents were in England, we endured yet another painful ordeal; however, it was the last. My father had a major stroke. He was hospitalized and was unable to walk or speak initially. But after intensive physical therapy for many weeks he was able to walk with the assistance of a cane, but his normal stamina never returned. This was the main reason that my parents did not go back: they would not be able to manage on their own in Iraq with Dad being in that condition.

In fact in Iraq in those days there were so many young men maimed from the war, the hospital wards were full of the disabled and wounded; if Dad had been there, no one would have given him any therapy or attention. The typical Ba'ath argument would have been: How many of your children died in the war? What did you give for the war? And you are an old man, you cannot serve us in the war, and so on. They would never have appreciated his years and decades of service to his country, his wealth of knowledge and the hundreds of young people whom he taught and inspired. They would never have shown any respect for his old age and his illness. So my parents stayed in England for a while and my father had good medical care there.

My Mom and Dad spent the few remaining years of their lives in Europe struggling with their ailing health, achingly wishing to go back to Iraq and heartbroken at the deteriorating circumstances in the country. It was hard for them as older people to relocate abroad. Also, my father's condition required attending and nursing and he made some progress initially. But then he had one or two other strokes months later. He regressed and his condition became worse.

Since the onset of this illness and disability, my mother looked after him day by day. Mom had always looked after Dad well and surrounded him with love and devotion. She enjoyed the good times with him before and she stood by him during bad times and of course during his detention ordeal and the difficult times that followed. All the events they endured in Iraq brought them even closer. Mom had always been his loyal friend and ally. But her best had yet to come.

During his illness, she looked after him like no one had seen before. Mom looked after Dad with all her energy and existence and even beyond her capacity. I witnessed that as I was with them when his first stroke took place. I witnessed both her devotion to him as well as her own emotional crumbling because of what had happened to him. Although she was in tremendous pain and sorrow over what had happened to my father and she was afraid for his life and his well being, she did not show any of her fears to him and she demonstrated incredible resilience and stamina. That was the very extraordinary character of my mother. In spite of the defeat and sadness she felt at seeing my father in that condition, she kept on going. It was like the traumatic events had ignited all her power and energy.

She would get up every morning and go to the hospital and fully take care of my father as if she were his nurse or his doctor. She would keep him company, cheer him up and tell him about who of the relatives and the family had called and asked about him. At that time we were all living in different places, but I was there with them visiting. She cooked some of his favorite foods and brought them to him. She kept him company and talked to him all day long. She was pumping life into him. She wanted to stay with him at the hospital. But the hospital did not allow such overnight stays so she had to leave at the end of the day. Over the weeks, she was there with him all the time and prayed while he had all kinds of scans and tests done. She did not want him to suffer in any way or possibly be ignored by the hospital staff. Also, I think that he felt more secure with her being around. My mother devoted all her existence to making my father feel better.

The response of my mother to this trauma was unusual. On the one hand, she was emotional and sad over what had happened to my father and what had become of them and their lives. That sadness, however, was transformed into unbelievable resilience and strength, which was manifested in her keeping an upbeat spirit, in looking after my father, and in bringing happiness to him and to us whenever we saw her. Although she herself was hurting, she delivered to those around her love and brilliant inspiration. I think that it was a combination of her strong faith in God and her own love for and dedication to my father that made her behave that way.

It was such a phenomenal devotion. Day and night she looked after him. She even surprised and amazed the nurses and the doctors who were attending to him at the hospital. The hospital administration gave her an award for dedication of a family member looking after a patient. At the hospital, we had many visitors because many of my father's relatives were also in Europe; they came to visit him when they heard what had happened. One of my father's cousins, who was also an older man, saw how my mother was devoted to my father and how each time he came to visit, she was there helping Dad one way or another or just sitting with him and keeping him company. The man, Mr. Hadi, was so touched and inspired by how devoted my mother was to Dad. Mr. Hadi, who was quite an outspoken man with a unique charisma, praised my mother and paid her beautiful compliments to honor her sincere devotion. He even kissed her hands. He said I have to kiss the hands of this devoted lady who served Makki and who stood by him in bad times. Then he turned to my Dad and said: "You are such a lucky man to have Lydia who loves you so much." Both Mom and Dad were laughing. They enjoyed this compliment from him and had tears of love and happiness in their eyes.

My mother indeed gave all of herself and her energy and indeed her life to my father. Those days of her life were a testimony to persistence and perseverance and she delivered her best. It was unbelievable dedication. I had never seen such energy and resilience before and I did not know that there could be so much devotion shown by one spouse for another. It was a beautiful example of true love and sincerity between a couple who were so madly in love.

I think that it is easy to love your spouse in good times but the real test of love comes in difficult times. How much would you endure with your lover or with your spouse? and when do you give up and abandon him or her? I think that true love will endure difficulties. Superficial relationships, however, will soon collapse at times of crisis. No one can understand those sentiments unless they have loved someone with all their soul and all their being. Those days taught me a new meaning of love, a truer meaning of love. Those last few years that Mom looked after Dad made me understand for the first time the meaning of the term *soul mates*: that they are inseparable, and that when one is hurting, the other cannot possibly be happy because each is part of a whole.

While I was there with my parents during these events, I saw that my mother was working very hard to look after my father. So I tried my best to help her and to ease some of the responsibility for her. She adamantly refused my help in this regard. Sometimes, I forced her to stay home and rest one or two days, and I told her that I would go and do whatever was needed to look after Dad. She could not do it. She would be thinking about him and calling at the hospital all day. I used to tell her, Come on, go out by yourself to have some tea, or go shopping or just stay home and rest. But it was futile. She would refuse; she would come to the hospital and say that she could not enjoy anything knowing that Dad was ill and that he was not with her. Her devotion was one of a kind. It was suicidal.

Although she delivered her best during those years, this final lengthy trauma was too much for her both emotionally and physically, and she herself became ill with various ailments and pains and from a heart torn with from pain and traumatic events. I think my mother dealt well with immediate crises and she had inspiring strength, but when the agony lasted too long, she tired and her body could not tolerate it anymore. I think this is true in general for all people, that we cannot tolerate traumatic events for too long. I think that strong people can handle crises well and they maintain their world intact and steadfast. Frail people collapse immediately and despair as soon as some crisis hits. I think that my Mom definitely was the strong type. However, the crisis lasted too long and eventually she began to wear down. And although I think my mother was so resilient and tenacious I think she also was impatient. It was painful for her to be enduring traumatic events for that long. When my Dad was hospitalized for many weeks, I stayed with Mom during this time and she collapsed emotionally. It was as if she were living the events of 1973 again. She was in grueling agony. She was crying and mourning. I tried my best to cheer her up and to enjoy some moments with her but it was hard.

Even though Mom was strong and resilient, Dad was indeed her fortress and her lifelong companion. I think she derived a lot of her power and resilience from being with him and from the love they had and the good times they enjoyed early on. I did not know then that love could be so powerful. Mom loved Dad not just as a husband and a man but she loved his soul. It was like their souls were attached even though they were two individuals. That's why they shared so many feelings and sentiments. They were not only husband and wife, but also best friends. They derived so much strength and happiness from each other.

Mom kept remembering the good days with him and how he had looked after her well and the lavish and glamorous life she had had with him. Mom was grateful to Dad for their entire journey together. She constantly praised and thanked him for the wonderful time they had had in their earlier years. She told me so many stories about their trips and their parties and all kinds of happiness she had had with him. It was as if he had already delivered his best to her and now it was her turn. It was like fulfilling an unstated promise. It was unbelievable and most admirable devotion between husband and wife.

Throughout those few years, they both ached to go back to Iraq. They missed their home and gardens, their friends, their relatives, their books and photographs. They were in sorrow over what was happening in Iraq, what it had turned into, the war, the destruction, the loss of many young lives in the war, even some people whom they knew, and the horrors they kept hearing about from friends and visitors. They were dismayed at how things were deteriorating in Iraq. Moreover, they were lonely and did not feel at home. It was a big transition for them: being ill, not working, and having lost their possessions and wealth. All of these things brought them feelings of disappointment and dismay. They had grown tired of these pains and ordeals. They just wanted to rest and to have peace of mind. I am sad to say that both my parents had a broken heart during those weeks and months because of the loneliness, the illness and the bad news from Iraq. There were only few people their age where they stayed. It was very hard for older people to leave home for good, especially the way Mom and Dad left, in haste, leaving behind friends and contacts of a lifetime and so many valuable things. And it was not possible to see a way back.

However, their best consolation was that they delivered all of us out of Iraq and it gave them peace of mind that we were away from the Ba'ath regime. It was what kept them alive. But, like all parents, they continued to worry and look to our needs. There were now new sets of challenges to deal with for all of us. Even though we were out of Iraq finally, we were all so far from each other. There were visa restrictions, we did not have valid passports, and so on. We could not see each other easily. In a way, we were all struggling to put a foot forward in our new environments. Although my brothers and sisters and I all adapted quickly to our new lives outside of Iraq, and indeed we were grateful that we were safe and sound, there were many challenges to be dealt with in our new lives; for example, living in a new environment and learning the ropes. It was not that easy and each of us had his or her own set of daily problems to deal with. But we all managed.

My parents also had some especially happy moments in the midst of all the new difficulties and the worry they endured: the births of their grandchildren. Their only joy now was to see us and their grandchildren. They were so happy to see all those new babies and it occupied their life a little. They liked being grandparents and this was their best consolation. They were happy that we were alive and safe compared to what would have happened to us had we stayed in Iraq. They were looking for our happiness and livelihood. They kept saying repeatedly that they accepted everything that they endured because it gave us children a chance at life, a new life away from the Ba'ath regime. That was a source of the utmost happiness for them.

* * *

In a chill November dawn, a police car from the hospital stopped at a small apartment in London. It was dropping my brother Haider home. He had been gone all night and into the early morning hours. He had just come from the hospital where my mother had passed away a couple of hours earlier.

He had gone with her when the ambulance picked her up, and he waited by the emergency room where she was being cared for. She had suffered a heart attack. Haider was sitting in the waiting room. He was praying and praying that she would be back. Now he remembers only that, praying and wishing that she would be back. There was silence, but many thoughts and sounds were pounding in his mind. During such moments one cannot feel anything. For him, many went by. But they seemed so long.

Suddenly the doctor walked out and came to tell him the bad news, that she was gone. Haider was in shock for several moments. He experienced immense sorrow. He could not move. He could not speak. He tried to get up. He felt that his body would not move, his legs would not support him. I think that we can all say that we have felt such feelings of sorrow, of denial, and of feeling incapacitated when we have lost someone whom we love and rely on. These feelings are awful and no one can tolerate them, especially when they hit the first time in your life—you probably were not even aware of such feelings and such weakness in your heart. I think no one is ready ever for such a moment. Although Haider is my older brother and he had endured all the former family events like all of us, I think he had those same fragile emotions that we all have in such events. He was in shock. He just sat in the same spot for a while until he could recover himself. He went in where my mother was lying. He prayed and recited Alfathia—a prayer recited by Muslims when someone dies—and other verses of the Holy Quran. He sat there for a while with anguish, and then he realized that the mission of telling the rest of us that Mom had passed away had fallen to him. He left the room and the hospital police gave him a ride home.

As the car drove along, Haider could not think, he could not talk. He felt like he was incapacitated, unable to speak, unable to move. He hoped the ride would last forever so that he would not have to face my sister Dalia and my Dad who were both home. When Haider arrived back at the apartment, it was like he was stepping into a fire; he did not know what to say to my sister or my Dad. He did not know how to break the news to the rest of us. He walked a few steps and he saw Dalia waiting outside by the door. She was waiting for him anxiously, praying that Mom would be alive, that Mom would be back with Haider, that the inevitable had not happened.

Dalia had spent a strange day with Mom. She said it was as if Mom had known that she was going to die. It was apparent in her looks, her glowing face, her gestures, and her few words. Now Dalia was feeling strange and very anxious. Haider arrived and she let him in. Mom was not with him however. He looked at her. He held her and looked at her face.

"Dalia, how are you?" he said.

"Tell me ... she is gone, isn't she?"

He handed her a small brown envelope. She held the envelope with shaking hands. She knew that it was bad news. The envelope contained

Mom's wedding band, her diamond ring, and a pair of earrings, which had all been removed from her body after she had passed. Haider and Dalia crumpled to the floor; they cried outside at the door, silently. It was painful to cry silently as normally one would want to grieve and weep, and it is so hard to maintain a grip on your emotions in such a case. They had to be quiet because Dad was inside and they did not know what to tell him. Dalia and her four-year-old son had been visiting my parents for a couple of weeks. Her son, Ahmed, was excited to know his grand-parents and he became attached to my mother like any kid would to his grandmother. She took him on a trip in a London bus and she had bought him all kinds of little things. When Dalia and Haider quietly went back into the house, her son was there and he was asking for her and Mom. He had already gone to sleep before she became ill and left for the hospital. So he did not know why she was not home. He was looking for her and asking Dalia about his grandmother. It was heartbreaking. She did not know who to attend to: herself or her son or my brother.

The death of one you love never comes at a time when you are ready for it, especially when it is your parents. Even though we are rational and we know that one day death will come to us all, we are always stunned by it. The death of my mother was a devastating shock to all of us and to my father. She was not only his life, his river of hope, his moonlight in the dark and his lifelong love, she was also our fortress especially during the time that Dad had been ill and incapacitated. Throughout the few latter years, she was like a tent and a shield that we all hid under and took shelter beneath. She was like a fire that remained lit even during a storm.

In spite of her own illness and her terrible ordeal and the pain she felt as she saw my Dad deteriorating, she kept up strong spirits and will for the most part. She had incredible intrinsic resilience and tenacity. I think her persistence was unique. In spite of enduring many losses and hits and setbacks, she kept relying on God, she kept having hope, and she kept trying to help my father. She was like a fatally wounded soldier who keeps fighting until the last breath. She persisted while she was in pain. She had inspiring energy and she managed to create some happy moments here and there for Dad and all of us. She still cared for everyone and ener-gized us all in her strong spirit and faith; she was like a spiritual or emotional column that held us all up. We all relied on her love, strength and warm heart. Losing her was like having your spine severed, and it felt like the beginning of the end. In fact there is an expression in Arabic that renders the same meaning; it says: *My back is now broken.* It is said about some event that is devastating and that knocks you out and crushes you, such as losing someone whom you have relied on all your life through the toughest moments. Losing Mom was like that for all of us. Indeed, after her death life became so much harder. Perhaps life had always been that way, but I felt, and so did my brother and sisters, that hardship was around and all over and that perhaps we had simply been shielded by the love and prayers of Mom who managed to remain inspired and faithful in spite of the hardest of times.

* * *

It has been said that lovers want the company of each other so badly that they even wish to die together. I never thought this had any real meaning until my Dad passed away several weeks later. During those short weeks my sister Dalia and my brothers stayed with Dad to look after him. Each day that passed, after she was gone, he ached for her. He was in immense sorrow. He told my brother Amer: "Amer, you know I shall not last long without your mother. I cannot imagine being here for long without her. I am living my last days."

He wanted to be with my mother and he talked about her day and night. He remembered her gentle care and compassion and every detail about their lives. He remembered stories of their earlier years, how they had met, how they had gotten married, their trips, their honeymoon, their house, their children, and he wondered what she was doing now and where she was. He lamented his biggest loss of all. He often cried for her: "Lydia.... Darling.... You left me? How could you leave me? I want to be with you.... I am coming after you." He thought of her every hour. He was in anguish.

I had heard my parents say that they wished to die together because they loved each other so much and that life without one another would not be enjoyable. I had always ignored what they said and did not think about it. I had told them that I wished they would both live a long happy life and that I did not want them to die. I never thought that their wish would come true. It's like she was calling him and he went to her. It was the most amazing connection between two souls. A few days after his death, my sisters and I were in my parents' apartment cleaning up and collecting what was left of their simple belongings. I came across a letter that my father had written to my mother on their last anniversary several months before she died. With tears in my eyes and a heart torn to pieces, I showed the letter to my sisters. We all cried at this final manifestation of love. I could not believe that people could still be so much in love after thirty-six years of marriage and so much heartbreaking turmoil. The letter said:

My darling Lydia

When I remember our journey together of the past thirty-six years, the most beautiful memory is that of the few hours right after we said our marriage vows. When we went out for our first walk together as husband and wife and we sat at the banks of the river Tigris and we had our moments of love and we envisioned our future and dreams together. The fires of love, which you ignited in every corner of my heart, will stay lit for eternity. Our love will last until eternity because it arose from the essence of my soul and the essence of your dear soul. Lydia: I love you. The kind of love that I have for you has never existed among mortal beings and even among spirits. Only God Almighty knows this kind of love. There is no means on earth to measure my love for you. Darling: Your love is the only thing I possess in this life. And I do not wish for anything more. I want to be with you and our children and our grandchildren, all in our beautiful home and gardens having many happy days filled with love and embraces. I want to be with you forever. I will never have been with you enough. I shall always want to be with you more until eternity. This is because our love descended from the heavens into our hearts and it stayed there cherished and protected forever.

* * *

Somewhere in Baghdad lies our empty home. Just what's left of it: some walls, some rooms, some bricks, some trees. But there is no one there. There is no life, no people, no roses, no sunflowers, no grapes, no laughter, no pictures and no dolls. The flowers are dead, the trees are withering away and the fountains are rusted and dry. The house was looted. Many things were scattered and many things were stolen. There is dirt everywhere, it is abandoned, and it is left behind because it all mattered less.

But one hears loud echoes striking the walls and shaking the trees. Echoes of happier days and many eventful nights. And echoes of my parents' aching wish to visit their home once more before they died, echoes of their loving words and echoes of their many unfulfilled dreams: Dad's wish to have our weddings celebrated in his beautiful gardens; Mom's wish to give us her special treasures from her world travels. At night, their souls look down at the dark walls of the house seeking the colorful memories of many happy days ... of Mom's beautiful banquets, of the glittering lights and golden ribbons, of our water fights in the gardens, of the cold nights we cooked the chestnuts and the summer evenings of Baghdad. The winter rain pours over Baghdad as it always did before. The streets surrounding the house seen all the days of our dramatic life carry a silent testimony to the tragic events that we endured. Many neighbors and friends who lived through these events have perished or have attained old age by now. Maybe no one there remembers our family after so many years. The city of Baghdad is still there enduring more of the Ba'ath terror, many times more severe and atrocious than before.

In their fierce fight with the Ba'ath regime, my parents managed to deliver all their children abroad. That was their victory against the Ba'ath regime. It is their legacy. While they lost their possessions and property and endured a lot of pain themselves, they managed to extract us, their children, out of Iraq one by one and protect us from the wars and the military recruitments and the madness that was going on. It is like Baghdad was prey to a slow creeping fire that was engulfing everything and everyone. Mom and Dad acted quickly and took us out of that fire one by one while they got burned and hurt.

It was not an easy task. With all the difficulties and the restrictions, it was magic. It was like extracting water from a rock. It was a race against fate. It was nearly impossible. But they did it. It was quite amazing. They gave up many materialistic gains and they risked their lives and endured tremendous pain during their final days, so that they could protect our lives. They protected us from the grinding of the youth that took place at the hands of the Ba'ath regime. They did all this to protect their children from the menace of this regime. It is very humbling. The Ba'ath regime ended the lives of so many young people and I or my brothers or sisters could have been among those people had we stayed in Iraq.

It must have been sad and hard for my mother and my father to see how their life took a bad turn after the time of my father's arrest. Before then, they were on top of the world. They had a happy life, beautiful house, healthy children and tremendous success. They enjoyed themselves. And then, everything came crashing down so badly. Things did not get better. Having endured so much loss and pain themselves, I think that my parents were on a mission to salvage what was most dear to them, what mattered most to them. They magically and incessantly worked hard to get their children out of Iraq. They gave us another chance at life. For that, I am so grateful.

* * *

Epilogue

I got to know of the terror of the Baʿath regime of Saddam Hussein at the age of seven. The Baʿath regime harmed and terrorized my family. They treated us with cruelty and injustice. All because of their vicious greed for power and control, my childhood was marred by sad events. Because of them, my family suffered. Because of them, we endured so much pain. Because of them, I missed many months and weeks of being with my father. Because of them, I was displaced far away from my parents for many years.

Leaving my parents while I was so young was very hard on me. Its effects on my life are permanent. I was detached from my parents when I was fourteen and I was displaced thousands of miles away from them because of the political chaos in Iraq. Then, because of the war and travel restrictions on them and my own restricted travel capabilities such as the lack of a passport, in addition to perhaps negligence on my part, I only saw then six times after that for a total combined time of about nine months. They were six short visits here and there over a period of six or so years during which my father was ill and both of them were getting old and frail. Such little time to spend with one's parents: only fourteen years, seven of which were in the midst of Baʿath terror and turmoil, and nine short months more.

I just wish that I had seen more of them and learned more of their experience and knowledge. I wish that I had had the pleasure of chatting with them as an adult, consulting them on my personal issues, going out with them for tea. I wish that they had been there at my eighteenth birthday, my wedding, my graduation, my first job, and all the happy and difficult moments of life that I went through. They could not be there because of the war, because of their health, because of visa restrictions and because they had passed away. I wish that I had spent all my time with them during the moments they were alive. But death and fate are always ahead of us and they always take us by surprise.

We cannot complain about death. It is a destination that we all shall reach one day. It is the will of God, when we are born and when we die. Like many young people in this world, I was denied having my parents with me during many important moments in life. But I indeed was blessed and privileged to have known my parents briefly and to have known that they loved me dearly and they did everything in their capacity to protect me and bring happiness to my life, in spite of the chaos and madness of the political circumstances that existed around us. Their death left a scar in my life, like the death of parents would for any child. My scar hurts greatly though. Because I was separated from them so early against my will and against their will. It was the only choice. It was a cruel choice. It was an abrupt detachment after which I went through many steps of my life alone and without the benefit of their advice and presence.

It is a small consolation, however, that those few loving and happy years that I had with them in childhood have sustained my soul a long way. The love my parents instilled in me is powerful and does not wither away. I passionately cling to my few earlier years of happiness and stability and I remember them well. It is like having a reservoir of happiness that I live on like a bank account full of money. These happy memories have carried me through my life, through happy and sad moments. I cherish those days, and I am privileged to have had extraordinary parents and a few extraordinarily happy years in my early childhood upon which I built the rest of my life. In fact, I have been confronted with my own difficulties in life, like everyone else; but in my moments of extreme trial, where I faced my own struggles and was about to give up, the lively images of my parents in my mind and echoes of their loving and inspiring words brought me back to my senses and gave me another breath. Their love is indeed like a fire that does not die out.

Over the years, I have started my own small collection of artifacts, dolls, precious objects, and souvenirs. I have come to appreciate every gift that I get no matter how simple it is and know the story of every precious object I have, and who gave it to me or where I bought it from. Today, it gives me tremendous pleasure to set the dining table for a beautiful dinner with family and guests, to light candles and to decorate my dining table with lace and golden ribbons. Every time I do that, I remember my mother and the few times I helped her with this task. Every day in my life, I like to display all around me my happiness and my love for my husband and my family. I strive to look after my brothers and sisters like I am their godmother. All these things remind me of my mother and these small things are just a few of her beautiful reflections in my life.

Today, I have a maddening love for museums and poetry books, a love that my Dad instilled in me when I was a child. When I walked in the various museums that I have visited in many countries, it was like walking with Dad and listening to his stories all over again. Poetry and museums arouse especially joyous feelings and precious memories of special moments with my father. Today, when I look at violas and lavender-colored roses, they take me back to my walks with Dad along the pathway surrounding the house. When I see the fiery colors of the bougainvillea flowers, they take me back to my play days in the gardens. And although I am a grown woman in my thirties, I still enjoy going to bookshops and stationery shops to buy fancy paper and notebooks and pens. It is such a joyful thing for me to do, and it is so because I enjoyed it so much before when Dad took my sister and me to the bookshops of Baghdad and gave us money to buy such little things.

When I visited Niagara Falls, the Eiffel Tower and the Golden Gate Bridge, I remembered my parents' pictures of these places and the stories they told us about their adventures there. I still have aspirations to travel and see the rest of the beautiful wonders of the world that they visited and to walk along in their steps and to remember more of what they told me about each of these places. The pleasures I get from all these things take me back to my happy days with my parents and let me live all over again our life in Baghdad.

Although I feel like my parents and I passed each other by and we touched each other for a short time, it was a magical touch. It was a brief time that we spent together but it was so special. They left unique marks on my life and my soul. In the midst of all the sadness and agony that the regime inflicted upon us, I had a true loving connection with my parents and they managed to imprint happiness and firm love in my soul. Indeed it is the delicate love and care they surrounded me with throughout the years I spent with them, that I remember today and that has made me so strong and enduring.

The few times that I saw them, my parents were surprised by how quickly I had grown up, gone to college, finished college, gotten married. But they, especially my mother, felt very sorry that they had not been there for my sister and me. She had not liked being a mother from a long distance; she had wanted to be there with us daily, to take care of us, to ask us about school, to help us with our teenage life. She felt sad that she had not been there for me every day like most Moms. She felt sad that we had been forced to let go of each other.

I never thought that my parents were to blame for our cruel separation and I know that it was hard for them too. It was the circumstances that led us to be apart. They felt that they should have been close to us and present in our lives. They felt sad that they could not see us during important moments and transitions in our lives such as living in another culture, going to college. I truly believe that my parents did their best and they did everything humanly possible to take care of me and my sisters and brothers. I wish there were a way for me to let them know that.

Moreover, I myself have a struggle that I must deal with all the time. It is an anguish that has been with me since my parents passed away. It is a sorrow that I feel because I did not have a chance to serve my parents and to help them when they were old and frail. When they were in the midst of their crisis, I was a child or a teenager—how could I help? And when I became an adult, they were gone. I wish I had done something for them to help or to serve them or to make their lives easier in some way.

The legacy of these two elevated human beings lives on in the lessons they taught us: that you stand by the truth and by your principles; that you cannot bend your back to other human beings, to thugs or criminals or anyone, no matter how powerful they are; and that you must be clear and truthful in your own conscience and with God. This is a hard path to take in life. This is a path that is not sweet and is not lined with roses. But it is a worthy one. Their positive image and good name still live today among so many people of their generation who knew them and what beautiful human beings they were. Their legacy also lives on in the values they taught us, in the elevated morals that they lived by, and in their endless love and devotion to their children, a love that still holds us together even though we are thousands of miles away from each other.

Many beautiful images and thoughts of those days are still with me today, however short and brief those days may have been. They are a treasure that cannot be valued by any means. They are eternal and so powerful. The Ba'ath regime could not take those images, thoughts and feelings away because they are ingrained in my heart and planted in my soul and they are still there. The most beautiful thing I learned from the example of my parents is that love between husband and wife is the center of any family. It is a powerful force that held my parents together through so many traumas and so much injustice. Their love was solid and enduring and withstood traumatic events. Not only that, but love creates more love. It changes the surroundings, it is transmitted to those around you, your children and to their children and it brings more love. And now that they are gone, I think that not all was lost. Their resonating loving words and care are not lost, their kindness is not lost, and our memories are not lost.

It is the mercy of God Almighty that took my parents out of this life at that time so they would not see more pain, as the situation in Iraq has gotten worse, so much worse. That pain alone would have killed them. Over the following years, the recklessness and brutality of the Ba'ath government, which began with the events that happened to my parents nearly thirty years ago, escalated and became many times worse. It did not matter anymore whether you supported the Ba'ath and the revolution or not. Initially, the Ba'ath terrorized and preyed on a few families and a handful of individuals. Later, the Ba'athists became more aggressive and their terror broadened and became more severe. There were mass executions, mass graves, ethnic cleansing, the grinding of a myriad young men in two ill-fated wars, and indeed genocide of the Shia population of southern Iraq throughout the 1990s after the second Gulf War.

When you meet Iraqis in various countries in the diaspora you hear so many stories of sad departures. It is like an encyclopedia of sad stories that would break your heart and you wonder how anyone can endure so much pain and so much separation. For so many Iraqis, important events in their lives took place without their parents or their children or their loved ones. There are people who have not seen their families for ten years, twenty years, thirty years. There are people who could not go to attend to their dying parents in Iraq and who could not go to the funerals of their dead. There are families whose sons or daughters were detained in the early 1980s or the late 1970s and they still do not know their fate. They do not know whether they are alive or dead. The pain that Iraqis endured has seldom been surpassed in its severity and it almost sounds unreal.

Did I think then, when we left, that we would stay away that long for so many years, now twenty something years? No. Not at all. I do not know why but I thought it would be a transient absence. I never ever though that I would not see my friends again. I never though that I would not see my uncles and my aunts, our neighbors, my cousin and our relatives for twenty something years. I do think often about my friends at school and my teachers too. How many of them are still alive? How did they endure the first Gulf War or the second Gulf War? How many of them died in one of these episodes? How many of them became widows because of these wars or because of other terrors of the Ba'ath regime? How many of them are struggling to survive and find food and immunization for their children? And I wish that I shall see my friends one day and explain to them why we had to leave in haste, why I never could say good-bye to them and why I never wrote or kept in touch.

* * *

When Saddam Hussein seized the presidency in 1979 and announced his impending onslaught to the world in that dreadful speech in which he referred to Iraq as a land without people, the world community was not alarmed. No one cared that the Iraqi government was grinding its population. When Saddam's forces burned and demolished a whole small town (named Gizanne) northeast of Baghdad, no international condemnation of atrocities was heard and the world media did not even report the incident. Western companies continued their many commercial deals and contracts with Iraq. Throughout the 1970s and 1980s, no sanctions or response of any kind was leveled against the Iraqi government by the world community for killing thousands of Iraqi citizens and displacing hundreds of thousands of others. In 1998 the U.S. Congress finally passed the Iraq Liberation Act, legislation that supports democracy in Iraq. When you read that document, it is sad and disheartening to see that even when, finally, the crimes of this regime were acknowledged, Congress failed to mention the atrocities of the 1970s described in this book: shoving thousands of people in jail, murdering innocent families, horrific human rights abuses, and the deportation of hundreds of families. The Iraq Liberation Act mentions other crimes of the regime (rightfully so) such as invading Kuwait and waging war against Iran and others, yet unforgivably ignores the biggest of all crimes of this regime: its crimes against the people of Iraq.

The shameful silence and inaction of the world community and the greed of many western companies for profits gave legitimacy to this regime and crushed the dreams and hopes of millions of people in Iraq. Iraqis could never understand the indifference the world community showed towards their onslaught. There is a question that still begs for an answer. Why was it that when a few dozen people died in Tiananmen square in 1989, the world community was enraged and many demands were put on China to improve its human rights record, yet when the Ba'ath regime massacred thousands of people, there was silence from the world? Toward the end of the second Gulf War in March 1991, a wholesale slaughter of Iraqi civilians took place right in front of the coalition forces and as a result of the terms of the cease-fire between Iraq and the American forces. Many eyewitnesses on the battlegrounds during the war reported atrocities committed within a few kilometers of the coalition forces. During the cease-fire negotiations which ended the Gulf War officially, Iraq specifically asked for permission to fly helicopters. It is that ill-fated agreement, allowing the use of helicopters, which enabled the regime to transport Ba'athist military thugs to the various locations of the popular uprising against the central government. This mobility of Saddam's forces in the first moments of the revolt against him led to the genocide of the Shia population in the south and the horrors of mass killing and ethnic cleansing. The uprising was crushed by the Ba'ath regime, thanks to the coalition forces, and many massacres took place. The only witness left is the southern desert and the few people who remained alive.

I hope that everyone reading this book will realize that the atrocities committed by the Ba'ath regime against the people of Iraq far exceed, in magnitude, horror and severity, what the regime did in Kuwait or in other international incidents. What the Ba'ath regime did to Kuwait was wrong. But its severity was not even one percent of what the Ba'ath regime, aided ironically by many countries of the Gulf War II coalition, did to the people of Iraq. And we have only begun to know about these atrocities, as many of these events were never documented. Many people who lived through them have already died.

I also hope that this book is only the first of many that we shall begin to see, because the cry of humanity in Iraq now is too loud to ignore. The cry of humanity has gone on for too long. It has reached a level that can no longer be borne. It can be heard from the mass graves in which hundreds of Shia families were buried alive, from the torture chambers which housed innocent people, from all the parents whose sons perished in the wars, from the young men whom my father saw being executed at Abu Graib prison and from all the women who were raped by the Ba'ath gangs.

While it was morally right to stop the aggression of the Iraqi regime outside of its borders, it was shameful and immoral to ignore the human rights abuses that were taking place in Iraq. And it is eternally unforgivable to have aided this reckless brutal regime economically, militarily and through intelligence and logistics

Tragedy hit all in Iraq, every age and every family and every profession. Today all Iraqi families are hurting because of the death of their sons or daughters or brothers or fathers or mothers in the first Gulf War or in the second or in the prisons and torture chambers of the Ba'ath. And if they did not die in any of these calamities, then they are dying because of the poverty that hit Iraq due to the merciless U.N. sanctions and due to the continued brutality of the regime.

The Ba'ath regime, aided by regional and Western governments throughout the 1970s and 1980s, destroyed a beautiful country and reduced its proud, brilliant people, who have carried human civilization forward for millennia, into beggars, orphans, refugees, impoverished and hopeless. Today, every living soul in Iraq is hurting because of the lack of medicine, the lack of hope, the lack of electric power, the crimes and prostitution that escalated because of the poverty and the misery that society is going through. People are dying from hunger and lack of immunization and because of the contamination of even the water and the air they breathe. Troops of humanity, desperate and just trying to leave Iraq, are trapped in cargo ships on the oceans and the seas.

So many tragedies have taken place in Iraq about which hundreds of books must be written, *shall* be written.

Index